T0094593

The Life and Letters of Emily Dickinson

The Life and Letters of Emily Dickinson

Martha Dickinson Bianchi
and Emily Dickinson

MINT EDITIONS

The Life and Letters of Emily Dickinson was first published in 1924.

This edition published by Mint Editions 2021.

ISBN 9781513212128 | E-ISBN 9781513212029

Published by Mint Editions®

MINT
EDITIONS

minteditionbooks.com

Publishing Director: Jennifer Newens
Design & Production: Rachel Lopez Metzger
Project Manager: Micaela Clark
Typesetting: Westchester Publishing Services

For their enthusiasm, intuitive understanding, and
critical assistance, my gratitude to Ferris Greenslet,
Curtis Hidden Page, and Alfred Leete Hampson

M. D. B.

*A*Mystic akin only to Emerson." W.P. Dawson, the English critic, in his own anthology states without apology: "Among the American poets I have named two—Poe and Emily Dickinson." And it was another Englishman, Martin Armstrong, writing of her poetry in the London "Spectator" last January (1923), who concluded: "Mr. Conrad Aiken in his recent anthology of modern American poets calls Emily Dickinson's poetry 'perhaps the finest by a woman in the English language.' I quarrel only with his 'perhaps.'"

However the present volume may lift the veil, or presume to lead her shy reality into the light of mortal dawns again, Emily alone supplies the only clue to herself, the articles of her Faith—

The Soul's superior instants
Occur to Her alone,
When friend and earth's occasion
Have infinite withdrawn.

Or she, Herself, ascended
To too remote a height,
For lower recognition
Than Her Omnipotent.

This mortal abolition
Is seldom, but as fair
As Apparition—subject
To autocratic air.

Eternity's disclosure
To favorites, a few,
Of the Colossal substance
Of immortality.

The essential difficulty in presenting a Life of Emily Dickinson has been enhanced by the sacred pact observed with her chosen few, that all letters should be burned after her death. This excludes exactly those which might have held together the frail external incidents of her days, which seem so scantily supplied to those ignorant of the thronging events of the Spirit which eternally preoccupied her.

This present record is made up from family letters hitherto withheld, deathless recollections, and many sentences overheard from her own lips and *scrupulously set down as too unique to be squandered upon the passing moment. The Letters formerly printed have now been chronologically arranged, and as far as of intrinsic value, retained; others have been added from my article in the "Atlantic Monthly," and "The Single Hound," a volume composed entirely of poetic flashes sent to her brother's wife, my mother, on every gust of impulse.*

A high exigence constrains the sole survivor of her family to state her simply and truthfully, in view of a public which has, doubtless without intention, misunderstood and exaggerated her seclusion—amassing a really voluminous stock of quite lurid misinformation of irrelevant personalities. She has been taught in colleges as a weird recluse, rehearsed to women's clubs as a lovelorn sentimentalist—even betrayed by one American essayist of repute to appear a fantastic eccentric.

On the other hand, she has been named "the Feminine Walt Whitman" in at least one of the great universities; in another—

> *Of the Colossal substance*
> *Of immortality.*

MARTHA DICKINSON BIANCHI

Contents

PART I
LIFE

I

ANCESTRY

There was nothing in the parentage or direct heredity of Emily Dickinson to account for her genius. There was equally nothing to impede its course or contradict its authority. It claimed her without those dissenting elements of being which came to her from her ideally mated but completely opposite father and mother. Her parents did not interfere with her actual life and behavior, both because they never realized her preoccupation quite fully, and because they had no will to destroy the individuality of anyone of their three children.

Nothing could have been more alien to any of the Dickinsons than a desire to be peculiar—"queer" they would have called it—or to do what the later generation calls pose. Eccentricity consciously indulged in would have merely been reprimanded as bad manners. Their dignity was of the stiff, reserved type resenting the least encroachment on its individuality in character and privacy in habit—which they insured by conforming handsomely to the sense of their community, the laws of their state and country, and the will of God as expounded from pulpits of the white meeting-house in Hadley and later in Amherst, where the colonial train of Emily Dickinson's ancestors undeviatingly worshipped. There was no allowance made in her family for oddity— temperament had not been discovered yet. There was no exception to what was expected of each of the children alike, her sister Lavinia, her brother Austin, and herself. What Emily did succeed in evading and eluding and imagining and believing, and setting down for those who came after her to profit by, was her own performance, dictated by her own need for the solitude in which to write, and the time necessary for thought. She was spared none of her share in the household duties, nor did she wish to be.

Before one thinks of her as a poet and philosopher or mystic, one must in honesty remember her as an adoring and devoted daughter, a sister loyal to blows, a real nun of the home, without affectation or ritual beyond that of her gentle daily task, and all that she could devise of loving addition to the simple sum. To one who loved her it is unthinkable that she could ever be supposed to have consciously secreted herself, or self-consciously indulged in whim or extravaganza in living, which her fine breeding would have been the first to discard as vulgar and unworthy. It was her absorption in her own world that made her unaware often of the more visible world of those who never see beyond it. It was not that she was introspective, egoistic, and selfish—rather that she dwelt so far out in the changing beauty of Nature, in the loves and joys and sorrows of the dear ones she held closest, in the simple drama of the neighborhood, and most of all the stupendous and sometimes revealing wonder of life and death and the Almighty God thundered at her from the high pulpit on Sundays—and known so differently in her own soul the other days of the week—that she never thought of Emily Dickinson at all; never supposed anyone watched her way of living or worshipping or acting. She never had time in all the vivid, thrilling, incessant programme of night and day, summer and winter, bird and flower, the terror lest evil overtake her loved ones, the glory in their least success—never stopped in her flying wild hours of inward rapture over a beauty perceived or a winged word caught and spun into the fabric of her thought—to wonder or to care if no one knew she was, or how she proceeded in the behavior of her own small tremendous affair of life.

Her heredity is distinctly traced for nine generations in America. Her first local ancestor settled in old Hadley and a later generation was one of the founders of the church and town of Amherst. There were Dickinsons mentioned in Hadley among the first letters of the original Indian grants in 1659. And when in 1714 the order was given for five men to superintend the erection of a new meeting-house in the middle of two streets, one of them was a Dickinson. There was also an ancestor in the famous "Shays's Rebellion" in 1786. Before that, in England, the stock from which she came was clear for thirteen generations more. Further than that her father's curiosity or pride had never gone in research.

Her own grandfather, Samuel Fowler Dickinson, was the first of her direct line in Amherst. His connection with the establishment of Amherst Academy, from which the College later sprang, is familiar local history. In his fervor for "the in-bringing of the Kingdom" he foresaw the universal education of ministers, and calculated the millennium in the near future of "about seven years." He was educated at Dartmouth College, a man of sincere piety, and a generosity that was his financial ruin. In a letter from his sister, Emily's Aunt Lucretia, to his son Edward at Yale, the following passage occurs. It is dated 1821:

Father left in the yellow gig for the Bay Road this morning. He has gone to Boston by coach to see about getting a charter for something they propose to call Amherst College. He looked so fine in his white beaver and new great coat.

Until this ardent enthusiast, almost bigot, lost all the money he had not previously given away in his fanaticism for education and religion, the family throve and were favorably known for this world's prosperity as well as in matters of piety and attainment.

His oldest son Edward, who was the father of Emily, was brought up strictly and with a regard for the needs of the missionaries first. He was sent to Yale College, driven there, too, in the family chaise upon at least one trip mentioned in the family correspondence. The family letters during that period are happily at hand and throw a profound and touching atmosphere about these earlier days of education, when it was a sacred boon possible to the few through fierce sacrifice, often, on the part of those who gave it, and not to be entered into with less than a consecrated spirit of trust for those to whom it was to be returned, transformed into a wisdom that was to help save the world.

In one letter from Samuel, who was a deacon for forty years in the First Church and whose zeal was sleepless, to Edward, his son, this passage strikes its own contrast to modern fathers and sons.

December 17, 1819, he writes:

It is good news to hear of your good health and conduct. I rejoice to hear that the government of the college pleases you—that so much attention is paid to moral and religious instruction. Learning and science without morality and religion are like a man without a soul. They probably would do hurt rather than good. No man is a neuter in the world. His actions, his example, his concepts, his motives are all tending either to that which is good or evil.

He concludes:

Remember the importance of the present time and never forget our hereafter.

Your affectionate parent
SAMUEL FOWLER DICKINSON

Again, in 1819, he writes enclosing five dollars with which to discharge all obligations Edward may have entered into. He adds:

> Consider the importance of every action as going to form character. Always be manly but do not expend more than you can pay, remembering that nothing is spent without sufficient cause. There are necessary uses for all our money.

Again, later on:

> I hear the religious attention continues at New Haven. If, Edward, I could learn that you were among the number who had embraced the Saviour how joyful the news! Pray for a new heart. Never forget your morning and evening supplication for such mercies as you need, and most of all for your great salvation. You know we place much confidence in your upright and honourable deportment and your strict attention to every religious and moral duty.

Edward Dickinson grew up to be a rather haughty, austere man, shy and gentle, laconic and strict. He dressed in broadcloth at all times, and wore a black beaver hat glossy beyond compare with that of any young beau, and carried a handsome cane to and from his law office on the Main Street of his village. About his neck was wound a black satin stock pinned with a jet and diamond pin, with a lock of his wife's hair at the back. His hair was a dark auburn, and his eyes those that Emily repeated in time. He was on the Governor's staff as a young man and his honorable discharge with flattering mention of his services is still preserved.

He followed the family profession and went into the law, practising in Amherst, pleading at the Hampshire County Bar, settling the disputes of his friends and neighbors, and drawing the deeds that no modern court has ever been able to set aside or adjudge not binding. He was a pillar in the First Church, although he joined it later in life than was customary, and served its interests with utter fidelity. A gentleman of the old school he was, with a distinction that was elegance, and many a laborer, among the aged recalling him in their own boyhood, spoke with respect amounting to reverence of "The Old Squire." "What he said he meant," was deeply burned into his legend.

Only one of his daughter Emily's sparks of reckless fire flew from his sedate characteristics—his nearest approach to self-indulgence was his sly liking for a horse handsome and fleet. "I always intend to have the best horse in town," he said more than once, as he set off for the court in the shire town across the river. And his lifelong next neighbor, Deacon Luke Sweetser, made this no easy ambition. There was just a hint of the daughter's later flashes in her father's concession to this love of speed and shining form.

He admitted nothing in Emily as different from his other children, or from any daughter. He made no allowances for her—ever; and yet their unspoken intimacy went so deep it never came to the surface in words, but was never absent, diminished, or lost, or ceased to be even after his death had blasted her trust in life forever. "If Father is asleep on the lounge the house is full," she often exclaimed. It expressed their understanding.

That the Squire was a proud man no one doubted, but that his name was the first on any subscription to relieve want or disaster, and that his eyes were capable of suffusing at the pain of an animal or trouble of the human heart, related him to Emily's fire and dew quality.

His wife, Emily's mother, was an exquisite little lady of the old school long passed into mythology. She was the daughter of Alfred Norcross, of Monson. The family were well-to-do and she was educated and finished off at a school for young ladies at New Haven, very much in repute in her day. Upon her marriage, no railroad then reaching Amherst, her dower was brought by several yoke of brindle oxen. Her mahogany was claw-footed and pine-apple cut; her silver had the basket of flowers on the handles; her bandboxes are still in the family possession—monstrous gay affairs, with scenes of Mount Vernon on one side and Paris on the other.

Emily Norcross Dickinson feared and honored her husband after the manner of the Old Testament. She trembled and flushed, obeyed and was silent before him. He was to her Jehovah, and she was to him the sole being to whom he entrusted the secrets of his inmost heart. His letters to her were discreet, respectful, "frosty but kindly"—ending always with the assurance of his remaining her "most ob't servant, Edward Dickinson."

On one occasion he wrote that he should see her at Northampton, being with the Governor as aide-de-camp, "which will," he hopes, "not be less agreeable to her than to him." A courtly pair, with not one glimmer of their transgressing Emily's future escape from all their well-known landmarks of thought and divination.

The society of their village was also stately, and they later played their part therein, being often sought, or, as the time-worn little notes still show, "Solicited, to an evening party" by this or that prominent household, as "Self and Lady," a form shared by even as pompous a host as Judge Delano, of Northampton. In 1821 Lucretia also stated, "There have been some splendid parties this Winter in town—one at the Strong's to which there were more than fifty invited." The lace shawls and India shawls, the gold-banded china and English blue, are mute witness to the social importance and obligation of the family, who did their part, whether any enjoyment was wrested from their conscientious performance or not, in keeping up the county standards of entertainment and hospitality.

It is impossible to derive Emily from either her stately father or her fluttering little mother, always timorous, always anxious. Treasured among the daughter's most cherished papers, was found the little yellow certificate of her mother's exemplary conduct as a girl at school:

> Miss Emily Norcross, for punctual attendance, close
> application, good acquirements, and discreet behavior merits
> the approbation of her preceptress.
>
> E. P. Dutch

The aunts seem to have been the Greek chorus of the family, dire in their fatal appearances. Her Aunt Elizabeth, Emily pronounced "the only male relative on the female side of my family." They were all married at a distance and imminent hourly for prolonged visitations. These invasions concluded the family circle, together with the uncles who were less disastrous to the plans of the children because they left sooner and paid less attention to them.

And out of this human stock and precision of living came the little girl whose soul flew up and away like the smoke from the high chimneys of her home under the tall pines.

II

CHILDHOOD

Emily Norcross Dickinson, named for her mother, was born December 11, 1830, in Amherst, Massachusetts, in the old house said to have been the first erected of brick in Amherst.

Her brother Austin and her younger sister Lavinia were the other children of the home, both possessed of marked ability and varied temperament.

Austin grew up to manhood with much of Emily's poetic quality, fiercely suppressed—a lover of trees and beauty, one with Nature—like her, a hero-worshipper, a partisan, and a lover of all the rare and noble books whose faded brown Ticknor and Fields first editions still stand in deserted ranks on the bookshelves of his own library in his former home at Amherst. He graduated from Amherst College in 1850, and in 1854 from the Harvard Law School, and was admitted to the Hampshire County Bar. When he was about to leave Amherst to accept a legal partnership in Detroit, his father, overcome by the impending separation, offered to build him a home if he would remain. So all the adventurous hopes were stifled, and immediately upon his marriage he took up the practice of law as his father's partner in the old office, since burned, which held many treasures of local history as well as a remarkably fine law library consulted far and wide throughout the region.

His marriage to the "Sister Sue" of Emily's lifelong adoration brought an outside element into the family, which bred some critical hours. Brought up by a Knickerbocker great-aunt in a more cosmopolitan atmosphere, Susan Gilbert's first celebration of Christmas in Amherst with wreaths of laurel in the windows almost upset the family apple cart, and Emily's brother was accused by the scandalized Puritan neighbors of having married a Catholic.

But in all and for all his father was on her side, and came regularly all his life each Sabbath morning for a surreptitious cup of stronger coffee than home thought wise. It was just this freer aspect of life in "Sister Sue" that fascinated Emily and cast such a spell over her from the first. The old house under the tall pines, rebuilt in 1813, and the new house built after a whim of Austin's in the style of an Italian villa, advertised the abyss that lay between the two generations.

The sister, Lavinia, was hardly less brilliant than Emily, but upon her, very early, depended the real solidarity of the family. A coquette from her cradle, very pretty, with a piercing wit and a rather bandit tongue, it became her lot to cover Emily's delinquencies and support her mother's gentle reign, increasingly enfeebled in spite of herself by the dominating daughter, and the powerful family maidservant who grew old along with them for almost forty years of unbroken service. It was Lavinia who knew where everything was, from a lost quotation to a last year's muffler. It was she who remembered to have the fruit picked for canning, or the seeds kept for next year's planting, or the perfunctory letters written to the aunts. It was Lavinia who leaped into the breach, when those unexpected guests drove up at nightfall—tearing her hair over a discrepant larder behind the scenes, but advancing all smiles and self-congratulation to receive the unwelcome invaders as they came up the double set of stone steps and into the front hall.

If Emily had been less Emily, Lavinia might have been more Lavinia. As it was, Lavinia carried the family honor to her grave as a sacred but rather acrid burden, and a few angels may have wept over her load when she laid it down, for sake of the self-renunciation its integrity implied. It was Lavinia who was thrown to the lions of every phase of dreary social duty, as she threw herself to those same beasts of anxious household routine. Always a brilliant mimic, a wit and wag, none could surpass her in her representations of the family circle, and in imitating the bass viol of the country choir her skill was supreme. She was said to be able to make her nose turn up at will, if her caricature demanded it, and when nothing aroused her animosity there was no one more amusing—not even Emily herself, whose bodyguard she became in their early thirties. Each had her own inner intimacies, and her own admirers in due time, and many they shared, but there is loving tribute due to the younger sister who must have always felt Emily's peculiar genius as distinguishing her apart and above, and who proudly stood aside for her while many, many sought her out. They were so vividly Martha and Mary that it seems trite to call up the parallel: Lavinia with her wearing rectitude in household affairs, Emily with her sublime disregard of all detail; one living in the seen, the other in the unseen and scarcely to be imagined; both in adoring subjection to their parents, both jealously involved in their only brother's success and happiness.

And among them an outsider, differing in tradition and upbringing, Austin's wife, with her broader youth and fulfilled happiness.

There is an artless painting of the three children, done by some itinerant painter, that gives them all three, at about the time their father's letters began to mention them by name as little individuals; hoping "Emily took care of her baby sister"—a hope faintly to be justified, perhaps—and "that Austin filled the wood box as he was told."

In the portrait Emily holds a book, but if her gaze was sibylline, it was beyond the vagrant artist's power to portray, and she stares out as frankly as her younger sister, who clutches a stiff rose, and leans against her rather indifferent red-lipped brother with his jaunty air of superior pleasure in being the boy of the trio. Just the real New England family, one sees them, a young father and mother, with perhaps a degree more of prosperity and education and noble ideals to bless themselves with than the majority of those about them, and an endowment of native refinement deeply engrained.

The children went to the public schools like all the other children of their time in New England towns. Helen Fisk, the daughter of Professor Fisk, and later to be known as "H. H." ("Helen Hunt"), so familiar in American literature, was their favorite playmate. There is a note still extant from Mrs. Fisk, in reply to one from Emily's mother, begging that Helen may play with Emily and Vinnie under the syringas. It reads:

> Professor Fisk will lead Helen over to play with Emily
> beneath the syringas, this afternoon. In case it prove not
> convenient to send her home, he will call for her in the chaise
> toward nightfall, before the dew falls.

What a picture of innocent pastime it leaves—little girls playing house under the sweet flowering syringa, to the hum of the bees, and safely restored to the family fold before the dew falls.

They went berrying and chestnutting; on grand occasions they drove in the pompous family cabriolet, lined with cream-colored broadcloth, with high doors and oval windows at the sides and back and framing in unexpected sections of horse and sky, as they moved, and from which the old-fashioned landscape looked formal and strange. Usually it was to spend the day with a relative at some distance or to attend a family funeral. There is no record of any less sedate amusement, but the child

Emily got thrill enough out of the orioles nesting in the cherry tree, or the exploits of her pets, or the dark excitement of the great barn where in the afternoon the sunbeams piercing through a crack in the roof observed her as she hunted for the eggs hidden so skilfully from her deep eyes. The robins came back and the crows in the tall pines called to her almost by name. She was so truly one of Nature's children herself that the daffodils dancing immemorial under the apple trees on the eastern slope of the dooryard every spring were as her own little guests returning. Except for her quickened sense of all beings, all creatures, all beauty, she differed little from other little girls of her time and town.

When she was sixteen the girl who was later to become her "Sister Sue" came to visit in Amherst, and then began the life that never ceased, of budding poetry and letters, affection and art, sympathy and love that surpassed the love real sisterhood often carelessly overlooks. Henceforth in all their girlish banditry, their secret frolics, their confidences, their love-affairs, their griefs and illnesses and disappointments, it was she of whom Emily always spoke as "Sister Sue," who shared the overflow of the real hidden life of that unique genius in her stiff, clean, God-fearing New England home. When her mother's astonishment and amazed concern summed itself up in a shrill cry, "Why, Emily! How can you talk so!"—or when her father evidenced displeasure by taking his hat and cane and passing out the door in silence, leaving an emptiness indicative of reproof, a wordless censure more devastating to her than any judgment day—it was to Sister Sue she fled for safety. Her timid imaginings were horrors worse than any actual event or punishment could ascribe.

There is no legend in the family that her father ever reproved her or called her to account in her various mishaps with duty. Probably his habitual dealing with culprits was after his own wisdom of criminals, and he knew her nature well enough to administer only his stern silence in her case.

Up to the time of her going away to school she was of rather precocious mentality, somewhat sentimental and given to girlish outpourings written in the accepted verbosity of the style of the mid-century (1845). Her flowers already claim a distinct part in her life. It is interesting to note also that at fourteen she announces herself as a Whig. She is interested in all the village happenings and when her father gives her a piano her life becomes crowded. She goes to singing school quite rapturously, and makes an herbarium of great variety and beauty, spending many afternoons off on the hillsides for her wild specimens. In one of her earliest letters preserved she makes fun of the future, saying, "I am growing handsome. I expect I shall be the belle of Amherst when I reach my seventeenth year. I don't doubt but that I shall have perfect crowds of admirers at that age—but away with my nonsense." All of which shows her a natural, silly, happy girl.

She has her garden and her house plants now and delights in her first real music lessons. She also is embroidering a book mark, which she admires. "It is an arrow with a wreath about it—very beautiful." She does her hair up now and admits "it makes me look different." The pieces she learns are "The Grave of Bonaparte," "Lancers Quickstep," and "Maiden, Weep No More." She learns to make bread and stays out of school, as she is not strong, and needs more physical exercise. The winter of 1846 finds her out of school, but reciting German, "as Mr. C., has a large class and Father thought I might never have another opportunity to study it." Her Christmas presents interest her vividly and she describes them at length in her letters to her friends. She says:

> I had a perfume bag and a bottle of attar of rose to go
> with it, a sheet of music, a china mug, with forget-me-not
> on it, a toilet cushion, a watch case, a fortune teller, and an
> amaranthine stock of pin cushions and needle books which in
> ingenuity and art would rival the works of Scripture Dorcas.
> Also an abundance of candy.

In September of 1846 she made her first visit to Boston, alone. The ride in the cars she found delightful and the visit upon her aunt full of excitement. She went to Mount Auburn, Bunker Hill, the Chinese museum, attended two concerts and a horticultural exhibition; was taken, as she herself declares, "On top of the State House and almost everywhere else you can imagine!"

All the next spring she was fitting to go to South Hadley Seminary, studying algebra, Euclid, ecclesiastical history, and reviewing arithmetic. She was always in love with her teachers at that time, quite regardless of their being men or women, but whatever there was fanciful or romantic in her girl imagination she was surely grounded as firmly in the uncompromising fundamentals of education as her Puritan father saw fit to have her. Her anticipations were boundless and she only feared the sky would fall before the plan was realized. It had been in her dreams for a long time, yet she felt that it was part of her own nature always to anticipate more than to realize; a curious instinct in one so entirely normal with life just opening before her.

Her brother Austin had entered Amherst College the year before, and at his first commencement she describes herself as "now very tall and wearing long dresses." One of her quaintest sentences slips in here between childhood and girlhood: "I have perfect confidence in God and His promises—and yet I know not why, I feel the world has a predominant place in my affections."

The sweet secluded pleasures she shared—those pensive yet wistful glances at life, with shy though resolute eyes—may best be understood from one of her letters just a few days before she went to South Hadley in the fall of 1847. A picture this, scarcely to be reproduced:

> Mattie Gilbert was here last evening and we sat on the front door steps and talked about life and love and whispered our childish fancies about such blissful things, the evening was gone so soon—and I walked home with Mattie beneath the silent moon and wished for you and heaven. You did not come darling, but a bit of heaven did—or so it seemed to me. As we walked silently side by side and wondered if that great blessedness which may be ours sometime is granted now to some. Those unions, dear Susie, by which two are one, this sweet and strange miracle.

A perfectly normal young heart responding to the natural wondering of impending maturity.

She is perfectly natural, too, in her religious emotions, with all the literal childishness about heaven, reminding her Susie enviously in another letter, that while she has parents and a sister in heaven, Emily's are on earth, until, carried away by her imagination, she exclaims— "Oh, I wish I had so many dear friends as you in heaven!"—a naïve cry, quickly amended, "I could not spare them now, but to know they had got there safely and should suffer no more!" she explains, in a mood that was always her own in later years, longing to spare those she loved.

Of course at this stage she sentimentalizes as all young girls do and should, and pours out her soul to her girl friend:

> I know I was naughty to write such things, and I know I
> could have helped it if I had tried hard enough, but I thought

my heart would break and I knew of nobody here that cared anything about it—so I said to myself—we will tell Susie. You don't know what a comfort it was. Susie can count the big true hearts by clusters—full of bloom and blossoms amaranthine, because eternal.

At the close she adds:

I send you a kiss shyly—if there's anybody around, don't let them see.

Yet even these simplest outpourings have each some flash redeeming from mere commonplace of her age.

One such glimpse of her variability of expression occurs in the following:

I have thought of you all day and I fear of but little else and when I was gone to Meeting you filled up my mind so full I couldn't find a chink to put the worthy pastor in, when he said "Our Heavenly Father," I said "O darling Sue!" When he read the One Hundredth psalm I kept saying your precious letter over to myself, and Susie, when they sang it would have made you laugh to hear one little voice piping to the departed. I made up words and kept singing how I loved you—and you had gone away—while all the rest of the choir were singing the Halleluyah! I presume nobody heard me because I am so small, but it was a comfort to feel I might put them all out singing of you. I am not there though this afternoon, because I am here, writing this letter to you.

What a darling vision she makes of herself, shy and small and heart-broken for her idol, singing against the volume of the established order of worship at the top of her little chirp, intrepid of consequences if overheard. Something of the later dissenting Emily is foreshadowed in every gesture of her early mind.

The daily four-horse stage that ran between Amherst and Northampton left quite early in the morning, and brought up with much cracking of the whip before the post-office at exactly five in the afternoon. There were no trains or trolleys or motors in those days, so she was driven to South Hadley in state, by her father, and left there alone for the first time in her life out in the strange, wide world; the Holyoke range shutting her away from all the geography of her previous existence more obdurately than any remote distance of modem latitude and longitude could devise.

III

School Days

In the fall of 1847, Emily entered South Hadley Female Seminary, which was at that time a unique establishment of learning, one of whose avowed objects was to provide mates for the missionaries sent out to the foreign field. It was in advance of the other Young Ladies' Seminaries in scope and grade, and had been founded by Mary Lyon with a zeal for service that infected all the fellowship of her co-workers. Her assistants drove over the hills far and near, day and night, summer and winter, collecting the necessary funds; many a woman still living remembers the words of her mother—"Put the kettle on, Miss White is turning in. She will be tired out, and want to spend the night"; for Ashfield supplied one of the most devoted pillagers of the neighborhood treasuries, and Great-Aunt Hannah White was known and served wherever she went on this mission of endowment.

At first Emily was desperately homesick and thought she should not live. She explained it touchingly by saying, "You see I have such a very dear home." Owing to the long list of applicants Miss Lyon had raised the standards of admission; the examinations were severe and had to be done in a specified time or the unfortunate was sent home. The nervous strain affected Emily with her excitable nature, until she exclaims, "I am sure I could never endure the suspense I endured during those three days again for all the treasure of the world!"

There were three hundred girls, and she found the teachers kind and attentive, the table better than she supposed possible for so many, the atmosphere pleasant and happy. "Things seem more like home than I anticipated," was her feeling, after the first natural strangeness wore off. Each girl was required by the curriculum to do her share of the domestic work, and Emily did not find hers difficult, which was "to carry the knives from the first tier of tables at morning and at noon, and at night to wash and wipe the same quantity of knives." She repeats often that "Miss Lyon and all the teachers try to do all they can for the comfort and happiness of the girls," and she found the girls themselves surprisingly anxious to make each other happy also with "an ease and grace quite unexpected."

She wrote out for her family the following list of her day's occupations, which seems calculated to outwit Satan of idle hours to fill!

> At six o'clock we all rise. We breakfast at 7. Our study hour begins at 8. At 9 we all meet at Seminary Hall for devotions. At 10.15 I recite a review of Ancient History in connection with which we read Goldsmith and Grimshaw. At 11 I recite a lesson on Pope's Essay on Man, which is merely transposition. At 12 I practise calisthenics, and at 12.15 I read until dinner which is at 12.30. After dinner from 1.30 till 2, I sing in Seminary Hall. From 2.45 till 3.45 I practise upon the piano. At 3.45 I go to Sections, where we give all our accounts for the day; including absence, tardiness, communications, breaking silence, study hours, receiving company in our rooms and ten thousand other things which I will not take time to mention.

At half-past four they all went into the Seminary Hall and received advice from Miss Lyon in lecture form. They had supper at six and retired at eight forty-five after a long silent study period. Unless their excuse for failure in any of these things was good and reasonable, they received a black mark, which they very much disliked against their names. Emily's family came to see her and filled her with delight: her brother Austin, then a sophomore at Amherst, causing quite a flutter among the girls and even a young teacher or two, but she counted the days until Thanksgiving, with all the rest.

This first Thanksgiving at home and her drive over the mountain with her brother was momentous to her. She was thrilled by the "first sight of the spire of the venerable meeting-house rising to her delighted vision." It was in the rain and the wind of late November, but never had Amherst looked so lovely to her. All were at the door to welcome her, "from mother, with tears in her eyes, to Pussy—who tried to look as gracious as was becoming her dignity." They went to church and heard their dear Parson Colton, and had dinner and callers, and four invitations out for the evening! Only two could be accepted—to her great sorrow. At seven they all went to a delightful evening at Professor Warner's, and later the young folk went down to the home of another friend, where they played games, had a candy scrape, and enjoyed themselves "until the clock pealed out—Remember ten o'clock, my dear, remember ten o'clock." After they returned, her father wishing to hear the piano, she "like an obedient daughter played and sang a few tunes, to his apparent gratification."

Monday came all too soon to drag her back, but she soon lost herself in her studies again. Silliman's Chemistry and Cutter's Physiology were first-term studies; both of which she found intensely interesting, and with the second term began what was called English composition. In this her work differed from the rest, showing a marked originality from the first. The last half of the year she had also astronomy and rhetoric, completing the Junior studies.

After her return the little minor note, later so characteristic, comes in when she writes her brother she is getting along nicely in her studies and is "happy, quite, for me." She finished her examination in Euclid without a mistake. Always she was counting the weeks—"Only 22 weeks more!" between her and home; imagining them there, missing herself among them. December 11, 1847, she writes to them on her seventeenth birthday, but it was contrary to the rules to allow the pupils to go home during the term, and only nine weeks before her release she was refused by a teacher who seemed stunned by her request to drive the eight miles over the mountain with her brother. Cramped, curbed, repressed in every natural desire or impulse, her youth seems to us, now, responsible for her later almost wilful love of solitude and the habit of repression, but at the time it was a universal condition applying no less to all her young companions who were more stolidly unconscious of any counter-emotions.

But if Thanksgiving was radiant, Christmas was gloom in comparison, and the legend of Emily's insurrection is one of the best in the family archives. It was only a day in advance that Miss Lyon announced, at morning devotions, that Christmas would be recognized as a fast. The girls were not to leave their rooms through long, definite hours and were to meditate to order. After laying down this unseductive programme she added that the school might rise in token of responsive observation. The school did rise—all except Emily and her roommate. The school sat down and Miss Lyon, appalled by such flagrant disregard of the decent required pieties, enlarged upon her programme. At the end of which she added that if there were any so lost to a sense of the meaning of the day as to wish to spend it otherwise, they might stand that the whole school might observe them. And be it said to her eternal glory, of the two terrified objects of her anathema Emily stood alone.

The derelict took the afternoon stage home, causing panic in her family by such a spirit of 1776, but the matter was finally arranged, and she was allowed to be returned, unconvinced and unrepentant.

When one of South Hadley's ardent lovers asked permission in recent years to raise a tablet to her memory there, the question hovered amusingly as to her heresy of youth. It would be interesting to know what Miss Lyon thought of her with her conflicting elements of shyness and fixed certainty of right and wrong, which established her own code regardless of her superior's opinion.

From a mere child Emily had been a newspaper reader, and heard much discussion of politics and world affairs at her father's table. She missed this during her cloistered life with mere femininity, and once in an outburst of smothered intelligence wrote her brother Austin—in mock despair—

> Please tell me who the candidate for President is! I have
> been trying to find out ever since your last visit, and have not
> succeeded. I know no more about the affairs of the outside
> world here than if I were in a trance. Was the Mexican War
> terminated? Is any nation about to besiege South Hadley?

Certainly the term "feminist" was unheard of then, but in this alert young mind there was a latent tendency stirring already toward indignation at being counted as *non compos* in a man's world of reality. A friend who wrote her of meeting Daniel Webster at this time provoked the retort, "You don't know General Briggs, and I do, so you are no better off than I."

In an echo of this same spirit she exclaimed at the end of a letter to Susan Gilbert at Baltimore, the year before her marriage in 1856:

> P.S. Why can't I be a delegate to the great Whig Convention?
> Don't I know all about Daniel Webster and the Tariff and
> the Law? Then, Susie, I could see you during a pause in the
> session, but I don't like this country at all and I shan't stay
> here any longer! *Delenda est* America! Massachusetts and all!

From another letter written later in the same year:

> I count the days. I do long for the time when I can count the
> hours—without incurring the charge of *Femina insania*. I

made up the Latin, dear Susie, for I could not think how it went in Stoddard and Anderson!

But if South Hadley in the forties denied political interest to women, it suppressed any idle amatory inclination with an equally firm hand, though not altogether successfully. The sending of those "foolish notes called Valentines" was forbidden by Miss Lyon under penalty. But according to Emily, she was outwitted by an elaborate system of bribery including the village postmaster, and some hundred and fifty were received in that February of '49 in spite of the prohibitory edict.

In May, owing to a temporary bad cough that terrified her father, Emily was taken home, much against her will, but kept up with her studies and was able to return to South Hadley at the beginning of the summer term. Meantime she was reading every sort of prose and poetry, mentioning as her especial favorites, "Evangeline," "The Princess," "The Maiden Aunt," "The Epicurean," and "The Twins and Heart," by Tupper.

With this exception she was always well, and delighted in nothing more than long wanderings in the woods with her young friends. She knew exactly where the first faint arbutus clung to the grey rock under a protecting bank in Pelham, and the wet, inaccessible spot the rare yellow violets chose as their home in the South Amherst swamp; the columbine and adder's-tongues had their own haunts fixed in her mind, and she could walk straight to the trillium, the bloodroot, even the pink lady's-slipper, as if their homes had street and number. There was no faint frail evidence of the shy New England spring that was not rejoiced over by this flower-sister, hardly less a creature of Nature than they.

After leaving the Seminary for good, in 1848, she reëntered the Amherst Academy: as the wit of the school, becoming humorist of the comic column of a paper edited by the girls of the school, called "Forest Leaves." Her life was stirred by all the mild gaieties of Amherst, the little social ripples which came at long intervals and which she anticipated with the rest. A party at Professor Tyler's, or the rumor of one to come at Professor Hazen's, filled them all with girlish zest, and Commencement always threw the town into a spasm. "Everything will soon be all in a buzz," was her way of expressing the universal premonitory excitement, that caught her like the rest.

One letter hitherto unprinted gives her mood after coming home to stay:

> Sunday—I haven't any paper, dear, but faith continues firm. Presume if I met with my deserts I should receive nothing. Was informed to that effect today by a dear Pastor. What a privilege it is to be so insignificant! Thought of intimating that the Atonement was not needed for such atoms. I think you went on Friday. Sometime is longer than the rest and some is very short. Omit to classify. Friday, Saturday, Sunday! Evenings get longer with the Autumn, that is nothing new. The asters are pretty well. How are the other blossoms? Vinnie and I are pretty well, Carlo comfortable, terrifying man and beast with renewed activity, is cuffed some, hurled from piazza frequently where he has the patent action, as I have long felt. I attended church early in the day. Professor Warner preached; subject Little Drops of Dew. Estey took the stump in the afternoon. Aunt Catherine Sweetser's dress would have startled Sheba. Aunt Bullard was not out, presume she stayed at home for self-examination. Accompanied by Father they visited the grave yard after service. These are stirring scenes! You know the chink your dear face makes. We would not mind the sun dear, if it did not set. How much you cost! I will never sell you for a price of silver. I'll buy you back with red drops when you go away. I'll keep you in a casket. I'll burn you in the garden and keep a bird to watch the spot.

Another little picture of their earliest girlhood remains in her own recording, "Vinnie sits sewing like a fictitious seamstress," and Emily is imagining a Knight at the door for her; they talk of growing old and Emily naïvely adds:

> Vinnie thinks twenty must be a fearful position for one to occupy. I tell her I don't care if I am young or not. I'd as lief be thirty!

Again she gives a domestic interior with a word.

We cleaned house—Mother and Vinnie did—and I scolded because they moved my things. I can't find much I used to wear. You will conceive I am surrounded by trial.

Later that same fall she writes:

The bells are ringing, Susie, North, East and South and your own village bell and the people who love God are expecting to go to meeting; don't you go Susie, not to their meeting, but come with me this morning to the church within our hearts, where the bells are always ringing and the preacher whose name is Love shall intercede for us. They will all go but me—to the usual meeting house, to hear the usual sermon, the inclemency of a storm so kindly detaining me.

But life had other diversions than church-going that first summer after Emily left South Hadley, and even the grim funerals of the remoter branches of the Dickinsons had a silver lining for her guilty satisfaction. One of her most madcap escapades occurred one lovely afternoon when, after being driven decorously to the burial of some unknown kinswoman in old Hadley, Emily ran from the open grave with her favorite cousin, a rather dashing young beau from Worcester—connived at his taking her home the long way round through Sunderland, full seven miles in the wrong direction, via his shining buggy and fast black horse, so fast, in fact, that when her parents and retribution caught up with her, she had capped her infamy by being securely locked in her own room at home. Perhaps today it does not sound so very rash and unforgivable— the gay young cousin, the joy of motion, and the seductive beguilement of the sunshine beneath the lacy elms full of bird-songs may plead for the culprit—but before the eyes of her immediate connections it was a misdemeanor at a scene of decent burial quite beyond imagination, and leading to untoward fears for her future state. She was wept over by her mother and ignored quite conspicuously by her father, who saw doom for her plainly; but her spirit was about as easy to chasten as a dawn. As well correct the bobolink for his madrigal or the meadow grass for bowing in the breeze! And so the incident was closed without much evidence of its instructive value against like dereliction under equally provocative circumstances.

In December she wrote to Sue:

> There is a tall pale snowstorm stalking through the fields and
> bowing at my window. I shan't let the fellow in! Went to
> church today in second best and boots, sermon from Dr. D.
> on unbelief. "Another Esau." Sermons on unbelief ever did
> attract me.

Her shyness, her shrinking from anything she could not explain or
reason with, comes out in her droll description of going to church alone
when her family were called to an obliging funeral which gave her a day
of rare liberty. She says she went in circles puzzling Euclid:

> When I reached the steps I smiled to think of my geometry
> during the journey—how big and broad the aisle looked,—
> full huge enough before,—as I quaked along up and reached
> my usual seat. There I sat and sighed and wondered I was so
> scared, for surely there was nothing I need fear in the whole
> world,—yet there the phantom was, though I kept resolving
> to be brave as Turks and bold as Polar bears, it would not
> help me any. After the opening prayer I ventured to look
> around. Mr. Carter immediately looked at me. Mr. Sweetser
> attempted to do so, but I discovered Nothing, up in the
> sky somewhere, and gazed intensely at it for quite a half an
> hour—
>
> How I did wish for you or Vinnie and Goliath or
> Sampson to pull the whole church down—requesting Dr. D.
> to step into Miss K.'s until the worst was past. Professor
> Aaron Warner—Professor of Rhetoric in Amherst College—
> preached this afternoon. I shall be disappointed if Horace
> Walpole does not address us this evening. If you stay away
> another Sabbath the Secretary of War will take charge of the
> Sabbath School. The singing reminded me of the legend of
> Jack and Jill allowing the bass viol to be typified by Jill, who
> literally tumbled after, while Jack, i.e., the Choir, galloped
> insanely on.

She never went back to South Hadley, for although the cough of
the winter before had entirely succumbed under the merciless family

dosing, her father decided to keep her at home for a year under his own supervision. Already he must have been aware of her brilliant intellect and the powers of her imagination extraordinarily evidenced in all she said or did. As yet there was no hint of her later reclusive tendency, and she sent her young friends off into fits of laughter over her impromptu stories, while her familiarity with the Bible gave her an ease at apt quotation appalling to her elders in its secular application—and jocular yet never of irreverent intent. One who loved her said of her, "Physically timid at the least approach to a crisis in the day's event, her mind dared earth and heaven. That apocrypha and apocalypse met in her explains her tendency so often mistaken for blasphemy by the superficial analyst."

Whatever her docile mother thought about this most unique offspring, whatever her observant father hoped from his older daughter, it was summed up in silence by his decision that Emily should remain at home.

The next years of her life were accordingly passed like those of the other young people of Amherst in the forties, as far as the external went. On what strange adventures she was already led by the wings and fins of her soaring and diving mind even she could not and would not have told.

IV

SOCIAL LIFE AT AMHERST SEVENTY YEARS AGO

1848—1853–54

There could have been little in the social life of Amherst seventy years ago to thrill a being like Emily Dickinson. Yet from eighteen to twenty-three she was a social creature in the highest sense, though she complains of often wearying of their house crowded daily with rich and poor, high and low, who came—and so rarely went—as a matter of course, without any warning or invitation, after the manner of that hospitable period, when gig or chariot might turn in at the great gate at any hour, depositing guests for a meal or the night or a long visit as it might happen. One of her contemporaries has left, in what Colonel Higginson once called "the portfolio literature of New England," a sketch of it all which gives, even with the most glowing intention, a rather scanty and very restricted story, lit by a solitary lantern here and there.

There were for Emily the elementals of all girlhood, of course. She evinces interest in her clothes, speaks of new ones in which she presumes she shall appear like an embarrassed peacock; complains of her brother Austin who returns from a trip to Baltimore to see her beloved Susie, as follows:

> Asked what you wore and how your hair was fixed and what you said of me—his answers were quite limited. "You looked as you always did" . . . Vinnie enquired with promptness if you wore a basque—"No, you had on a black thing." Dear, you must train him, 'twill take many moons in the fashion plates before he will respect and speak with proper deference of this majestic garment.

There were the inevitable, inescapable family visits, too, already mentioned, when any hour of any day might behold a chaise at the door and helplessness within the house before the impending calamity. On one occasion when a family of four descended upon them without warning, Emily expressed her feelings as to the sweetness of the young daughters, and the tediousness of their father, concluding:

> Cousin P. says he might stay round a month visiting old acquaintances if it wasn't for his business. Fortunate indeed for us that his business feels the need of him or I think he would never go. He is a kind of mixture of Deacon Haskell, Calvin Merill, and Morton Dickinson; you can easily guess how much we enjoy his society.

It was one autumn evening, when the Hollands had driven over unexpectedly to pass the night, that her mother, anxious for their every comfort, offered one solicitous suggestion after another, until Emily, always exasperated by repetition, cried—"O Mrs. Holland, don't you want to hear me say the Lord's prayer? Shouldn't you like me to repeat the Declaration of Independence? Shan't I recite the Ten Commandments?"

She had a cousin who came over from Sunderland to spend a day—"Father and Mother being on a little journey"—when just such deviations from regularity were apt to occur. Her friend Vaughn Evans, the Southerner who brought a warmer note into her life, stayed on after Commencement, and they had many long talks; and the brilliant young Henry Root—an uncle of the present President of Johns Hopkins University—whose charm and handsome grace was a fable that followed him down the century, came to see her often. She says it was to hear Susie's letters, and insists, she admires him, but lets him come only to give him this pleasure. It was at this point in her life that she began to be called down to entertain callers, and she confesses she went with sorry grace. In the July of 1851 she heard Jenny Lind sing at Northampton and cared more for her than her voice or manner of singing.

Before Emily ceased to mingle with the other young people, she shared the lectures upon which the village throve. The professors all gave of their best; John Lord, who was considered a wizard of style and manner, persuaded to any conclusion by his perennial charm; and Richard Dana, father of the poet Dana, and even wise men from Europe occasionally appeared. It was one of the pleasant pastimes of the young ladies of that day to attend, escorted by some attractive Senior, before whose class they were always given, the walk and escort often blurring in the young brains the cloudy values of information.

The sketch of "Society in Amherst Sixty Years Ago," to which allusion has been made, was written for the family remembrance by her sister-in-law, just before her own death in 1913. In this, there are many quaint illuminations of the life Emily Dickinson shared with the rest. From it we learn:

> The social life at Amherst in those early days was no less unique in grace and simplicity than that of Northampton, though differing always in certain social habits held contraband by piety and conscience in Amherst. The harmless cards and dancing common there were not even so much as mentioned at Amherst as suitable or even possible occupations for immortal beings, until a quite recent date. Yet sixty years ago, dear moderns, one could have discovered in the small circle of Amherst as beautiful girls, or "young ladies," as they were then called, as ever graced any drawing room. There were as accomplished and well poised matrons, as chivalric young men,—nay, men both old and young, as full of high purpose and generous achievement as could be found in any town, university or commercial.

Under President Humphrey and also under President Hitchcock, Amherst College and Amherst were one. The village, being smaller then, was fully represented at all the college levees, as the receptions were then called, and entered warmly into all college affairs, lectures, and literary occasions. Emily must have played "blind-man's buff" with the rest, in the first President's house, where the high mantel in the kitchen was the rather perilous retreat of the taller boys, since they were safe there from the nervous clutches of the girls, when, aware of great shrinkage in numbers, they pulled up their blinders to bring the culprits down to justice. The Senior Levee given by the President to the graduating class was the event of the year; occurring in August at the close of the term. To this Emily went with all friends of the Senior Class, and all the village beside, and was one of those strolling couples, no doubt, that, wishing to escape ostensibly the modest glare of the astral lamp within, wandered up and down the rural sidewalks in front of the house.

The sketch referred to goes on in more sprightly fashion:

There was never dancing, never vaudeville. I confess
there were flirtations, whatever that was—in odd corners,
especially under the stairs in the front hall, where a Puritan-
backed sofa covered in horsehair, guiltless of cushions, was
converted into a rather stiff Arcadia. There was music
always, with the piano—Miss Jane Gridley, daughter
of the notable Dr. Gridley, the medical genius of the
region, sang in a strikingly clear voice with a really artistic
rendering "Oh, Summer Night!" And in effective contrast
to her metropolitan culture and ease the sweet winsome
"Oh, Wert Thou in the Cauld Blast," would follow, sung by
Emily Fowler, granddaughter of Noah Webster, afterward
Mrs. Gordon L. Ford, of Brooklyn, a wizard in person
and power. There was the diversion of refreshments, with
a refreshment-table, as it was called then, and President
Hitchcock being strongly and frankly in favour of early hours,
only intruders lingered after ten o'clock at his parties; though
with unaffected hospitality the gentle host appeared to ignore
the late mad hour as it approached.

Weeks before this climax of the year the young ladies were
in a modest agitation over it; arranging becoming gowns with
charming refinement and economy. As the Summer was so
nearly over, to these same young ladies at least, there was a
sort of collapse after the party and a little feeling of gloom in
the earlier drawing in of evening with the sad-voiced crickets,
and a rather pensive waiting for the return of the students.
But never was the slightest utterance given to that effect,
lest maiden modesty blush for such dependence upon these
fascinating comrades. For many years the dress that satisfied
feminine vanity was of the simplest. Soft merino dresses
of gentle shades were worn entirely for all ordinary visiting,
black silk for stately occasions of the elders. In Summer the
young ladies wore sprigged muslins, not too prudish as to
cut at the throat. As the season grew chilly, sashes of scarlet
ribbon were added, with knots of red berries festooned on the
shoulders and drooping gracefully from the hair. Often quite
heavy wreaths of myrtle leaves were bound about the head,
giving a classic touch, as of filleted martyrs or Parnassian
victims! No one smiled over the simplicity of these toilets

or coveted richer or more elaborate effects. The girls were so pretty and winsome they dominated externals. During the visit of some world-famous *savants* from Europe, the stony-hearted scientists became enthusiastic over the unusual number of beautiful and attractive girls they met there.

President Stearns's family were all intimately friendly with the Dickinson family and their entertaining was less general, a little more stately, than their predecessors'. With their administration came a touch of the worldly in the general appearance of the president's house, always so plain and simple before. Rich odd cabinets, carved chairs and treasures sent home from a son in India, as well as inherited silver of aristocratic pattern, lent an air of elegance agreeable and suitable. Quoting again:

> There was little social variety sixty years ago; never dinners, a rare evening party perhaps, and sometimes the small friendly suppers, or tea parties. The parlors of Deacon Luke Sweetser set the standard of elegance and struck the grand note in these affairs. There was more light, more inherited silver, a certain pomposity on the part of the hostess, who always received in purple gloves, and with a long dipping backward curtsy, a relic of her gay education at boarding school. She waved aloft a feather fan sent her from a thousand miles up the Nile by a missionary friend, and after supper Syrian relics were handed about, musky curios of Arab and Greek,— lentils, from the Holy Land, husks,—"such-as-the-swine- did-eat,"—inlaid coffee cups, attar of rose bottles, sent home by their niece the wife of the Rev. Daniel Bliss, founder of the Protestant College at Beyrut, Syria. Later came music, Lavinia Dickinson singing "Are we almost there? said the dying girl," "Coming Through the Rye,"—and a local Basso of a profundity beyond all known musical necessity after prolonged urging giving "Rocked in the Cradle of the Deep," with such sustained power that the glasses tinkled in the cupboard from the jar. Later everybody sang "America" and "Auld Lang Syne," and all in a glow the party broke up with the host standing at the top of the stone steps holding an oil lantern in the air for his guests' safety,—at that time the only beacon in Amherst.

The diversions of these days were pallid and calm, leading almost inevitably back to the religious activities of the church. There was an occasional lecture, there were the Wednesday evening prayer meetings, and the Sewing Society once a fortnight, clergyman and husbands coming in for tea. In mid-winter there were usually six weeks of protracted meetings. The picture deepens while one reads on:

> As the snow lay two or three feet deep on the level those wintry days, Amherst with no street lights, no trolleys, no railroads, telephone and movie undreamed of, seemed to my perverse young mind, animal spirits and vigorous happiness, a staring, lonely, hopeless place,—enough to make angels homesick. The lugubrious sound of the church bell still rings in my winter dreams.

Emily always declared she was sure the Baptist bell would ring in the Day of Judgment, and more and more she turned to the warmth of her home within, and the little conservatory where her ferns and yellow jasmine and purple heliotrope made an atmosphere more tropical for the dwelling of her imagination. The scent of her cape jasmines and daphne odora is forever immortalized to those who breathed it, transporting them back to the loveliness of her immortal atmosphere.

The Tyler home was another one distinguished for unstinted hospitality. The stranger, the foreigner, rich and poor were welcomed there; missionaries, statesmen, scholars, and when Charles Sumner was in Amherst he found with them the only welcome afforded an abolitionist—for the aristocratic salvation of the Nation, as it was then held, lay in the choice of the old Whig Party. How slowly they yielded, those handsome stubborn gentlemen in velvet collars and beaver hats, to the emancipating chariots of the God of battle and Abraham Lincoln!

But even in these repressed lives stolen pleasures were sweet, and it is a relief to be told that

> Emily Fowler had what she called P.O.M. meetings at her house, impromptu dances,—if our floundering attempts to get through a Virginia Reel, or Lancers could be called that— to the sharp voice of an attenuated piano! It was great fun and seemed real,—beside it was contraband. Just across the Connecticut river good people played cards and loved God,

while this side such recreation was wicked as Juggernaut or idols! For secrecy's sake, the name "Poetry of Motion meetings," to be sure. Once only were they surreptitiously invited to gather at the home of the dignified pair who were to be away for the night, and would therefore remain in blest ignorance of this departure on the part of their young people, Emily and Austin, from the moral code of those days. All went merry as a marriage bell. The revellers danced late and with quite an abandon. But trifles light as air are time proven betrayers,—the slight scarlet thread of Jezebel, Newton's apple, Fulton's tea-kettle, "Great oaks from little acorns grow!" It was the lion's tail on the hearth rug in the parlor of this strict home that convulsed domesticity for twenty-four hours and led to discovery at last. Taken up to relieve the dancing toes from clumsy entanglement in the fringe, it was put back in the flurry of righting up in the morning before the parents' return, regardless of the lion's anatomy and jungle grace. He was a big brown fellow set off by a vague green background of some appropriate sort. The silly half-frightened young folk had replaced him, but completely reversed, so that his majestic tail was turned up where it should have turned down, and all his members were topsy-turvy accordingly! Only too soon after the return the maternal shriek,—"Why, girls, girls! What has happened? The lion's tail is upside down!" proved the forerunner of a little private judgment day. But eventually the mother was "managed" and recommended "not to trouble Father with it"!

One can hardly realize at the present time the importance of the two great events of the year in Amherst mid-century. These were, of course, Commencement Day and the annual Cattle Show in October. Both took place all over the Village Green.

Cattle Show was an affair of bucolic sweetness and simplicity, which Emily loved afar; especially the strains of military music on the air, at intervals. It was begun with an address by some distinguished person, and this was followed by a prayer of thanks for the ingathering of the crops. The procession then formed at the Amherst House, an inspiring band leading the way, while mounted escorts, with a military hint in dress and style, cavorted hither and thither. The ploughing match was of intense interest, held just west of the church on the Hadley road. Draft matches were held on the west side of the green or common. The exhibition of horses included the entire space of the common and down the Main Street. Deacon Luke Sweetser, Seth Nims, and Emily's father, Squire Dickinson, were invariably owners of fine horses, and they drove about on these occasions sitting very straight in the backless open buggies, reins taut, and the high showy heads of their steeds refusing the senseless check. People turned to look after them—and in these latter days one might not irreverently exclaim, "Where are the horsemen and the chariots thereof?"

From early morning on Commencement Day, the common was the camping-ground for fakirs' tents, peddlers' carts, every imaginable sort of vendor, and most delightful of all girls and boys in the Sunday best from Shutesbury and Pelham and all the region about, hand in hand, with arms entwined, enjoying the outdoors part of the show, and the wonderful if to them meaningless array in the old village church. Everybody was there—wonderful young men declaiming even more wonderful pieces on the big stage, where all the Trustees in stiff collars and stiffer dignity were sitting with other important men of the Valley, listening to the eloquence displayed and sizing up the orthodoxy. The most conspicuous places always were deferentially reserved for the returned missionaries, those idolized sons of the college, for whose sacred and brave ideals the institution was prayed into being.

Edward Dickinson, with his Trustee tea party, held on the Wednesday night of Commencement Week for forty years, was too pronounced a feature of those days to be forgotten or omitted. Friends were received all over the house and grounds from six to eight. A supper was handed about with most remarkable tea and coffee. Here one could always find Governors and Judges, interesting missionaries, famous professors from our best colleges, editors of high repute, fair women and brave men. This became such a time-honored affair that one was often heard to say in the hurried good comradeship of the week, "Oh, I will see you again at the Dickinson tea party."

The social functions of Commencement Week today seem rather lacking in high effect as one recalls how the Governor and his staff in uniform, with spurs clanking, blended and contrasted with the sombre black all about the piazzas and under the old pines of three generations' growth. Governor Banks was said to be the handsomest, most martial of them all. Governor Bullock was another memorable figure, with high fine bearing, rather stiffly elegant, and always complete *suaviter in modo*, as he quoted his classics on any small mellow justification. Later on in her life Emily Dickinson forsook her usual seclusion at these times, and radiant as a flying spirit, diaphanously dressed in white, always with a flower in her hand, measured her wit and poured her wine amid much excitement and applause from those fortunate enough to get near her.

V

"THE END OF PEACE"

1853–55

While Emily was passing through the first quiet years between her school days and her momentous visit to Washington and Philadelphia, there were passages in several letters from her which revealed something of her inner experience.

It was just before her twentieth birthday that she wrote:

> You and I have been strangely silent upon one topic, Susie. We have often touched upon it and as quickly fled away,— as children shut their eyes when the sun is too bright for them. I have always hoped to know if you had no dear fancy illumining all your life, no one of whom you murmured in the faithful ear of night, and at whose side you walked in fancy the livelong day. How dull *our* lives must seem to the bride and the plighted maiden,—whose days are fed with gold and who gather pearls of evening,—but to the wife, Susie,—sometimes the wife forgotten,—our lives perhaps seem dearer than all others in the world. You have seen flowers at morning satisfied with dew, and these same sweet blossoms at noon with their heads bowed in anguish before the mighty sun,—think you that thirsty blossoms will need nought but dew? No, they will cry for light and pine for the burning noon, though it scorches them, scathes them; they have got through with peace. They know that the sun of noon is mightier than the morning and their life is henceforth for him. Oh, Susie, it is dangerous and it is all too dear,—those simple trusting spirits and the spirits mightier we cannot resist! It does so rend me, the thought of it,—when it comes, that I tremble lest at sometime I too am yielded up. You will forgive my amatory strain,—it has been a very long one.

She writes again in fun, with a touch of the same foreboding, however, "I miss the grasshoppers much—but suppose it is all for the best—I should become too much attached to a trotting world," betraying a poignant certainty of her own stifled capacity for life that persists like an organ note held down, torturing the silence with its insistence. Even from extreme youth her unconscious philosophy seems to have been one of renunciation before the temptation was presented; the fear of loving what she could not have driving her to self-imposed abnegations. As if she knew by intuition all the possible devastation of love as well as all the loneliness without it—she seems to have fled within herself like an eremite to his altar. A premonition of the beauty and mystery and power of living seems to have grappled with her—another angel wrestler without face or familiarity—and all but worsted her, before she was confronted by her own actual ordeal.

Every fatal possibility seems to have hovered about her, every small day been big with monstrous approachings. Her intimate letters at this time, too sacred for revealing, show her as one who fled from a suspected wonder lest seeing it she faint to possess it and be lost. She knew and trembled for her own guess at life—was loath to admit it, lest failing it she lose hold on all there was left. She put so much of her own supernatural imagination into a person or event or just the ordinary weather, that few if any other minds could have conceived the voltage of her impressions or reactions. To her the death of some nameless neighbor opened an abyss of conjecture; a sudden fire, though it might be only a small shed burning behind a yellow barn, set the elements loose and sent her off into the Book of Revelation and the Day of Judgment. A perfidy always distracted her, whether national or private—disloyalty she could never conceive or admit. As with Keats her "angel nerves" were ill adapted for any higher vibrations than the old house afforded with its safe routine, quite electric enough for her sensitive transmission.

Always, when a circus was to pass her window in the first grey dawn on its hooded way from town to town, she sat up all night to watch for it, thrilled by its wild vagrancy, its pathos, its utter sophistication: hungry for sensation, starving for a world she later shunned, with a vague dread of its haunting power over her. Characteristic of her shy hidden self is her explanation:

> *If the archangels veil their faces—*
> *Sacred diffidence my own attitude.*

And again:

> Perhaps there is never quite the sorcery that it is to surmise—
> though the obligation to enchantment is always binding.

So the years following her South Hadley experiences passed externally uneventful, until in 1853 Emily spent a winter in Washington with her father, who was in Congress for two terms to serve a special cause, and not from personal political ambition. He took his family and they stayed at Willard's, where Emily was at once recognized as unique by men much her senior. Her father had misgivings as to her being willing to go, as already she shrank peculiarly from being away from home, but his wish seems to have inspired her. There are many tales of her repartee still remembered.

She is said to have astonished some of her father's friends by her insight into men and affairs, and created quite a sensation by her wit. One story of her, handed down in the family, was of her asking a prim old Chief Justice of the Supremest sort, when the plum pudding on fire was offered—"Oh, Sir, may one eat of hell fire with impunity here?" To Susan at home she writes, "Would you rather I would write you what I am doing here, or whom I am loving there?"

She was charmed by the sweet softness of the spring, soft as summer there—the darling maple trees in bloom and grass green in sunny places—and could hardly realize it was winter still at home. It makes the grass spring in her heart, she writes, and the linnet sing to know that one she loves is coming there, and for one look of this friend she would give all the pomp, the court, the etiquette of the world. She becomes perversely fixed in her own notion that those who are of the earth will not enter heaven. The jostle and turmoil and scramble confuse her. She met many people, and after the fashion of the day walked a long time up and down in the hall of the hotel with some of them in the evenings. She was excused from some of the gaiety on the plea of fatigue, but at that was far gayer than she had ever been before in her life. Her passivity to her father's wish comes out in a postscript to the effect:

> We think we shall go to Philadelphia next week, though
> Father has not decided. Eliza writes everyday and seems
> impatient to have us. I don't know how long we shall stay
> there or in New York. Father has not said.

It was on a visit to this same Eliza, in Philadelphia, that Emily met the fate she had instinctively shunned. Even now, after the many slow years she has been removed from us in the body, her spirit hinders the baring of that chapter in her life which has been so universally misunderstood, so stupidly if not wantonly misrepresented. All that ever was told was a confidence to her Sister Sue, sacredly guarded under all provocation till death united them—the confiding and the listening—in one abiding silence.

Certainly in that first witchery of an undreamed Southern springtime Emily was overtaken—doomed once and forever by her own heart. It was instantaneous, overwhelming, impossible. There is no doubt that two predestined souls were kept apart only by her high sense of duty, and the necessity for preserving love untarnished by the inevitable destruction of another woman's life.

Without stopping to look back, she fled to her own home for refuge—as a wild thing running from whatever it may be that pursues; but only a few days later Sister Sue looked up from her sewing to see Lavinia, pallid and breathless from running, who grasped her wrist with hurrying hand, urging: "Sue, come! That man is here!—Father and Mother are away, and I am afraid Emily will go away with him!" But the one word he implored, Emily would not say. Unable to endure his life under the old conditions, after a short time he left his profession and home and silently withdrew with his wife and an only child to a remote city, a continent's width remote, where echo at least could not mock him with its vain outcry: dying prematurely, the spell unbroken.

And Emily went on alone in the old house under the pines. On the wall of her own room hung a picture in a heavy oval frame of gold—unexplained. That was all, to the visible score. Only once is there any evidence of her breaking a silence like that of dead lips, when she inexplicably urges a friend to name a new little son by the name never like any other to her ears. And a little later she ends a note to the same mother, "Love for the child of the bravest name alive." Always afterward she called him so, whether the family adopted the suggestion or not, finding a strange little comfort, perhaps, in the mere naming of the name.

From this time on she clung more intensely to the tender shadows of her father's house. She still saw her friends and neighbors from time to time, but even then her life had begun to go on in hidden ways. "I am not at home," she often said; or, "When I was at home"—and only one faithful heart understood that love to her had been home for an instant, and that she lived in its remembrance, while her little form flitted tranquil through the sunny small industries of her day, until night gave her the right to watch with her flowers and liberated fancies. The dead of night and the closed door were ever to her synonyms of release.

Her father never opposed her slightest preference, and there was never the least recognition in the family of any lasting effect from the much-envied fatal sally into the great world beyond the purple rim of the home horizon. Whatever may in after years have been supposed or surmised was but the idle gossip of any country village provoked by any woman unmarried—especially a gifted girl like Emily Dickinson, whose family were so warmly included in all the society of her time. It was spoken of her father that to him compromise was disloyalty. One of her own sentences sums it all up for his daughter, "Alleviation of the irreparable degrades it." She was as truly a nun as any vowed celibate, but the altar she served was veiled from every eye save that of God.

Her becalmed days in the years immediately following found their best understanding and comfort in her brother's home across the lawn. To her Sister Sue she writes at this time:

> I rise because the sun shines and sleep has done with me. I brush my hair and dress and wonder what I am and who made me so,—and then I help wash the breakfast cups, and— anon wash them again, and then 'tis afternoon and ladies call,—and evening and some members of another line come in to spend the hours, and then the day is done. And prithee what is life? The supper of the heart is when the guest is gone!

Another scrap at the same date runs:

> The definition of beauty is that definition is none; of heaven easier, since heaven and He are One.

Again:

> Susan—We both are women and there is a Will of God.
>   Could the dying confide Death, there would be no dead.
>   Wedlock is shyer than death.
>   Thank you for tenderness.

And during her first ecstasy of renunciation:

> *Title divine is mine*
> *The Wife without*
> *The Sign.*
> *Acute degree*
> *Conferred on me—*
> *Empress of Calvary.*
> *Royal, all but the*
> *Crown—*
> *Betrothed, without the Swoon*
> *God gives us Women*
> *When two hold*
> *Garnet to garnet,*
> *Gold to gold—*
> *Born—Bridalled—*
> *Shrouded—*
> *In a day*
> *Tri-Victory—*
> *"My Husband"*
> *Women say*
> *Stroking the melody.*
> *Is this the way?*

EMILY

In her own words, Emily had "got through with peace."

And since there is no portrait of her, except one made from her child face in the group mentioned, and another of extreme youth rather too freely restored to give much idea of her, perhaps it would not be amiss to quote the likeness in words from the preface to the volume of her verse called "The Single Hound":

It has been told often of her that she wore white exclusively. She had said herself in one of her letters to an inquisitive friend who had never yet seen her and importuned for a hint of her outward self,—that her eyes were the color of the sherry left in the glass by him to whom she wrote. Her hair was of that same warm bronze-chestnut hue that Titian immortalized, and she wore it parted on her brow and low in her neck, but always half covered by a velvet snood of the same tint,—such as the Venetian painters loved to add as a final grace to their portraits of their most beloved and beautiful women. Her cheek was like the petal of the jasmine, a velvety white never touched by a hint of color. Her red lips parted over regular little teeth like a squirrel's, and it was the rather long upper lip that gave to the mouth its asceticism and betrayed the monastic tendency in her, that austerity of the senses of which she was probably quite unaware. If this combines nature and art and mysticism in one, too bewilderingly to reproduce any definite impression, it is the fault of that face—as animate in memory as it is still in dreams.

She had a dramatic way of throwing up her hands at the climax of a story, or one of her own flashes. It was entirely spontaneous, her spirit seemed merely playing through her body as the aurora borealis through the darkness of a Summer night.

Fascination was her element. She was not daily bread, she was star dust. Her solitude made her and was part of her.

VI

"A HEDGE AWAY"

1856–62

E mily's only brother, Austin, was married on July 1, 1856, and from that time she was part of every incident in his household. Her first little note to his wife, with which "The Single Hound" is prefaced, expressed her feeling perfectly:

> *One sister have I in our house*
> *And one a hedge away—*
> *There's only one recorded*
> *But both belong to me.*

In the years following that crucial visit to Washington and Philadelphia, her life moved on without external change, except that she imperceptibly but increasingly withdrew from outside festivities and public appearances and became less accessible to all save her chosen few. But her brother's marriage brought a thrilling new element into her life, and she continued to flit across the intervening lawns behind the bulwark of high hemlock hedges long after all other visits had definitely ceased. The narrow path "just wide enough for two who love" ran luringly between, whether her light flashed across the snow to them under a polar moon, while she sat up to watch over her flowers and keep them from freezing, or past the rosebushes of a midsummer, where the moths were at their amorous trafficking.

Emily's own conservatory was like fairyland at all seasons, especially in comparison with the dreary white winter cold outside. It opened from the dining-room, a tiny glass room, with white shelves running around it on which were grouped the loveliest ferns, rich purple heliotrope, the yellow jasmine, and one giant Daphne odora with its orange-bloom scent astray from the Riviera, and two majestic cape jasmines, exotics kin to her alien soul. She tolerated none of the usual variety of mongrel house plants. A rare scarlet lily, a resurrection calla, perhaps—and here it was always summer with the oxalis dripping from hanging baskets like humble incense upon the heads of the household and its frequenters.

When her brother's first son was born, named for his grandfather, her flying little greeting to him—delivered at her sister's pillow—was:

Is it true, dear Sue?
Are there Two?
I shouldn't like to come
For fear of joggling Him!
If you could shut him up
In a coffee cup,
Or tie Him to a pin
Till I got in,
Or make Him fast
To Pussy's fist,
Hist! Whist!
I'd come!

—EMILY

Later, with her little niece, and the golden-haired arch-darling of both houses—the transitory child, Gilbert, who only came and flashed a mere eight years and went on—Emily was just another child like them, only endowed with subtle powers of the high gods to produce unexpected rewards and avert disastrous consequences. No treat could be offered anyone of the three like that of being left in her care while the grown-up family wandered. As they grew older, she made companions of them, talked to them as equals, trusted them with her choicest interests. To them her increasing solitude never seemed strange; love gave them understanding. Had she worn wings instead of her simple white frocks, they would have taken it quite for granted.

Until she was obliged to go to Boston for treatment of her eyes in 1864 and again in 1865 the events in Emily's life were counted as with Shakespeare's clock—"by heart-throbs, not by hours."

As her brother's family grew up, she accepted them one by one, an individual relation existing between each of the three and her fairy self. When her little niece began her first attempts to write her own fancies in verse, Emily's response came quickly back, "I was surprised, but why? Is she not of the lineage of the spirit?" She always alluded to the youngest son, Gilbert, as "Thy Son, our Nephew." As she put the world further from her their triple alliance increased in intimacy. She hailed them as treading where she dared not venture, bade them come back and tell her their adventures, was curious about their thoughts and tiny events which gave her escape from her own limited environment, which she loved, yet endured.

Though she dwelt only "a hedge away" from their home, she had the habit of sending her constant thought to them in her tiny notes as other people would have spoken them. The gambol of her mind on paper was her pastime. Sometimes her mood was one of sheer extravaganza—like this:

Friday Noon

Dear Friend

I regret to inform you that at three o'clock yesterday my mind came to a stand, and has since then been stationary Ere this intelligence reaches you I shall probably be a snail. By this untoward Providence a mental and moral being has been swept ruthlessly from her sphere. But we should not repine—"God moves in a mysterious way his wonders to perform," and if it be his will that I become a bear and bite my fellow men, it will be for the highest good of this fallen and famishing world. If the gentleman in the air will please stop throwing snowballs, I may meet you again. Otherwise it is uncertain. My parents are pretty well. General Wolf is here. We are looking for Major Pitcairn in the afternoon stage. We were much afflicted yesterday by the supposed removal of our cat from time to eternity. She returned however last evening, having been detained by the storm beyond her expectations.

We need some paths up our way, shan't you be out with the team?

Yours till death
Isaiah

The stately old barn was an equine palatial structure, sheltering horses, cows, pigs, hens, and pigeons, with wings for musty carriage houses, and leaning ramparts of loft where swallows darted and doves eternally gurgled. The animal traffic out there had a charm for Emily, and her wit often pranked with its daily round. Wanting her nephew once to the rescue she sends this:

NED
Dennis was happy tonight and it made him graceful. I saw him waltzing with the cow and suspected his status. You told me he had not tasted liquor since his wife's decease— then she must have been alive at six this evening. I fear for the rectitude of the barn. Love for the Police.

EMILY

Her Christmas offering of iced plum cake and candy was once sent in the afternoon and with it this apology:

SISTER
Please excuse Santa Claus for calling so early, but gentlemen 1882 years old are a little fearful of the evening air.

And in the early days of the very last spring of her life, to Gib the characteristic lines:

Not at home to callers
Says the naked tree—
Jacket due in April.
Wishing you good day.

There are still endless little notes sent in every possible phase of her mood. Comments on books she read, cries of the heart, dashes of wit; and when her habit of writing became confirmed, poems for suggestion, or criticism. From the time Emily had taken the dare of thirty, that "frightful age" spoken of with bated breath in their teens by her sister Lavinia, the notes were often those same poems afterward published, sent either as an expression of an emotion she wished to share, or with a request for criticism.

In an article upon her unpublished letters to her brother's family, which appeared in the "Atlantic Monthly," it has been told of her that these notes

contained numberless phrases of universal truth, written though they were by this shy recluse in her retired New

England home, intrenched by lilacs and guarded by bumble bees. . . She had her finger on the pulse of events and noted phenomena unerringly, with her own comment. Whenever stirred, by whatever cause, she trapped her mood, then waited for her messenger, as vigilant as any spider. . . Emily Dickinson differed from all the women letter-writers of France and England in her scorn of detail, scarcely hitting the paper long enough to make her communication intelligible.

The following brief note is quoted from the same source:

> *Opinion is a flitting thing*
> *But truth outlasts the sun,*
> *If then we cannot own them both,*
> *Possess the oldest one.*

And this one:

> *When we have ceased to crave*
> *The gift is given*
> *For which we gave the earth*
> *And mortgaged heaven,*
> *But so declined in worth—*
> *'Tis ignominy now to look upon.*

Life had for her an infinite and increasing fascination. "Are you sure we are making the most of it?" she wrote on a slip of paper and sent over by hand just because she was quick with the thrill of another day. Again she sent the following:

Dear Sue
    A fresh morning of life and its impregnable chances and the dew for you!

Emily

Other quotations from the same articles show her response to every appeal.

To the faithful absence is condensed presence. To the others,— but there are no others.

So busy missing you I have not tasted Spring. Should there be other Aprils we will perhaps dine.

I must wait a few days before seeing you. You are too momentous,— but remember dear, it is idolatry, not indifference.

Her notes to the three children were their keen delight, and preserved by them beyond all their other treasures. No one but their Aunt Emily could have written, "Emily knows a man who drives a coach like a thimble and turns the wheel all day with his heel. His name is Bumble Bee!" At the close of a letter to her older nephew away on a visit as a child, she writes:

DEAR NED-BIRD
 It will be good to hear you again. Not a voice in the woods is so sweet as yours. The robbins have gone, all but a few infirm ones,—and the Cricket and I keep house for the frost. Goodnight little brother. I would love to stay longer. Vinnie and Grandma and Maggie all give their love. Pussy her striped respects.
Ned's most little AUNT EMILY

When sending him a tiny pie:

DEAR NED:
 You know that pie you stole? Well, this is that pie's brother. Mother told me when I was a boy, that I must turn over a new leaf. I call that the foliage admonition. Shall I commend it to you?
EMILY

On the birthday of her little niece she sends a knot of her choicest flowers and this word of greeting—

DEAR MATTIE
 I am glad it is your birthday. It is this little bouquet's birthday too. Its Father is a very old man by the name of Nature, whom you never saw. Be sure to live in vain, dear. I wish I had.
EMILY

The following chronicle came to Gilbert's mother after the rescue of a favorite cat by his Aunt Lavinia:

Memoirs of little boys that Live

"Weren't you chasing Pussy?" said Vinnie to Gilbert.
  "No, she was chasing herself."
  "But wasn't she running pretty fast?"
  "Well, some fast and some slow," said the beguiling villain. Pussy's Nemesis quailed. Talk of hoary reprobates! Your urchin is more antique in wiles than the Egyptian sphinx. Have you noticed Granville's letter to Lowell? "Her Majesty has contemplated you, and reserved her decision."

It was, as Colonel Higginson once observed later on, a pretty rarefied atmosphere for children, but they regarded their Aunt Emily as a magical creature, and were brought up on her stabbing wit, her condensed forms and subtle epigram, and felt a lively contempt for people who said they could not understand her when their mother sometimes read out sentences or poems of hers to the curious who begged to hear something she had written. They felt she was always on their side, a nimble as well as a loving ally. She never dulled their sunshine with grown-up apprehensions for their good, or hindered their imagination, but rather flew before, like Aurora, straight out into the ether of the impossible, as dear to her as to them.

The following she sent to Ned after some reputed indiscretion reported of him by harder hearts:

> *The cat that in the corner sits*
> *Her martial time forgot—*
> *The rat but a tradition now*
> *Of her desireless lot,*
> *Another class reminds me of—*
> *Who neither please nor play,*
> *But—"not to make a bit of noise"*
> *Adjure each little boy!*

P.S. Grandma characteristically hopes Neddy will be a good boy. Obtuse ambition of Grandma's!

EMILY

On returning a photograph of a child in Greenaway costume:

That is the little girl I meant to be and wasn't; the very hat I meant to wear and didn't.

One verse she sent them that particularly hit their fancy was:

> *That butterfly in honoured dust*
> *Assuredly will lie,*
> *But none will pass his catacomb*
> *So chastened as the fly.*

One sent at Christmas with a beautifully iced cake was:

> *The Saviour must have been a docile Gentleman*
> *To come so far, so cold a night*
> *For little fellow men.*
> *The road to Bethlehem—*
> *Since He and I were boys—*
> *Has levelled—but for that 'twould be*
> *A rugged billion miles.*

To Ned after being severely stung by a hornet:

DEAR NED
  You know I never *did* like you in those "yellow-jackets"!
                                                        EMILY

To Gilbert, a child in kindergarten then, she sent this, accompanied with a dead bee:

THE BUMBLE BEE'S RELIGION

For Gib to carry to his teacher from Emily

> *His little hearse-like figure*
> *Unto itself a dirge,*
> *To a delusive lilac*
> *The vanity divulge*

> *Of industry and morals*
> *And every righteous thing,*
> *For the divine perdition*
> *Of Idleness and Spring.*
> *"All liars shall have their part." Jonathan Edwards.*
> *"And let him that is athirst come." Jesus.*

She furthered their childish love of mystery and innocent intrigue on every occasion, purloining for them any treat from the family supplies she could lay her fond hands upon.

Once with sweets smuggled over to them came these laconic instructions:

> Omit to return box. Omit to know you received box.
>
> Brooks of Sheffield

At another like occasion:

> The joys of theft are two; first theft; second superiority to detection. How inspiring to the clandestine mind. "We thank thee, Lord, that Thou hast hid these things!"

She did a deal of brilliant trifling apropos of local events. On the death of the wife of a doctor she disliked she writes:

> DEAR SUE
>   I should think she would rather be the Bride of the Lamb than that old pill box!
>
> EMILY

With a cape jasmine sent to a guest of her niece as yet unknown to her (Sara Colton Gillett) she writes:

> M. will put this little flower in her friend's hand. Should she ask who sent it, tell her—as Desdemona did when they asked who slew her—Nobody—Myself.

After the death of a strictly dull acquaintance with no vital spark visible she writes:

Now I lay thee down to sleep,
I pray the Lord thy dust to keep,
If thou should live before thou wake,
I pray the Lord thy soul to make!

This scrap is Emily at her most audacious:

My Maker, let me be
Enamoured most of Thee—
But nearer this
I more should miss!

In a panic lest some cherished plan fall through she sent this:

Boast not myself of tomorrow, for I "knoweth not" what a noon may bring forth.

This, too, is Emily to the core:

Cherish power dear; remember that it stands in the Bible between the kingdom and the glory because it is wilder than either.

The instances cited are characteristic of varying moods. Her passion for brevity always deducted relentlessly. She refuses an invitation thus:

Thanks, Sue, but not tonight. Further nights.

Emily

After some flashing pleasure given her she replies:

Don't do such things. Your Arabian Nights unfits the heart for its arithmetic.

Emily is sorry for Susan's day. To be singular under plural circumstances is a becoming heroism.

Susan knows she is a siren and at a word from her Emily would forfeit righteousness.

A spell cannot be tattered and mended like a coat.

No message is the utmost message, for what we tell is done.

To lose what we have never owned might seem an eccentric bereavement, but Presumption has its own affliction as well as claim.

The things of which we want the proof are those we know the best.

Where we owe but little we pay. Where we owe so much it defies money we are blandly insolvent.

Has *All* a codicil?

In a life that stopped guessing, you and I should not feel at home.

Tasting the honey and the sting should have ceased with Eden. Pang is the past of peace.

"To multiply the harbors does not reduce the sea," defines her constancy.

"Emblem is immeasurable, that is why it is better than fulfillment, which can be drained"—reveals her elusive quality.

And how much she crowded into one sparse sentence when she said:

Danger is not at first, for then we are unconscious, but in the slower days.

Her letters sent when her family were really at a distance are never like those of anyone else, and usually reflect the day and season more than any personal happenings. Across one runs this postscript:

Father's sister is dead, and Mother wears a black ribbon on her bonnet.

But usually they were more like this, one chosen at random:

Nothing is gone, dear, or no one that you know. The forests are at home, the mountains intimate at night and arrogant at noon. A lonesome fluency abroad, like suspended music.

Further on in the same letter:

Come home and see your weather; the hills are full of shawls. We have a new man whose name is Tim. Father calls him "Timothy" and the barn sounds like the Bible.

Twilight touches Amherst with his yellow glove. Miss me sometimes, dear, not on most occasion, but in the Sometimes of the mind.

The small heart cannot break. The ecstasy of its penalty solaces the large.

Emerging from an abyss and reëntering it, that is Life, dear, is it not?

There were no so gay hours in Emily's life as those spent at her brother's home when there were guests of their own inner circle, who revelled in her companionship. For her own life never lacked its joy in comedy nor was her spirit quenched by its most subduing contact with the elemental tragedy that was constant to her thought. When Mrs. Anthon, of London, and Samuel Bowles, of the "Springfield Republican," were there they played wild games of battledore and shuttlecock in the long winter evenings; Emily convulsing their onlookers by her superfluous antics added to their game. She improvised brilliantly upon the piano all sorts of dramatic performances of her own, one she called the Devil being particularly applauded.

It was on one of these winter nights of revel that they forgot the hour and suddenly, unwarned by the approaching beams of his lantern across the snow, became aware of her father's presence in their midst, to enquire the meaning of such prolonged hours. Emily is said to have drooped and disappeared before him like the dew, without a sound, but with a wicked glance or gesture to assert her unreconcilement to the proceedings.

Her sister Sue recognized her genius from the first, and hoarded every scrap Emily sent her from the time they were both girls of sixteen. Their love never faltered or waned. Emily pictures their first meeting and its changelessness:

As much now as when love first began—on the step at the front door, under the evergreens.

One of her very last pencilled lines was this:

With the exception of Shakespeare you have told me more knowledge than anyone living. To say that sincerely is strange praise.

EMILY

Sometimes Emily addressed her as "You from whom I never run away"; and again she exclaims:

> Susan! I would have come out of Eden to open the door for you if I had known you were there. You must knock with a trumpet as Gabriel does, whose hands are small as yours. I knew he knocked and went away—I did not dream you did!
>
> EMILY

And again:

> To see you unfits for stabler meetings. I dare not risk an intemperate moment before a banquet of bran.

The decision to publish "The Single Hound," the poem of their lifetime, was determined by a faded little note of her early twenties:

> DEAR SUE
>
> I like your praise because I know it knows. If I could make you and Austin proud someday, a long way off, 'twould give me taller feet.
>
> EMILY

She never told her family of her writing, and this is the only mention of any secret ambition to have her work known even on a day "a long way off." The first poem dated, that she sent to Sister Sue, was in 1848, and probably the last word she ever wrote was her reply to a message from her—

> My answer is an unmitigated *Yes*, Sue.
>
> EMILY

VII

LATER YEARS WITH BOOKS AND FRIENDS

From the time Emily was thirty her life can only be told by the development of herself. Any mere chronicle of events would leave out all that made her and her surviving poems.

Yet if there were few startling happenings to record, to her there was nothing otherwise. If art is as Mérimée once declared "exaggeration apropos"—she was an incomparable artist at life. To her there was a prodigality of excess in each thrill of the returning common day. Her spirit found its own nectars in spite of her loneliness for all her brother's home so vividly illustrated—in spite of the dearth of music, painting, and the stimulus others took for granted as necessary for any lasting accomplishment.

A brilliant and ardent admirer of her work said recently: "The truest vision I ever got of the great Napoleon was in hearing a great artist sing the 'Two Grenadiers.' That is the only way possible of expressing Emily Dickinson—by indirections, through her own *milieu*, her contacts with others, and the impressions she set down in her writings." There is hardly a soul left now who knew her or ever saw her, and only one of her own family surviving to depict her as not only a poet and mystic, but a beloved person, moving from window to window to watch the day's retreat or the change of light on Pelham hills, or flitting across from house to house, a dear familiar spirit of delight in either.

As early as 1862 she had visibly withdrawn from the outside world, even humoring her moods until those she professed to love saw her less often when they came to the house. As one has said of the shortening afternoons of early autumn, "There was less of the Toreador spirit in her now"; though she was always the ecstatic, daredevil, shy paradox, supreme and incomparable, to those who found her. Once she seems puzzled by some slight coldness on the part of a friend—exclaiming, "Odd that I who run from so many cannot brook that one turn from me!" Yet she confessed that her ideal caller—like ideal cat—was always just going out of sight!

Her books and friends went together in her later life; books first, perhaps. But it was her own work done in secret and often at midnight—"Death's and Truth's Unlocking Time"—that "kept the awe away" and led her on. She confessed it to herself and hardly another. Most of her earliest friends remained her closest friends to the end; as she expressed it, "I never sowed a seed in childhood unless it was perennial—that is why my garden lasts." Those girls of her earliest choosing, Abby Wood, Eliza Coleman, Abiah Strong, Martha Gilbert, Emily Fowler, and Helen Fisk—all married and gone away from her—she cherished and was true to as the years gave her also Kate Anthon, Maria Whitney, Mrs. Bowles, and others drawn to her through her brother's family.

She had her own peculiar exclusive rights in the family friends also, the Hollands of Springfield, the Lords of Salem, her father's friend Mrs. Eastman, who lived abroad and wrote to them on thin paper with the letterhead of magical foreign places, sealed with enormous seals, and made them incredible presents of coral and mosaics and those cameos so coveted by that generation, when she made her rare visits upon them. The Hollands were intimates of the entire family, and until the death of Dr. Holland in 1881 the families visited back and forth familiarly, Emily going to them after she had ceased to accept invitations even from her own cousins in Boston. Dr. Josiah Gilbert Holland was one of the founders of "Scribner's Magazine" in 1870 and became one of its editors; leaving Springfield, where he had been engaged on the "Republican" for many years, to live in New York. At his home, "Bonnicastle," named from the hero of his first novel, his friends were constantly entertained and a sorry gap in the lives of the entire Dickinson family was made by the change. Dr. Holland—who afterward came to be widely known as J. G. Holland—made a valuable contribution to local American history in his two-volume "History of Western Massachusetts." He also wrote a number of novels, "Arthur Bonnicastle," "The Bay Path"—a colonial tale, one of his first—followed by the "Titcomb Letters," "Nicholas Minturn," "Sevenoaks," etc., and several volumes of poems, of which "Bitter-sweet," "Kathrina," and "The Mistress of the Manse" were those most popular. After his work called him to New York to live, he often returned to the Dickinson home for rest and refreshment and inspiration. Richard Watson Gilder, later editor of the "Century Magazine," remembered being taken there by him, as a lad, but "did not see Miss Emily," a fact he bewailed in later years.

Judge Otis P. Lord, of Salem, was her father's friend, but into his childless heart of rigorous justice Emily flashed as an unconscious aurora on a polar night and their friendship was of the most deep and lasting quality. At her request his letters and the little souvenirs he had given her were burned at her death, held by her too sacred for other fate. Says the formal biographer appointed to draw up the resolutions upon his death for the Commonwealth of Massachusetts: "In him the people lost a fearless, vigorous, upright magistrate of great learning and unquestioned integrity and purity; a man of marked individuality and power. His fame belongs to the Commonwealth. For nearly a quarter of a century he served it as a judge of its highest tribunal with distinguished ability; a positive force in the administration of justice." Pompous in manner, elegant in speech, he was to the younger generation the embodiment of the Supreme Court. His face was haughtily handsome, and beneath his slow, awe-inspiring reserve of manner lay a sense of humor to which his little friend Emily pierced unceasingly. Her approach was sure on the high themes of Shakespeare, his favorite author re-read and known by heart by them both, but their enjoyment of the comedy of everyday was also broadly akin. They saved scraps of current nonsense for each other, and these clippings flew back and forth between the grim court-house in Salem and the little desk by her conservatory window, where Emily oftenest sat.

There was a certain kind of wit she labelled "the Judge Lord brand." One specimen of it especially relished by both remains still pinned to her tiny workbox. It is yellow with age, in a type quite bygone and evidently cut from the county paper. It is marked in her own handwriting—"Returned by Judge Lord with approval!"

NOTICE!

My wife Sophia Pickles having left my bed and board without just cause or provocation, I shall not be responsible for bills of her contracting.

SOLOMON PICKLES

NOTICE!

I take this means of saying that Solomon Pickles has had no bed or board for me to leave for the last two months.

SOPHIA PICKLES

Another story which they repeated, liking its portentous inference lacking fact, was this; the Nurse speaks first.

"Nurse," says he, kind of high and haughty-like, "what is your opinion?"

"Doctor," says I, kind of low and deferential-like, "I am of your opinion."

"And what was his opinion?" asked the listener.

"Lord bless you, my dear, he hadn't any!"

Her brother's children never forgot the Sunday when he repeated at the dinner table a few of the hymns of his upbringing, their teeth chattering at his rendition of

"My thoughts on awful subjects roll—
Damnation and the Dead!"

Emily had about this time quite a spicy affair with a young law student in her father's office, an habitué of the house who was bewitched with her and certainly added quite an amount of variety, if only as another objective for her own mental sallies. He became a confirmed bachelor, but she assailed him with a valentine unique in that Saint's calendar, and he brought her many books, among which were the first copies of the Brontë girls' strange stories, from "Jane Eyre" to "Wuthering Heights" and the "Tenant of Wildfell Hall."

The Civil War, for which Amherst furnished a proud quota, must have crashed in on the seclusion of Emily's thought, thrilling her as drum and fife—but the personal realization of it did not come to her until Fraser Stearns, son of President Steams, was killed at the battle of Newbern in 1862.

This was her first intimate reaction to the universal tragedy, and she wrote poignantly of it to more than one friend; also of trying to do all in her power to comfort his family—especially the young sister, Ella (afterward Mrs. James Lee, of Boston), of whom she was always devotedly fond.

It was in 1862 also that her literary philandering with Colonel Thomas Wentworth Higginson began through a stray note of admiration from her for his article in the "Atlantic Monthly" on the "Procession of the Flowers," sent her by Sister Sue. Her family viewed the ensuing correspondence between them as a diverting interlude rather than a serious instruction, for, though she addressed him as "Dear Master" with an outward show of docile humility, she never changed one line to please him. He heard from her in camp during the Civil War, which he entered in a volunteer regiment in 1863, and it was in the September of that same year that her eyes necessitated her going to Boston for serious treatment, which abbreviated her correspondence almost to entire elimination for sometime.

From the close of the war until 1868 their relations seem to have remained as a comedy version of Browning's "Statue and the Bust." Their letters were all they knew of each other. For one reason or another he was prevented from visiting Amherst and she was disinclined to leave home, even to visit her relatives in Boston. His letters to her, and there were many of them, she labelled to be burned upon her death; her chivalry outrunning his publication of her little impulsive notes to him, published with his own comment. One of his somehow did escape into Sister Sue's papers, and in this, dated May, 1868, he says eagerly:

> Sometimes I take out your letters and verses, dear friend, and when I feel their strange power, it is not strange that I find it hard to write and that long months pass. I have the greatest desire to see you, always feeling that perhaps if I could once take you by the hand I might be something to you; but till then you only enshroud yourself in this fiery mist and I cannot reach you, but only rejoice in the rare sparkles of light. Every year I think I will go to Amherst and contrive to see you somehow, but that is hard, for I am obliged to go away for lecturing, etc., often and rarely can go for pleasure. I would gladly go to Boston at any practicable time to meet you. I am always the same toward you, and never relax my interest in what you send to me. I should like to hear from you very often, but feel always timid lest what I write should be badly aimed and miss that fine edge of thought which you bear. It would be so easy to miss you. Still you see I try. I think if I could once see you and know that you are real I might fare better. It brought you nearer to know you had an actual uncle—though I can hardly fancy two beings less alike. I have not seen him for several years, though I have seen a lady who once knew you, but could not tell me much. It is hard for me to understand how you can live so alone—with thoughts of such a rarity coming up in you and even the companionship of your dog withdrawn. Yet it isolates one anywhere to think beyond a certain point, or have such flashes as come to

you—so perhaps the place does not make much difference. You must come down to Boston sometimes? All ladies do. I wonder if it would be possible to lure you to the meetings on the thirtieth of every month at Mrs. Sargent's, 13 Chestnut Street, at ten A.M., where somebody reads a paper and others talk or listen. Next Monday Mrs. Emerson reads and then at three and a half P.M. there is a meeting of the Woman's Club at 3 Tremont Place, where I read a paper on the Greek Goddesses. That would be a good time for you to come, though I should still rather have you come on someday when I shall not be so much taken up, for my object is to see you, more than to entertain you. I shall be in Boston also during anniversary week, June 25th, or will the Musical Festival in June tempt you? You see I am in earnest. Or don't you need sea air in Summer? Write and tell me something in prose or verse, and I will be less fastidious in future and willing to write clumsy things rather than none.

Ever your friend—

P.S. There is an extra meeting at Mrs. Sargent's that day and Mr. Weiss reads an essay. I have a right to invite you and you can merely ring and walk in.

To which she replied in a letter full of gratitude and grace, but as Shakespeare's Imogen might have spoken, "I do not cross my father's ground to any house or town." In August of the same year 1870 he went to see her at Amherst instead. After this until her death their friendship and correspondence continued uninterrupted.

Her cousins Louisa and Fannie Norcross, relatives on her mother's side, were her beloved always. The winters they spent at the Hotel Berkeley in Boston, when she was with them at brief intervals, she never ceased to look back upon lovingly, even wistfully—and they, too, were of her elect from whom she never ran away. Her Southern cousin, Perez Cowan, a Carolinian, was another of her favored relatives, for whom she had a real affection. His softer accent, genial manner relieved of the New England stiffness, loosened her shy tongue and appealed to her eager imagination. His coming was always "a tropic," though she could never be prevailed upon for a return visit upon any of the family "below the frost line."

Her correspondence with Mr. C. H. Clarke, whom she met but once, continued until just before death, another evidence of the inclusive quality of her human sympathy.

Emily's childhood intimacy with Helen Hunt Jackson, later the author of "Mercy Philbrick's Choice," "Ramona," etc., was one of her dearest pleasures. "H. H.," as her books were signed, would be driven into town with a pair of smashing grey horses, which were dramatically walked up and down before the house, while the two charmers visited together behind the closed blinds. From girlhood Helen looked up to Emily as something supernatural, and Emily returned her adoration, calling Helen a witch, but never succumbing to her repeated requests for material for publication. Helen Hunt was herself a siren who enchanted all men's hearts—a hopeless coquette from her youth up, worldly where Emily was secluded, expressive while Emily was reserved, a charmer of charmers, who never let go her hold on the hand of the little girl she played with under the syringas, and never lost a chance to come back and warm herself at the fire of that deathless altar.

What they talked of none can ever know, for the door was shut upon their hours together, and not one member of the family ever dared invade. Their partings overheard were like those of desperate final sundered souls; but both were dramatic of temperament and to Emily the darkness was denser always after the radiant passage of one of her chosen. Helen always preferred Emily in genius and power, and considered herself but a small spark beside her. Her generosity of appreciation was boundless and well grounded. Her letters from Emily, as well as hers to Emily, were believed to have been burned at last in accordance with their own agreement.

"Mercy Philbrick's Choice" in the No Name Series was attributed to Emily, but denied in a single white glance of repudiation from Emily that such could be thought possible. One poem "H. H." did publish at her own risk, but Emily never knew it until the book appeared called "A Masque of Poets." She could not even dimly understand Helen's merry protestation that it was fun to make people wonder and keep them guessing. She did not want them even to suspect about her— guessing was the last of her inclinations toward herself. Mr. Sweetser's looking at her in the old church was all she wanted of publicity, bless her! That was almost more even than she could endure.

Helen out in the world, courted, quoted, envied, a beauty always, full of social ease and grace, brought the world, like an attar of fantastic blend, to her little white-robed hostess, who gave in return her heart's devotion and a deeper glance at life and trust than any Society could ever teach or bestow. "When you are dead you will be sorry you were so selfish!" Helen threw back at her gaily, when she had again refused to meet somether friend proposed. It was through Helen Hunt that her friendship with Mr. Thomas Niles began, after her poem "Success" was pirated, and though she wrote to him and sent him a poem now and then he could never induce her to publish. Emily had spirit relations with her living, actual neighbors, much such as are now broadcasted through the air, sending her notes on special occasions, or with flowers or some of her exquisite cookery in return for their little attentions to her hidden presence. It is impossible to cite them all; the Jenkinses, the Mathers, the Bliss family, returned from Syria for the education of the sons, were those nearest. Most of them she seldom saw; they hardly expected her to see them. Royalty was never more intact, though her methods were so simple, her spirit guileless of it as guile. Mrs. John Anthon, with just a touch of Irish blood in her veins, was a gay madcap of a girl, solemnized by cruel sorrow later in life, but always witty and of blessed sympathy and humor. From their first meeting, when as Kate Scott she was living in the old Fenimore Cooper mansion at Cooperstown, Emily's heart "voted for her." Living abroad as she did, she brought the very breath of life during her rare visits, and was one of the dwindling few Emily never refused to see, going over to her brother's home when she was there, long after her earlier stages of seclusion.

Maria Whitney was a friend of her maturer years, but another sacredly treasured one. Their visits were also in the darkened library, hand in hand on the little sofa by the fire, and with them, two intellects met as equals. Miss Whitney was the sister of Professor William Whitney, of Yale, and another brother was Professor Josiah Whitney, of Harvard. She lived at Northampton in the original Jonathan Edwards house, under the majestic Jonathan Edwards elms, and was in many ways Emily's antithesis—keen, scientific, agnostic, schooled in German criticism, a cool thinker, influenced by her brother's ideas, saying calmly: "It is a great grief to me that I cannot accept the Christian faith"; subjected to church admonishment for wearing a red silk petticoat on her return from years of study in Europe; later a professor of old German in Smith College, a woman of unusual attainments and profound convictions, rational, calm, true as steel to friend or conviction, who turned to Emily to probe for her deeper than the schools had been able, and out-soar the obstacles that hindered her own mind.

Grey-eyed, pale, keen, crisp of tongue from the habit of clean thought and the study of languages other than her own, their apparent contrast mated unerringly, and they never missed a chance to match discoveries or compare revelations. In those days a free-thinker, a materialist, was almost a felon. For a woman to profess such scepticism was daring beyond credibility. The sincerity of the troubled inability "to believe" was undoubted in this case, and it must have set Emily off on boundless conjecture, encountered at such close and resolute range.

But after all her faithful devotion to her friends of girlhood is cited, those she professed profligate-hearted from start to finish of her solitary life, there was but one to whom she entrusted the secret of herself. Many instances are in existence still of her referring to her sister-in-law's judgment in all literary matters. The poem called "A Syllable" in the published collection was originally written with a second verse:

> *Could any mortal lip divine*
> *The elemental freight*
> *Of undeveloped syllable*
> *'Twould crumble with the weight,*
> *The prey of unknown zones,*
> *The pillage of the sea,*
> *These tabernacles of the mind*
> *That told the news to me.*

The poem which published reads "A modest lot, a fame petite," originally had a first verse sent with it:

> *A little bread, a crust, a crumb,*
> *A little trust, a demijohn,*
> *Can keep the soul alive—*
> *Not portly, mind!*
> *But breathing, warm,*
> *Conscious, as old Napoleon*
> *The night before the crown!*

The resemblance of these first four lines to the now popular quatrain of Omar Khayyám is noteworthy, as Emily so far as can be proved never saw the translations of Fitzgerald, though they were published in England in 1858. Her Sister Sue never saw them until the Houghton

Mifflin & Company American edition in 1888, two years after Emily's death; nor were they among her books.

She was always eager to respond to Susan's criticism, and when the first pencilled copy was sent over of the poem, "Safe in their alabaster chambers," it was returned with profound admiration, but this comment, "The second verse is not frosty enough yet." To which Emily replied next day:

Perhaps this would suit you better, Sue?

Grand go the years in the crescent above them,
Worlds scoop their arcs
And firmaments bow,
Diadems drop and Doges surrender
Soundless as dots on a disc of snow.

Is this frostier?

Springs shake their sills
But the echoes stiffen,
Hoar is the window and numb the door,
Tribes of Eclipse in tents of marble
Staples of Ages have buckled there.

The first variant was chosen, and so appears as a third stanza, in Volume One of the published poems. "In this Wondrous Sea" was sent to Susan in 1848 when she was but eighteen, signed "Emilie": after the whim of her girlhood.

The poem entitled "The Master," as written "To Sue," reads, "He fumbles at your soul," line first; in line first of the second stanza, "Prepares your brittle nature"; adding two lines at the end:

When winds take forests in their paws,
The Universe is still.

The critical estimate of Emily's thought and her ultimate place in American literature must be left to one more wise, better qualified, and less near her actual bewildering personality. It may be pardonable to hint at her sagacity of words, in a few instances, since George Meredith says, "We are in truth indebted for expression to those who phrase us." She sorted and tested them as a wine-taster in his cellar. They came, for the most part, but often another came too; they came tandem and in pairs, shouting at her to be chosen. The joy of mere words was to her like red and yellow balls to the juggler. The animate web for the inanimate thing, the ludicrous adjective that turned a sentence mountebank in an instant, the stringing of her meaning like a taut bow with just the economy of verbiage possible, the unusual phrase redeemed from usage by her single selected specimen of her vocabulary—all this was part of her zestful preoccupation. For example:

It was like a breath from Gibraltar to hear your voice again, Sue. Your impregnable syllables need no prop to stand.

I dreamed of you last night and send a carnation to endorse it.

Your little mental gallantries are sweet as chivalry—which is to me a shining word, though I don't know what it means.

The dictionary was no mere reference book to her; she read it as a priest his breviary—over and over, page by page, with utter absorption. Emile Hennequin said, "Words are visions, visions ecstatic, visions chimerical, without models, without objects; ideals rather than images, desires rather than reminiscences." And Emily:

SUSAN—

A little overflowing word,
That any hearing had inferred
For ardor or for tears.
Though Generations pass away,
Traditions ripen and decay,
As eloquent appears.

EMILY

Although she never went to live in it except in spirit, the world was Emily's real neighborhood. George Eliot's works she called "that lane to the Indies Columbus was trying to find." Longfellow, Tennyson, the Brownings, Socrates, Plato, Poe, and the Bible sift through her conversation; Keats and Holmes, Ik Marvel, Hawthorne—"who appals and entices"—Howells and Emerson, Sir Thomas Browne, De Quincey,

George Sand, Lowell—whose "Winter" enthralled her for days at a time she declared—and perhaps differently from all the rest the Brontës, all three, Charlotte, Anne, and Emily! Shakespeare always and forever, Othello her chosen villain, with Macbeth familiar as the neighbors and Lear driven into exile as vivid as if occurring on the hills before her door. She "watched like a vulture for Cross's 'Life' of his wife," the criticism and joy of literature running through her letters as her conversation.

She always read Frank Sanborn's letters in the columns of the "Springfield Republican" for their reflection of the art and literature of his period, and was glad a friend heard Rubinstein for her, adding "he makes me think of polar nights." She mentioned her sister as "Vinnie, spectacular as Disraeli and sincere as Gladstone," and alludes to "a new pussy the colour of Bramwell Brontë's hair." One gets her feeling for Wordsworth by one of these oblique slants when she remembers her cousin's sitting-room at the Berkeley "as the poet's thought of Windymere."

"David Copperfield" was published when she was twenty-one, and Dickens was always a favorite of her father's, so that many of the expressions used in his stories became household words. "Donkeys, Davy," was flung back over Emily's shoulder as she fled from unwelcome visitors. The drollery of Dickens was congenial to her sense of the ludicrous, and "Barkis is willin'" was a message carried more than once by the children between her and their mother without any realization of its import.

She was keenly interested in the Egyptian campaign of Arabi Pasha against the allied French and English, alluding to his defeat at Tel-el-Kebir, after the bombardment of Alexandria, with a grasp of European affairs and interest in their great statesmen unique among the women of her day, who chiefly overheard their newspaper information at scattered male dictation. "Will you have Theophilus or Junius?" she offers Mr. Bowles for a birthday gift. He called her his Rascal—with a gleam in his eyes in speaking of her like that of freshets breaking loose. "Part angel, part demon," he said once, when she refused to see him after he had driven over from Springfield for that peculiar pleasure. It was his custom to bring to her the manuscripts of famous writers, before publication, and when he entertained Canon Kingsley, Bret Harte, Charles Dickens, or any other author of note, he would share his impressions of them first-hand with her; often reading her notes to him to those he considered able to follow her meteoric flights. She counted him among her brightest beacons, and when his Life and Letters was about to be published in 1885 wrote—

Dear Sue:

It seems like a memoir of the sun when the Noon is gone!
You remember his swift way of wringing and flinging away a
theme, and others picking it up and gazing bewildered after
him; and the prance that crossed his eyes at such times was
unrepeatable.

Emily was a fond reader of Ik Marvel. On receiving a copy of
"Dream Life" from her brother she wrote back:

It is not nearly so great a book as "Reveries of a Bachelor,"
yet I think it full of the very sweetest fancies, and more
exquisite language I defy any man to use. On the whole I
enjoyed it very much, but I can't help wishing that he had
been translated like Enoch of old, after his bachelor reverie,
and chariot of fire and the horsemen thereof were all that had
been seen of him ever after.

In the winter of 1857, Emerson was her brother's guest. There is no
mention of their having met—inexplicable as it seems—but in a note
to her Sister Sue after his departure she says, "It must have been as if he
had come from where dreams are born!"
She wrote to Sister Sue as if it were perfectly probable:

Dreamed of your meeting Tennyson at Ticknor and Fields
last night. Where the treasure is the heart is also.

When Howells first appeared in the magazine of which Dr. Holland
was editor, Emily wrote:

Doctor
How did you snare Howells?

Emily

His reply came back:

Emily
Money did it.

Holland

Her books and authors were a vital part of her happiness. On the walls of her own room hung framed portraits of Mrs. Browning, George Eliot, and Carlyle. If only Emily could have heard the question an old family retainer, assisting at the time of Emily's death, asked diffidently, after some hesitation, if they were "relatives on the Norcross side"; adding hastily, "I know they can't be Dickinsons, for I have seen all of them and they are all good-looking."

In writing her letters to friends at a distance, she seems to show an accumulated sadness which in her intercourse with those about her she rarely if ever permitted expression. No one of her family in either house ever associated her with sadness or any tendency toward indulgence of heaviness of spirit, though solemnity was her normal attitude toward life and like those golden Florentines "she was eternally preoccupied with death."

From the death of Samuel Bowles in 1878 life lost its original sense of certainty. And when her father died in Boston during the June of 1879, the very foundations trembled under her. He was stricken in the House of the Legislature, where he had gone to serve the local interests of his town, and died without recovering consciousness, at the Tremont House, before any of his family could reach him. Her brother Austin had to break the news to the three worshipping women of the end of that ideal unbroken family life, and it was for the effect upon Emily that the task was especially dreaded.

She describes it afterward in a line:

We were eating our supper when Austin came in. . . He had a despatch in his hand, and I saw by his face that we were all lost, though I did not know how.

For a time it seemed as if her mind could not sustain the blow. His death seemed to reverse all laws of nature or mind for Emily. No one who heard her repeated cry, "Where is he? I can't find him!" could ever forget it, or those days of abyss when her face wore a stricken expression of surprise that the world and stars could slip from their orbits and leave such confusion.

She never quite recovered her faith in life, and just a year later her mother was paralyzed. All through the long, tedious invalidism following, Emily ministered to her with a tenderness as to one also bound for the supernatural and to be cherished as a temporary guest of the heart, already half an angel. Two such calamities shook her belief in stability of this world of hers, where she had been the child of parents permanent and equal to all her natural demand of care and continuance. "The beginning of always is more dreadful than the close—for that is sustained by flickering identity," she wrote her Sister Sue.

Dr. Holland's death in 1881 was another link broken, followed by the loss of Judge Lord, who was now both father and friend.

In the autumn of 1883 her youngest nephew, Gilbert, died after an illness of only three days and shattered the goldenest intimacy she had left. He was a precocious and brilliant child. Emily idolized him from his birth and only after days of stricken silence recovered from the blow sufficiently to write his mother:

DEAR SUE

The vision of immortal life has been fulfilled. How simply at last the fathom comes! The passenger and not the sea surprises us. Gilbert rejoiced in secrets. His life was panting with them. With what a menace of light he cried, "Don't tell, Aunt Emily." My ascended playmate must instruct me now. Show us, prattling preceptor, but the way to thee! He knew no niggard moment. His life was full of boon. The playthings of the Dervish were not so wild as his. No crescent was this creature— he travelled from the full. Such soar, but never set. I see him in the star and meet his sweet velocity in everything that flies.

> *His life was like a bugle*
> *That winds itself away:*
> *His elegy an echo,*
> *His requiem ecstasy.*

Dawn and meridian in one, wherefore should he wait, wronged only of night, which he left for us? Pass to thy rendezvous of light pangless except for us who slowly ford the mystery which thou hast leapt across!

And during these years of increasing isolation it was to her work she turned for relief and renewal. She admitted she was besieged for poems, but held her peace, working because "it kept the awe away," though in other mood she confessed it "a bleak redeeming."

From the time of her father's death she never left the house, except to flit about the porch at dusk to water her frail plants—set just outside in summer—looking in her white dress like just another moth fluttering in the twilights. The red army blanket that was thrown down on the dewy grass to prevent her taking cold was the only bit of color associated with her, and the origin of the many fanciful tales of a red carpet spread before her when she went beyond the door.

It is at this time she wrote:

> There is no first or last in Forever. It is Centre there all the time. To believe is enough and the right of supposing.

She had never told her family of her writing and they never dared ask. She never showed what she wrote to them. Her timidity awed their love and New England reserve completed the deadlock. Once and only once her sister-in-law published a poem of hers incognita, and when she showed it to Emily, in the darkest, entirest privacy, was terrified for the result of her experiment—the little white moth being almost fluttered to death, all a-tremble and ready to die of the experience and be found on the floor next morning a mere hint of winged dust! She seemed to know the world from intuition, but to shrink from that which sends the soft bright-eyed things flying from us in the forest. All the while she was writing and selecting and tying up her poems in slender packages with a single thread, another Lady of Shalott at her subtler tapestries that were to amaze her readers when her little boat had drifted down to Camelot forever.

"There's substance here" might have been truly said of her mentality, even when the supernatural began to outweigh the actual in her consideration. This was no empty yearning after a lost romance, no idle acceptance of passivity. Up to the last, when blow after blow had stunned her, Emily kept her vital creative force intact. Watched over by her sister and what Mr. Henry James once called "an archaic Irish servant," she was with difficulty kept at home in the flesh those last years; seeing her brother's family at rarer intervals, and still sending her pencilled messages, among which are the few quoted at random:

> Great hungers feed themselves but little hungers ail in vain.
> Never mind, dear, trial as a stimulus far exceeds wine though it could hardly be prohibited as a beverage.

A promise is firmer than a hope. Hope never knew horizon. Awe is the first hand that is held to us. Hopelessness in its first film had not life to last. That would close the spirit, and no intercession could do that. Intimacy with mystery after great space will usurp its place. Moving on in the dark like loaded boats at night, though there is no course, there is boundlessness. Expanse cannot be lost.

> *Morning might come by accident, Sister,*
> *Night comes by event—*
> *To believe the final line of the card*
> *Would foreclose Faith,*
> *Faith is doubt, Sister.*
> *Show me Eternity, and*
> *I will show you memory—*
> *Both in one package lain*
> *And lifted back again.*
> *Be Sue while I am Emily,*
> *Be next what you have ever been—*
> *Infinity.*

VIII

Her Religion

The village church in the forties as described by her Sister Sue must have bred either mysticism or madness in a soul like that of Emily Dickinson.

> It stood on the hill at the head of the village common, swept by the four winds of heaven. Architecture was never thought of or mentioned in those days. The old village church with its Grecian pillars was late in its life a target for any lazy wit, but that it survived beheading once, and lived bravely on in spite of jests, and stands today with little external change—rather Grecian in effect—defying its malefactors, bespeaks its integrity of composition.

The original interior was truly an odd picture. There were high pews painted white, with doors fastened securely by brass buttons, affording something of a sense of tribal ownership and comfort in the owner's sentiment of worship. These doors were too often carelessly slammed, but that only set off the noise made by the sexton just as the sermon ended, throwing open the doors of the two cast-iron box stoves with violence and hurling strange-looking geometrical wood, called felly wood, into their vast satanic depths, so that the farmers and their families, who remained for afternoon service at one o'clock, might warm their half-frozen members and refill their foot stoves. During the noon interval, as they sat about the red-hot stove on the circular seats, neighborly visiting was indulged in, with low sad tones. A meagre lunch was drawn from the large yellow muffs to stay them up for the long later service, while from the same capacious quarter small soapstones were drawn to be re-heated for the cold drive home in the early winter dusk.

The light, much weather-stained walls, patched and cracked, were brought into bold relief by the heavy mahogany pulpit and the really immense red damask curtain dropped for a background. Whoever conceived and executed the plan of that end of the meeting-house must have been fresh from a mince-pie dream of Solomon's temple.

The pulpit was so high the minister was obliged to infer the effect of his sermon chiefly from the tops of the heads and bonnets before him, to the exclusion of more normal and favorable angles for sympathetic observation of human expression. Dr. Dwight, a nephew of President Dwight, of Yale College, held those ramparts of mahogany, accepting the call in 1850, on condition of a few practical changes to the reverend old building.

The concessions he begged were that the tin kettles hung from the long stovepipes that ran from the stoves down the side aisles to the chimneys in the opposite walls—kettles set to catch the black creosote that dripped from the pipe joints—might be abolished by some ingenuity; and that the big iron catches on the front doors be replaced by some design compelling less racket in the opening and closing. Also that there be some green baize doors, to be drawn when "the house," as everybody called it, was filling. Most people were on the whole not displeased by the changes, but one or two prominent persons exclaimed against such iconoclasms; remarking that we "were getting too refined." Dr. Dwight also influenced the congregation to remain seated during the last hymn, instead of rising and facing the choir. It was an old habit that died hard, and there was smiling among the youngsters the first Sunday it was tried, when one lone spinster spunkily preserved the honored custom.

But it was the supplanting of the bass viol by the organ that was most sternly resented and deplored. "It was a step toward Romanism." It was "a wicked outlay of money." Deacon Leland, although of musical repute, objected stoutly on the ground that it made his wife's head ache. And worse still the organist was a young and handsome girl. There was endless opposition to the new and heavenly aid to worship. Deacon Leland, Deacon Sweetser, and Deacon Mack, who did not dare be good and graceful too, preserved their John Calvin sternness until even their ice cracked under the new force.

There were sermons of mighty power preached from that tall pulpit, a memorable one by Dr. Swift, of South Hadley, "I heard Thy voice in the garden and was afraid," typical of the prevailing mood. His pronouncedly spiritual physique and solemn manner added to the supernatural awe of the text. Adam's apology, not then influenced or dissected by a short process of *reductio ad absurdum*, or minute German scholarship, became a shrinking experience of every listening soul from the white, ineffable, eternal God. At the close there was left only a wide cold planetary space, void of all save sin and its consequence. The stillness and sobs must have been proof of the power and excitement of his impassioned picture.

What the shy young heart of Emily Dickinson felt—whether she steeled herself not to think or no—no modern mind can safely conjecture. That she had a terror of God on the Sabbath, and loved his creatures and his sunshine with renewed dearness on Monday, is a pretty shrewd guess. The awful God of the sanctuary, and the God of her flowers, or the wood, or her friends was a reconcilement easily baffling to one wiser and older than she. She flouted the external glooms in her reactionary moods, made fun of the worthy saints of local fame, dashed into sacrilege and out again before she was caught, all the while dutifully accompanying her family with due meekness to the family pew, until the time came when she gradually was allowed to set up her own church within her own heart at home.

The form and substance of her religion were hardly on speaking terms. Her letters are full of flashes like this—called forth by one of the protracted seasons of revival called an awakening—"I know of no choicer ecstasy than to see Mrs. F roll out in crepe every morning, I presume to intimidate Antichrist." She scorned hypocrisy and writes to Sister Sue:

> *A counterfeit, a plated person I would not be,*
> *Whatever strata of*
> *Iniquity my nature under-lie*
> *Truth is good, health and safety is good—*
> *And the sky.*
> *How meagre is a lie!*
> *And vocal when we die!*
>
> PECKSNIFF

To her nephew, detained from church, she wrote:

> *Sanctuary privileges*
> *For Ned, as he is unable to attend—*
>
> *The Bible is an antique volume*
> *Written by faded men,*
> *At the suggestion of Holy Spectres—*

Subjects—Bethlehem—
Eden—the ancient Homestead—
Satan—the Brigadier,
Judas—the great Defaulter,
David—the Troubadour.
Sin—a distinguished Precipice
Others must resist,
Boys that "believe"
Are very lonesome—
Other boys are "lost."
Had but the tale a warbling Teller
All the boys would come—
Orpheus' sermon captivated,
It did not condemn.

EMILY

To NED—

The Devil, had he fidelity,
Would be the finest friend—
Because he has ability,
But Devils cannot mend.
Perfidy is the virtue
That would he but resign,—
The Devil, so amended,
Were durably divine.

EMILY

Often and often her best quips and most startling suggestions come in her allusions to the Bible, which she uses with a familiarity unknown to her time, and with a spirit of equality almost jocular; using words—to others of her same conventional training—unbelievably yoked. "As the Bible boyishly says—new every morning and fresh every evening"—is one of her adverbs forever fresh in the family quotation.

Paul took the marine walk at great risk.

"I have finished the faith," he said; we rejoice he did not say *discarded* it.

Vinnie is picking a few seeds, for if a pod die, shall it not live again?

More seriously she exclaims:

Gethsemane and Cana are a travelled route—
   So loved her that he died for her, says the explaining Jesus.

Could character be more shrewdly epitomized than by this terse antithesis:

To do a magnanimous thing and take oneself by surprise, if one is not in the habit of it, is precisely the finest of joys. Not to do a magnanimous thing, notwithstanding it never be known, notwithstanding it cost us existence, is rapture herself spurned.

The Church dominated all life, social and public, in Amherst in the mid-century, but the religion of Emily Dickinson was not a blend of any she received by inheritance or instruction. The gentle belief of her mother in a God who would hold back the rain until after the hay was in, or who sent the undesirable showers to prove the faith of his meek followers in his chastening for their good, or the fear of God that sent her forth in her best shawl of a pleasant afternoon to collect the annual missionary money for her church; her minute abstinence from all labor on the seventh day, her punctilious conscientiousness in rectitude and mercy, in deeds of kindness and faithfully restrained tongue, was too limited, too earth-bound for Emily. This guileless little being, timid, yet one of the most persevering of saints, gave little to her daughter which explains or defines. This pattern of a good and amiable housewife and mother had little exhibition in her offspring, except for the gentleness which was always a predominant characteristic, the supreme gentleness of action and feeling.

From her father there descended upon her the inward quality of her own outward grace. He was one of the most just, loyal and reserved souls that ever avoided cant or religious over-expression. He became a member of the village church rather late in life, having served its parish in almost all capacities. His confession of faith was a simply expressed desire "to be a better man," that was touching in the extreme to those who heard his clear and crisp statement at the evening meeting of his friends and neighbors. He was a man of sterling purity against whom no one ever had taken up a reproach, a friend of the entire community, a notable figure of the County Bar: fulfilling nobly his ideal, expressed in a letter to his wife dated March 19, 1828, a few weeks before their marriage. "Let us prepare for a life of rational happiness. I do not expect or wish for a life of *pleasure*! May we be happy and useful and successful, and each be an ornament in society and gain the respect and confidence of all with whom we may be connected."*

Emily, of course, attended church with her family and heard the long sermons of her day on "foreordination—whereby"—etc. The incident of her dear friend and parson, Dr. Dwight, attempting to convert her, remains as a cherished family annal, for she could never be brought to consider God as an enemy, or herself as hateful in his sight. What a contrast her own cry: "Could pathos compete with that simple statement,—'Not that we first loved Him, but that He first loved us'?" But the contribution to Faith that Emily Dickinson made to the world will someday be definitely recognized. Her way of loving God, knowing Him, serving Him, was as ancient as Brother Lawrence, as modern as William James. Brother Lawrence in the seventeenth century saying the smallest action for the love of God is all, and Emily saying, "The simplest solace with a loved aim has a heavenly quality," are really more than paraphrase. The similarity of their source of power parallels in his letters as well as its daily exhibition.

She had the soul of a monk of the Middle Ages bound up in the flesh of Puritan descent, and, from Heaven only knows where, all the fiery quality of imagination for which genius has been burned at the stake in one form or another since the beginning. She accepted the results of her training, as she shows in her attitude that if He be against us all other allies are useless! Even this is not so much resignation of the true brand as shrewd observation in result.

---

* *Springfield Republican*: "In his State, and particularly in its western section, he has long ranked among the few 'first citizens,' honored for his years and public services, respected for his sterling good sense and independence of character, revered for his spotless integrity and patriotic self-sacrifice to public duty, beloved even by all who came near to him for the simple truthfulness and chivalric tenderness that lay deep and broad in the base of his nature. He has left an example of service as a public-spirited citizen and faithful official that both in quality and quantity should alone make him an historic character in Massachusetts. He was indeed a New England Chevalier Bayard, without fear and without reproach. He possessed and exhibited that rarest and yet most needed of all qualities in these days of cowardly conformity and base complaisance,—*the courage of his convictions*. This was the essence of his life. This is his noblest bequest to his community and his State."

One of the students of her poetry—himself a preacher of brilliant reputation—writes of her: "Her power is really the unusual degree in which she reflects the divine. . . If her genius was inspiration, it was something to which every soul that is human has a claim, in some humble degree, to share; and the way in which she lived deserved study for the light it may throw upon what mankind can do to come into its own share of the same gift."

She was not a pantheist, though she saw each tree and bush "afire with God," and each revelation of twilight and dawn or starry sky as spread forth by the Eternal. Each personality had a dignity that lent it awe to her. She was respectful to every mortal as to every worm that crawls. She could mock or epigramize the mean or outrageous, but never inflict a false or wounding touch or thought upon a sincere and unspoiled nature.

Toward her family and her daily circle, servants, friends, chance comers, she was the spirit of loveliness incarnate. "Whatever it is, Emily will get it for you!" she vowed dramatically to her weeping children adorers, who fled to her in dismay in any incredible panic. The fruit of her religion was incessant sweet ministration; she was incarnate devotion, service; wanting nothing for herself except to give to someone else.

There must have been the most lofty, holy inspiration, indeed, to perfect such fragrant living. Like Saint Francis, she might have preached to the birds, and included not only "Sister Lark," but Bumble Bee, in her sermon. And when the immortal in her friends began, and when she approached death and the mystery of the superhuman, who shall attempt to follow her except by repetition of her own words, those phrases she brought back from her perpetual adorations of the Unknown, from her adventures in the dark ways of thought and spirit? She may not have had a consciously phrased conviction, such as her family called "creed"; she may not have connected the old First Church with what she called her "Father's House"; she certainly never considered God her judge or her enemy; but her faith was that of one who has never ceased to be a mortal. She was a part of God, and God was in her so truly that no outward effort was necessary nor was it to her possible to exaggerate the harmony between the Creator and His created child. The adjustment was never broken. She would have spoken to God more simply than to her honorable parent—with less constraint; would have been quite capable of offering God her sweetest flower or her frailest fern, sure of His acceptance.

While to her family religion was a sad and solemn duty, preparing them for death and presided over by a dread and awful Majesty, whose wrath was to be appeased by dreary observance and repeated incantations to remove the curse left by Adam hanging over their innocent and timorous heads—to Emily it was not so at all. They might take her to church and seat her decorously where they sat, like a silent shadow or an inappropriate sunbeam, but from the first word of the prayer till the last word of the benediction, though her body was present, only Emily knew where her soul spent those hours of motionless pause. Hiatus was an art with her, and one she fully employed. There may have been stepping-stones in the sermon that caught her back, in her daring the wide flood of her own fancy, but hardly more than that. The devil was her favorite character in the drama of piety, and she invented him even more deliciously than others presented him to her. In him she seemed to recognize an artless but joyous comrade of her own unrelated moments of wit. An untrammelled twain they two, at whom God winked, in true Old Testament fashion.

With a solemn undercurrent truly tragic, too searching and chill to contemplate unmoved, she had the inhuman, elfin strain that has nothing whatever to do with manmade rites or professions. There was a side of her that escaped, as a retiring sunbeam to its native sky, leaving mere chairs and tables on their certain spots in the drab pattern of the carpet left below.

"With reticence before and mystery behind,"

as Carman puts it, like the wind of which he is speaking, she passed through the heroic convulsions of that country church, unharmed and undetained.

The thought persists, though put aside repeatedly, of her possible reincarnation. How else did those hanging gardens of Babylon in her nature get themselves implanted? Characteristics of Richelieu—craving for the sultry Orient—how came these in the nature of a New England Puritan, nun and worshipper, mystic and philosopher, woman and eternal child? How else account for her?

Both personal memory of countless hours with her, and the open-minded re-reading of her poems and family letters lead to the conclusion that awe summed up her attitude toward religion and love toward life. She could write, "To die before one fears to die may be a boon," yet in one hour her wondering conclusion could be swallowed up in the near joy of a little exquisite service for a dear one. To those with whom she lived and her brother's family, she was all loveliness, all glimmering whiteness, all spirit—an avenging angel with a fiery sword against whatever evil befell them. Christ with the lashing words of contempt for the money-changers was her true spiritual progenitor then, and at all times she belonged by face and mien to the sweet fields of Nazareth and Cana of Galilee as truly as to the Egypt of Cleopatra and the generations yet unborn.

This may sound like a wild and contradictory claim, but Emily was a unique and universal being; all times, all sympathies, all hopes, all fears, all throbs of timeless hearts beat on in her. Only God and eternity and the dazzling thought of immortality were worth her while, though her patient little hands wrought out their daily ministries in dumb rectitude. She moved about with a rapt manner at her simplest duties, making the bread her father loved best from her hands, or the exquisite caramels she sent to her favored ones, and the large sunny kitchen, with its windows both to the east and west, saw her often standing with her listening manner, of Domremy, sharing "the voices," perhaps, of a less troubled, less martial throng of phantoms; apparitions of her own thought and fancy. This, it must be confessed, led sometimes to catastrophe, but flight was ever her imminent salvation and mute defense.

Only her wit flew over the walls that hedged her in. And this even beat against high heaven at times, but with never a sacrilegious intention and almost a certainty innate that even her Father in heaven could be trusted to enjoy her sally into the uncharted dark where angels dared not go. She had a confidence in her, toward heaven, unlike any ever revealed. Though she said of Thomas that "his faith in anatomy was stronger than his faith in faith," her own faith in faith was stronger than any expression she either received or gave, in words.

After her father's death she went about always wondering where he could be, and even to her brother's children saying unforgettable things in her search for a clue to what, and where, he was, and "what kind" he had become. To more than one friend she wrote, "Footlights cannot improve the grave—only immortality." And no acting of tragedy in later years ever effaced the memory of her husky whisper, "Where is he? Emily will find him!"

It was of her mother after her death that she wrote later with less rebellion, "Like a flake gathered by the wind she is now part of the drift called Infinity. We don't know where she is, though so many tell us," expressing her maturing doubt of the infallibility of that high pulpit to divulge what her heart cried out to know. There was far more, then, that was native to Emily's feeling for the Eternal in the prayer of Saint Augustine:

> *"O Truth who art Eternity!*
> *And Love who art Truth!*
> *And Eternity who art Love!*
> *Thou art my God, to Thee do I*
> *Sigh night and day."*

While her work still fascinated her, there came a morning in June, 1884, when without warning Emily was smitten as her father before her, and though she lived for two years after,

> *"The green world went on a sudden blind,"*

and it was impossible for her to write more than an occasional pencilled note. She wrote her Sister Sue at this time, "You must let me go first, Sue, because I live in the sea always now, and know the road."

When the better days came, she still took out her writing and made her last corrections, playing with her beloved iridescent words to the last, but, in her own words, reminiscent of an oft-repeated family caution, "it was already growing damp"—"I must go in, the fog is rising," she warned, at the end of her briefest last message. Perhaps she was too elemental, too close to the very basis of being, to belong to mere humanity.

It was on May 16, 1886, that her family gave her back to immortality with a strange relief, as of setting a winged thing free. At the simple funeral in the old house, Colonel Higginson read a poem of Emily Brontë's, the last words she ever wrote, prefacing it by saying:

"This poem on Immortality was a favorite of Emily Dickinson, who has just put it on—if she could ever have been said to have put it off."

> *"No coward soul is mine,*
> *No trembler in the world's storm-troubled sphere:*
> *I see Heaven's glories shine,*
> *And faith shines equal, arming me from fear.*

"O God within my breast,
Almighty, ever-present Deity!
Life—that in me has rest,
As I—undying Life—have power in thee!

"Vain are the thousand creeds
That move men's hearts: unutterably vain;
Worthless as withered weeds,
Or idlest froth amid the boundless main,

"To waken doubt in one
Holding so fast by thine infinity;
So surely anchored on
The steadfast rock of immortality.

"With wide-embracing love
Thy spirit animates eternal years,
Pervades, and broods above,
Changes, sustains, creates, and rears.

"Though earth and man were gone,
And suns and universes ceased to be,
And Thou wert left alone,
Every existence would exist in Thee!

"There is not room for Death,
Nor atom that his might could render void;
Thou—Thou art Being and Breath,
And what Thou art may never be destroyed!"

On an improvised bier of pine boughs, entirely covered by a pall of blue sand-violets which fell so low it swept the grass on either side as they passed, she was borne in a soft white coffin by laborers, who had all worked upon her father's land and reverenced her almost as the Madonna, across the few intervening fields carpeted with the young summer flowers, followed only by those closest to her, to the old cemetery where her father and mother had preceded her. A singularly lovely and fitting ending of her visible journey into the mortal world.

In her own room stood the old mahogany bureau, filled with her friend's letters marked to be burned unread, and her own manuscript poems. Her sacred wishes were carried out by her family to the utmost—until they came to her own work. It seemed to them too much to ask of them to destroy this wealth of her inner genius, with its gift for the world of poets and kindred natures throughout all time. They knew that Emily Dickinson belonged not alone to them. And in rescuing her work from destruction to which she destined it in her naïve panic before impending discovery, they were sure their decision would have been justified even by her if she could have foreseen their meaning to later generations. Her sister Lavinia, her brother Austin, were the ones to decide—technically—but it was the Sister Sue who realized that there had been visions of her own continuing in this world through her written words, long animating the quiet performance of daily routine by the white-robed little poet-philosopher, mystic, flitting about the old house under the tall pines. That the verdict of the world would have been Treason, had they acted otherwise, has been abundantly proved.

They have all gone that same green path she took, now, and it remains for the last living member of her own family to submit Emily's work to the final judgment of others, and her life, as far as it concerns others, as a beautiful inspiration. For which may her shy soul pardon the revelation; may it never be a betrayal to her spirit, still so vivid and real that to grieve her would be the supreme act of blasphemy against the Holy Ghost, which truly was her guest on this earth. Wherever she is, whatever she knows, may she *know* this!

The following appreciation, written by her brother's wife at the time of Emily Dickinson's death, for the "Springfield Republican," was requested by Colonel Higginson for the introduction to the first volume of her poems, but was withheld, and remains to be the last confirming witness of a contemporary.

Miss Emily Dickinson of Amherst

The death of Miss Emily Dickinson, daughter of the late
Edward Dickinson, at Amherst on Saturday, makes another
sad inroad on the small circle so long occupying the old family
mansion. It was for a long generation overlooked by death,
and one passing in and out there thought of old-fashioned

times, when parents and children grew up and passed maturity together, in lives of singular uneventfulness unmarked by sad or joyous crises. Very few in the village, except among older inhabitants, knew Miss Emily personally, although the facts of her seclusion and her intellectual brilliancy were familiar Amherst traditions.

There are many houses among all classes, into which her treasures of fruit and flowers and ambrosial dishes for the sick and well were constantly sent, that will forever miss those evidences of her unselfish consideration, and mourn afresh that she screened herself from close acquaintance. As she passed on in life, her sensitive nature shrank from much personal contact with the world, and more and more turned to her own large wealth of individual resources for companionship, sitting henceforth, as someone said of her, "in the light of her own fire." Not disappointed with the world, not an invalid until within the past two years, not from any lack of sympathy, not because she was insufficient for any mental work or social career—her endowments being so exceptional—but the "mesh of her soul," as Browning calls the body, was too rare, and the sacred quiet of her own home proved the fit atmosphere for her worth and work. All that must be inviolate. One can only speak of "duties beautifully done"; of her gentle tillage of the rare flowers filling her conservatory, into which, as into the heavenly Paradise, entered nothing that could defile, and which was ever abloom in frost or sunshine, so well she knew her subtle chemistries; of her tenderness to all in the home circle; her gentlewoman's grace and courtesy to all who served in house and grounds; her quick and rich response to all who rejoiced or suffered at home, or among her wide circle of friends the world over. This side of her nature was to her the real entity in which she rested, so simple and strong was her instinct that a woman's hearthstone is her shrine.

Her talk and her writings were like no one's else, and although she never published a line, now and then some enthusiastic literary friend would turn love to larceny, and cause a few verses surreptitiously obtained to be printed. Thus, and through other natural ways, many saw and admired her verses, and in consequence frequently notable persons paid her visits, hoping to overcome the protest of her own nature and gain a promise of occasional contributions, at least, to various magazines. She withstood even the fascinations of Mrs. Helen Jackson, who earnestly sought her coöperation in a novel of the No Name series, although one little poem somehow strayed into the volume of verse which appeared in that series. Her pages would ill have fitted even so attractive a story as "Mercy Philbrick's Choice," unwilling though a large part of the literary public were to believe that she had no part in it. "Her wagon was hitched to a star"—and who could ride or write with such a voyager? A Damascus blade gleaming and glancing in the sun was her wit. Her swift poetic rapture was like the long glistening note of a bird one hears in the June woods at high noon, but can never see. Like a magician she caught the shadowy apparitions of her brain and tossed them in startling picturesqueness to her friends, who, charmed with their simplicity and homeliness as well as profundity, fretted that she had so easily made palpable the tantalizing fancies forever eluding their bungling, fettered grasp. So intimate and passionate was her love of Nature, she seemed herself a part of the high March sky, the summer day and bird-call. Keen and eclectic in her literary tastes, she sifted libraries to Shakespeare and Browning; quick as the electric spark in her intuitions and analyses, she seized the kernel instantly, almost impatient of the fewest words by which she must make her revelation. To her life was rich, and all aglow with God and immortality. With no creed, no formulated faith, hardly knowing the names of dogmas, she walked this life with the gentleness and reverence of old saints, with the firm step of martyrs who sing while they suffer. How better note the flight of this "soul of fire in a shell of pearl" than by her own words?

> *Morns like these, we parted;*
> *Noons like these, she rose;*
> *Fluttering first, then firmer,*
> *To her fair repose.*

—S. H. D.

PART II

LETTERS OF EMILY DICKINSON

1845–1886

Letters of Emily Dickinson

To Mrs. Strong
(When Emily was but fourteen)

AMHERST, *Feb.* 23, 1845

DEAR A.,

After receiving the smitings of conscience for a long time, I have at length succeeded in stifling the voice of that faithful monitor by a promise of a long letter to you; so leave everything and sit down prepared for a long siege in the shape of a bundle of nonsense from friend E.

. . . I keep your lock of hair as precious as gold and a great deal more so. I often look at it when I go to my little lot of treasures, and wish the owner of that glossy lock were here. Old Time wags on pretty much as usual at Amherst, and I know of nothing that has occurred to break the silence; however, the reduction of the postage has excited my risibles somewhat. Only think! We can send a letter before long for five little coppers only, filled with the thoughts and advice of dear friends. But I will not get into a philosophizing strain just yet. There is time enough for that upon another page of this mammoth sheet. . . Your *beau idéal* D. I have not seen lately. I presume he was changed into a star some night while gazing at them, and placed in the constellation Orion between Bellatrix and Betelgeux. I doubt not if he was here he would wish to be kindly remembered to you. What delightful weather we have had for a week! . . .

I wish you would come and make me a long visit. If you will, I will entertain you to the best of my abilities, which you know are neither few nor small. Why can't you persuade your father and mother to let you come here to school next term, and keep me company, as I am going? Miss——, I presume you can guess who I mean, is going to finish her education next summer. The finishing stroke is to be put on at Newton. She will then have learned all that we poor foot-travellers are toiling up the hill of knowledge to acquire. Wonderful thought! Her horse has carried her along so swiftly that she has nearly gained the summit, and we are plodding along

on foot after her. Well said and sufficient this. We'll finish
an education sometime, won't we? You may then be Plato,
and I will be Socrates, provided you won't be wiser than
I am. Lavinia just now interrupted my flow of thought by
saying give my love to A. I presume you will be glad to have
someone break off this epistle. All the girls send much love
to you. And please accept a large share for yourself.

From your beloved
EMILY E. DICKINSON

Please send me a copy of that Romance you were writing at Amherst.
I am in a fever to read it. I expect it will be against my Whig feelings.

TO THE SAME

AMHERST, May 7, 1845

DEAR A.,

It seems almost an age since I have seen you, and it is
indeed an age for friends to be separated. I was delighted to
receive a paper from you, and I also was much pleased with
the news it contained, especially that you are taking lessons
on the "piny," as you always call it. But remember not to get
on ahead of me. Father intends to have a piano very soon.
How happy I shall be when I have one of my own! Old
Father Time has wrought many changes here since your last
short visit. Miss S. T. and Miss N. M. have both taken the
marriage vows upon themselves. Dr. Hitchcock has moved
into his new house, and Mr. Tyler across the way from our
house has moved into President Hitchcock's old house.
Mr. C. is going to move into Mr. T.'s former house, but the
worst thing old Time has done here is he has walked so fast
as to overtake H. M. and carry her to Hartford on last week
Saturday. I was so vexed with him for it that I ran after him
and made out to get near enough to him to put some salt
on his tail, when he fled and left me to run home alone. . .
Viny went to Boston this morning with father, to be gone
a fortnight, and I am left alone in all my glory. I suppose
she has got there before this time, and is probably staring
with mouth and eyes wide open at the wonders of the city.

I have been to walk tonight, and got some very choice wild flowers. I wish you had some of them. Viny and I both go to school this term. We have a very fine school. There are 63 scholars. I have four studies. They are Mental Philosophy, Geology, Latin, and Botany. How large they sound, don't they? I don't believe you have such big studies. . . My plants look finely now. I am going to send you a little geranium leaf in this letter, which you must press for me. Have you made you an herbarium yet? I hope you will if you have not, it would be such a treasure to you; 'most all the girls are making one. If you do, perhaps I can make some additions to it from flowers growing around here. How do you enjoy your school this term? Are the teachers as pleasant as our old school-teachers? I expect you have a great many prim, starched up young ladies there, who, I doubt not, are perfect models of propriety and good behavior. If they are, don't let your free spirit be chained by them. I don't know as there (are) any in school of this stamp. But there 'most always are a few, whom the teachers look up to and regard as their satellites. I am growing handsome very fast indeed! I expect I shall be the belle of Amherst when I reach my 17th year. I don't doubt that I shall have perfect crowds of admirers at that age. Then how I shall delight to make them await my bidding, and with what delight shall I witness their suspense while I make my final decision. But away with my nonsense. I have written one composition this term, and I need not assure you it was exceedingly edifying to myself as well as everybody else. Don't you want to see it? I really wish you could have a chance. We are obliged to write compositions once in a fortnight, and select a piece to read from some interesting book the week that we don't write compositions.

We really have some most charming young women in school this term. I shan't call them anything but women, for women they are in every sense of the word. I must, however, describe one, and while I describe her I wish Imagination, who is ever present with you, to make a little picture of this self-same young lady in your mind, and by her aid see if you cannot conceive how she looks. Well, to begin. . . Then just imagine her as she is, and a huge string of gold beads encircling her neck, and don't she present a lively picture; and then she is so bustling, she is always whizzing about, and whenever I come in contact with her I really think I am in a hornet's nest. I can't help thinking everytime I see this singular piece of humanity of Shakespeare's description of a tempest in a teapot. But I must not laugh about her, for I verily believe she has a good heart, and that is the principal thing now-a-days. Don't you hope I shall become wiser in the company of such virtuosos? It would certainly be desirable. Have you noticed how beautifully the trees look now? They seem to be completely covered with fragrant blossoms. . . I had so many things to do for Viny, as she was going away, that very much against my wishes I deferred writing you until now, but forgive and forget, dear A., and I will promise to do better in future. Do write me soon, and let it be a long, long letter; and when you can't get time to write, send a paper, so as to let me know you think of me still, though we are separated by hill and stream. All the girls send much love to you. Don't forget to let me receive a letter from you soon. I can say no more now as my paper is all filled up.

Your affectionate friend
EMILY E. DICKINSON

TO THE SAME
(Written in 1845; postmarked Amherst, August 4)

Sabbath Eve

DEAR A.,

I have now sat down to write you a long, long letter. My writing apparatus is upon a stand before me, and all things are ready. I have no flowers before me as you had to inspire you. But then you know I can imagine myself inspired by them, and perhaps that will do as well. You cannot imagine how delighted I was to receive your letter. It was so full, and everything in it was interesting to me because it came from you. I presume you did not doubt my gratitude for it, on account of my delaying so long to answer it, for you know I have had no leisure for anything. When I tell you that our term has been eleven weeks long, and that I have had four studies and taken music lessons, you can imagine a little how my time has been taken up lately. I will try to be more punctual in such matters for the future. How are you now? I am very sorry to hear that you are unable to remain in your school on account of your health, it must be such a disappointment to you. But I presume you are enjoying yourself much to be at home again. You asked me in your last letter if old Father Time wagged on in Amherst pretty much as ever. For my part, I see no particular change in his movements unless it be that he goes on a swifter pace than formerly, and that he wields his sickle more sternly than ever. How do you like taking music lessons? I presume you are delighted with it. I am taking lessons this term of Aunt S——, who is spending the summer with us. I never enjoyed myself more than I have this summer; for we have had such a delightful school and such pleasant teachers, and besides I have had a piano of my own. Our examination is to come off next week on Monday. I wish you could be here at that time. Why can't you come? If you will, you can come and practise on my piano as much as you wish to. I am already gasping in view of our examination; and although I am determined not to dread it I know it is so foolish, yet in spite of my heroic resolutions, I cannot avoid a few misgivings when I think of those tall, stern trustees, and when I know that I shall lose my character if I don't recite as precisely as the laws of the Medes and Persians. . . You gave me a compliment in your letter in regard to my being a faithful correspondent. I must say I think I deserve it. I have been learning several beautiful pieces lately. The 'Grave of Bonaparte' is one, 'Lancers Quickstep,' and 'Maiden, weep no more,' which is a sweet little song. I wish much to see you and hear you play. I hope you will come to A. before long. Why can't you pass commencement here? I do wish you would. . . I have looked my letter over, and find I have written nothing worth reading. . .

Accept much love from your affectionate friend,
EMILY E. D.

Thursday, Sept. 26, 1845

DEAREST A.,

As I just glanced at the clock and saw how smoothly the little hands glide over the surface, I could scarcely believe that those self-same little hands had eloped with so many of my precious moments since I received your affectionate letter, and it was still harder for me to believe that I, who am always boasting of being so faithful a correspondent, should have been guilty of negligence in so long delaying to answer it. . . I am very glad to hear that you are better than you have been, and I hope in future disease will not be as neighborly as he has been heretofore to either of us. I long to see you, dear A., and speak with you face to face; but so long as a bodily interview is denied us, we must make letters answer, though it is hard for friends to be separated. I really believe you would have been frightened to have heard me scold when Sabra informed me that you had decided not to visit Amherst this fall. But as I could find no one upon whom to vent my spleen for your decision, I thought it best to be calm, and therefore have at length resigned myself to my cruel fate, though with not a very good grace. I think you do well to inquire whether anything has been heard from H. I really don't know what has become of her, unless procrastination has carried her off. I think that must be the case. I think you have given quite a novel description of the wedding. Are you quite sure Mr. F., the minister, told them to stand up and he would tie them in a great bow-knot? But I beg pardon for speaking so lightly of so solemn a ceremony. You asked me in your letter if I did not think you partial in your admiration of Miss Helen H., ditto Mrs. P. I answer, not in the least. She was universally beloved in Amherst. She made us quite a visit in June, and we regretted more than ever that she was going where we could not see her as often as we had been accustomed. She seemed very happy in her prospects, and seemed to think distance nothing in comparison to a home with the one of her choice. I hope she will be happy, and of course she will. I wished much to see her once more, but was denied the privilege. . . You asked me if I was attending school now. I am not. Mother thinks me not able to confine myself to school this term. She had rather I would exercise, and I can assure you I get plenty of that article by staying at home. I am going to learn to make bread tomorrow. So you may imagine me with my sleeves rolled up, mixing flour, milk, saleratus, etc., with a deal of grace. I advise you if you don't know how to make the staff of life to learn with dispatch. I think I could keep house very comfortably if I knew how to cook. But as long as I don't, my knowledge of housekeeping is about of as much use as faith without works, which you know we are told is dead. Excuse my quoting from Scripture, dear A., for it was so handy in this case I couldn't get along very well without it. Since I wrote you last, the summer is past and gone, and autumn with the sere and yellow leaf is already upon us. I never knew the time to pass so swiftly, it seems to me, as the past summer. I really think someone must have oiled his chariot wheels, for I don't recollect of hearing him pass, and I am sure I should if something had not prevented his chariot wheels from creaking as usual. But I will not expatiate upon him any longer, for I know it is wicked to trifle with so revered a personage, and I fear he will make me a call in person to inquire as to the remarks which I have made concerning him. Therefore I will let him alone for the present. . . How are you getting on with your music? Well, I hope and trust. I am taking lessons and am getting along very well, and now I have a piano, I am very happy. I feel much honored at having even a doll named for me. I believe I shall have to give it a silver cup, as that is the custom among old ladies when a child is named for them. . . Have you any flowers now? I have had a beautiful flower-garden this summer; but they are nearly gone now. It is very cold tonight, and I mean to pick the prettiest ones before I go to bed, and cheat Jack Frost of so many of *the treasures* he calculates to rob tonight. Won't it be a capital idea to put him at defiance, for once at least, if no more? I would love to send you a bouquet if I had an opportunity, and you could press it and write under it, The last flowers of summer. Wouldn't it be poetical, and you know that is what young ladies aim to be now-a-days. . . I expect I have altered a good deal since I have seen you, dear A. I have grown tall a good deal, and wear my golden tresses done up in a net-cap. Modesty, you know, forbids me to mention whether my personal appearance has altered. I leave that for others to judge. But my (word omitted) has not changed, nor will it in time to come. I shall always remain the same old sixpence. . . I can say no more now, as it is after ten, and everybody has gone to bed but me.

Don't forget your affectionate friend,
EMILY E. D.

TO THE SAME

January 12, 1846

. . . Haven't we had delightful weather for a week or two? It seems as if Old Winter had forgotten himself. Don't you believe he is absent-minded? It has been bad weather for colds, however. I have had a severe cold for a few days, and can sympathize with you, though I have been delivered from a stiff neck. I think you must belong to the tribe of Israel, for you know in the Bible the prophet calls them a stiff-necked generation. I have lately come to the conclusion that I am Eve, alias Mrs. Adam. You know there is no account of her death in the Bible, and why am not I Eve? If you find any statements which you think likely to prove the truth of the case, I wish you would send them to me without delay.

Have you heard a word from H. M. or S. T.? I consider them lost sheep. I send them a paper every week on Monday, but I never get one in return. I am almost a mind to take a hand-car and go around to hunt them up. I can't think that they have forgotten us, and I know of no reason unless they are sick why they should delay so long to show any signs of remembrance. Do write me soon a very long letter, and tell me all about your school and yourself too.

Your affectionate friend
EMILY E. DICKINSON

To the same

Friday Eve (summer), 1846

My dear A.,

Though it is a long time since I received your affectionate epistle, yet when I give you my reasons for my long delay, I know you will freely forgive and forget all past offences.

It seems to me that time has never flown so swiftly with me as it has the last spring. I have been busy every minute, and not only so, but hurried all the time. So you may imagine that I have not had a spare moment, much though my heart has longed for it, to commune with an absent friend. . . I presume you will be wondering by this time what I am doing to be in so much haste as I have declared myself to be. Well, I will tell you. I am fitting to go to South Hadley Seminary, and expect if my health is good to enter that institution a year from next fall. Are you not astonished to hear such news? You cannot imagine how much I am anticipating in entering there. It has been in my thought by day, and my dreams by night, ever since I heard of South Hadley Seminary. I fear I am anticipating too much, and that some freak of fortune may overturn all my airy schemes for future happiness. But it is my nature always to anticipate more than I realize. . . Have you not heard that Miss Adams—dear Miss Adams— is here this term? Oh, you cannot imagine how natural it seems to see her happy face in school once more. But it needs Harriet, Sarah, and your own dear self to complete the ancient picture. I hope we shall get you all back before Miss Adams goes away again. Have you yet heard a word from that prodigal,—H.? . . .

Your affectionate friend
Emily E. D.

To the same

September 8, 1846

. . . Does it seem as though September had come? How swiftly summer has fled, and what report has it borne to heaven of misspent time and wasted hours? Eternity only will answer. The ceaseless flight of the seasons is to me a very solemn thought; and yet why do we not strive to make a better improvement of them? With how much emphasis the poet has said, "We take no note of time but from its loss. 'Twere wise in man to give it then a tongue. Pay no moment but in just purchase of its worth, and what its worth ask death-beds. They can tell. Part with it as with life reluctantly." Then we have higher authority than that of man for the improvement of our time. For God has said, "Work while the day lasts, for the night is coming in the which no man can work." . . .

To the same

Sabbath Eve, 1846

My dear A.,

When I last wrote you I was in Boston, where I spent a delightful visit of four weeks. I returned home about the middle of September in very good health and spirits, for which it seems to me I cannot be sufficiently grateful to the Giver of all mercies. I expected to go into the Academy upon my return home, but as I stayed longer than I expected to, and as the school had already commenced, I made up my mind to remain at home during the fall term and pursue my studies the winter term, which commences a week after Thanksgiving. I kept my good resolution for once in my life, and have been sewing, practising upon the piano, and assisting mother in household affairs. I am anticipating the commencement of the next term with a great deal of pleasure, for I have been an exile from school two terms on account of my health, and you know what it is to "love school." Miss Adams is with us now, and will remain through the winter, and we have an excellent Principal in the person of Mr. Leonard Humphrey, who was the last valedictorian. We now have a fine school. I thank you a thousand times for your long and affectionate letter. . . I found a quantity of sewing waiting with open arms to embrace me, or rather for me to embrace it, and I could hardly give myself up to "Nature's sweet restorer," for the ghosts of out-of-order garments crying for vengeance upon my defenceless head. However, I am happy to inform you, my dear friend, that I have nearly finished my sewing for winter, and will answer all the letters which you shall deem worthy to send so naughty a girl as myself, at short notice. . .

Write soon.

Your affectionate

EMILY E. D.

To HER BROTHER, WILLIAM AUSTIN DICKINSON
(South Hadley, Autumn, 1847)

Thursday Noon

MY DEAR BROTHER AUSTIN,

I have not really a moment of time in which to write you, and am taking time from "silent study hours"; but I am determined not to break my promise again, and I generally carry my resolutions into effect. I watched you until you were out of sight Saturday evening, and then went to my room and looked over my treasures; and surely no miser ever counted his heaps of gold with more satisfaction than I gazed upon the presents from home. . .

I can't tell you now how much good your visit did me. My spirits have wonderfully lightened since then. I had a great mind to be homesick after you went home, but I concluded not to, and therefore gave up all homesick feelings. Was not that a wise determination? . . .

There has been a menagerie here this week. Miss Lyon provided "Daddy Hawks" as a beau for all the Seminary girls who wished to see the bears and monkeys, and your sister, not caring to go, was obliged to decline the gallantry of said gentleman,—which I fear I may never have another opportunity to avail myself of. The whole company stopped in front of the Seminary and played for about a quarter of an hour, for the purpose of getting custom in the afternoon, I opine. Almost all the girls went; and I enjoyed the solitude finely.

I want to know when you are coming to see me again, for I want to see you as much as I did before. I went to see

Miss F. in her room yesterday. . . I love her very much, and think I shall love all the teachers when I become better acquainted with them and find out their ways, which, I can assure you, are almost "past finding out."

I had almost forgotten to tell you of a dream which I dreamed last night, and I would like to have you turn Daniel and interpret it to me; or if you don't care about going through all the perils which he did, I will allow you to interpret it without, provided you will try to tell no lies about it. Well, I dreamed a dream, and lo! father had failed, and mother said that "our rye-field, which she and I planted, was mortaged to Seth Nims." I hope it is not true; but do write soon and tell me, for you know I should expire of mortification to have our rye-field mortgaged, to say nothing of its falling into the merciless hands of a loco!

Won't you please to tell me when you answer my letter who the candidate for President is? I have been trying to find out ever since I came here, and have not yet succeeded. I don't know anything more about affairs in the world than if I were in a trance, and you must imagine with all your "Sophomoric discernment" that it is but little and very faint. Has the Mexican War terminated yet, and how? Are we beaten? Do you know of any nation about to besiege South Hadley? If so, do inform me of it, for I would be glad of a chance to escape, if we are to be stormed. I suppose Miss Lyon would furnish us all with daggers and order us to fight for our lives in case such perils should befall us. . . Miss F. told me if I was writing to Amherst to send her love. Not specifying to whom, you may deal it out as your good sense and discretion prompt. Be a good boy and mind me!

To the same
(South Hadley, November 2,1847)

Tuesday Noon

My dear Brother Austin,

I have this moment finished my recitation in history, and have a few minutes which I shall occupy in answering your short but welcome letter. You probably heard that I was alive and well yesterday, unless Mr. E. Dickinson was robbed of a note whose contents were to that effect. But as robbers are not very plenty now-a-days, I will have no forebodings on that score, for the present. How do you get along without me now, and does "it seem anymore like a funeral" than it did before your visit to your humble servant in this place? Answer me! I want much to see you all at home, and expect to three weeks from tomorrow if nothing unusual, like a famine or a pestilence, occurs to prevent my going home. I am anticipating much in seeing you on this week Saturday, and you had better not disappoint me! for if you do, I will harness the "furies," and pursue you with "a whip of scorpions," which is even worse, you will find, than the "long oat" which you may remember. . . Tell father I am obliged to him much for his offers of pecuniary assistance, but do not need any. We are furnished with an account-book here, and obliged to put down every mill which we spend, and what we spend it for, and show it to Miss Whitman every Saturday; so you perceive your sister is learning accounts in addition to the other branches of her education. I am getting along nicely in my studies, and am happy quite for me. Do write a long letter to

Your affectionate sister
EMILY

To MRS. STRONG

MOUNT HOLYOKE SEMINARY
Nov. 6, 1847

MY DEAR A.,

I am really at Mount Holyoke Seminary and this is to be my home for a long year. Your affectionate letter was joyfully received, and I wish that this might make you as happy as yours did me. It has been nearly six weeks since I left home, and that is a longer time than I was ever away from home before now. I was very homesick for a few days, and it seemed to me I could not live here. But I am now contented and quite happy, if I can be happy when absent from my dear home and friends. You may laugh at the idea that I cannot be happy when away from home, but you must remember that I have a very dear home and that this is my first trial in the way of absence for any length of time in my life. As you desire it, I will give you a full account of myself since I first left the paternal roof. I came to South Hadley six weeks ago next Thursday. I was much fatigued with the ride, and had a severe cold besides, which prevented me from commencing my examinations until the next day, when I began. I finished them in three days, and found them about what I had anticipated, though the old scholars say they are more strict than they ever have been before. As you can easily imagine, I was much delighted to finish without failures, and I came to the conclusion then, that I should not be at all homesick, but the reaction left me as homesick a girl as it is not usual to see. I am now quite contented and am very much occupied in reviewing the Junior studies, as I wish to enter the middle class. The school is very large, and though quite a number have left, on account of finding the examinations more difficult than they anticipated, yet there are nearly 300 now. Perhaps you know that Miss Lyon is raising her standard of scholarship a good deal, on account of the number of applicants this year, and she makes the examinations more severe than usual.

You cannot imagine how trying they are, because if we cannot go through them all in a specified time, we are sent home. I cannot be too thankful that I got through as soon as I did, and I am sure that I never would endure the suspense which I endured during those three days again for all the treasures of the world.

I room with my cousin Emily, who is a Senior. She is an excellent room-mate, and does all in her power to make me happy. You can imagine how pleasant a good room-mate is, for you have been away to school so much. Everything is pleasant and happy here, and I think I could be no happier at any other school away from home. Things seem much more like home than I anticipated, and the teachers are all very kind and affectionate to us. They call on us frequently and urge us to return their calls, and when we do, we always receive a cordial welcome from them. . .

You have probably heard many reports of the food here; and if so, I can tell you that I have yet seen nothing corresponding to my ideas on that point from what I have heard. Everything is wholesome and abundant and much nicer than I should imagine could be provided for almost 300 girls. We have also a great variety upon our tables and frequent changes. One thing is certain, and that is, that Miss Lyon and all the teachers seem to consult our comfort and happiness in everything they do, and you know that is pleasant. When I left home I did not think I should find a companion or a dear friend in all the multitude. I expected to find rough and uncultivated manners, and, to be sure, I have found some of that stamp, but on the whole, there is an ease and grace, a desire to make one another happy, which delights and at the same time surprises me very much. I find no Abby nor Abiah nor Mary, but I love many of the girls. Austin came to see me when I had been here about two weeks, and brought Viny and A. I need not tell you how delighted I was to see them all, nor how happy it made me to hear them say that "they were *so lonely.*" It is a sweet feeling to know that you are missed and that your memory is precious at home. This week, on Wednesday, I was at my window, when I happened to look towards the hotel and saw father and mother, walking over here as dignified as you please. I need not tell you that I danced and clapped my hands, and flew to meet them, for you can imagine how I felt. I will only ask you, do you love your parents? They wanted to surprise me, and for that reason did not let me know they were coming. I could not bear to have them go, but go they must, and so I submitted in sadness. Only to think that in 2½ weeks I shall be at my *own dear home* again. You will probably go home at Thanksgiving time, and we can rejoice with each other.

You don't (know) how I laughed at your description of your introduction to Daniel Webster, and I read that part of your letter to cousin Emily. You must feel quite proud of the acquaintance, and will not, I hope, be vain in consequence. However, you don't know Governor Briggs, and I do, so you are no better off than I. . . A., you must write me often, and I shall write you as often as I have time. . .

From your affectionate

EMILY E. D.

Saturday, P.M.

My dear Brother Austin,

. . . I finished my examination in Euclid last evening, and without a failure at anytime. You can easily imagine how glad I am to get through with four books, for you have finished the whole forever. . . How are you all at home, and what are you doing this vacation? You are reading "Arabian Nights," according to Viny's statement. I hope you have derived much benefit from their perusal, and presume your powers of imagining will vastly increase thereby. But I must give you a word of advice too. Cultivate your other powers in proportion as you allow imagination to captivate you. Am not I a very wise young lady?

I had almost forgotten to tell you what my studies are now—"better late than never." They are Chemistry, Physiology, and quarter course in Algebra. I have completed four studies already, and am getting along well. Did you think that it was my birthday yesterday? I don't believe I am *seventeen*! . . .

From your affectionate sister
EMILY

To Mrs. Strong

Jan. 17, 1848

. . . You will probably think me foolish thus to give you an inventory of my time while at home, but I did enjoy so much in those short four days that I wanted you to know and enjoy it too. Monday came so soon, and with it came a carriage to our door, and amidst tears falling thick and fast away I went again. Slowly and sadly dragged a few of the days after my return to the Seminary, and I was very homesick, but "after a storm there comes a calm," and so it was in my case. My sorrows were soon lost in study, and I again felt happy, if happiness there can be away from "home, sweet home."

Our term closes this week on Thursday, and Friday I hope to see home and friends once more. I have studied hard this term, and aside from my delight at going home, there is a sweetness in approaching rest to me. This term is the longest in the year, and I would not wish to live it over again, I can assure you. I love this Seminary, and all the teachers are bound strongly to my heart by ties of affection. There are many sweet girls here, and dearly do I love some new faces, but I have not yet found the place of a *few* dear ones filled, nor would I wish it to be here. I am now studying Silliman's Chemistry and Cutter's Physiology, in both of which I am much interested. We finish Physiology before this term closes, and are to be examined in it at the spring examinations, about five weeks after the commencement of the next term. I already begin to dread that time, for an examination in Mount Holyoke Seminary is rather more public than in our old academy, and a failure would be more disgraceful then, I opine; but I hope, to use my father's own words, "that I shall not disgrace myself." What are you studying now? You did not mention that item in your last letters to me, and consequently I am quite in the dark as regards your progress in those affairs. All I can say is, that I hope you will not leave poor me far behind. . .

Your affectionate sister
EMILY E. DICKINSON

TO HER BROTHER AUSTIN
(South Hadley, about February 14, 1848)

Thursday Morn

MY DEAR AUSTIN,

You will perhaps imagine from my date that I am quite at leisure, and can do what I please even in the forenoon, but one of our teachers, who is engaged, received a visit from her intended quite unexpectedly yesterday afternoon, and she has gone to her home to show him, I opine, and will be absent until Saturday. As I happen to recite to her in one of my studies, her absence gives me a little time in which to write.

Your welcome letter found me all engrossed in the study of sulphuric acid! I deliberated for a few moments after its reception on the propriety of carrying it to Miss Whitman, your friend. The result of my deliberation was a conclusion to open it with moderation, peruse its contents with sobriety becoming my station, and if after a close investigation of its contents I found nothing which savored of rebellion or an unsubdued will, I would lay it away in my folio, and forget I had received it. Are you not gratified that I am so rapidly gaining correct ideas of female propriety and sedate deportment? After the proposed examination, finding it concealed no dangerous sentiments, I with great gravity deposited it with my other letters, and the impression that I once had such a letter is entirely obliterated by the waves of time.

I have been quite lonely since I came back, but cheered by the thought that I am not to return another year, I take comfort, and still hope on. My visit at home was happy, very happy to me; and had the idea of in so short a time returning been constantly in my dreams by night and day, I could not have been happier. "There is no rose without a thorn" to me. Home was always dear to me, and dearer still the friends around it; but never did it seem so dear as now. All, all are kind to me, but their tones fall strangely on my ear, and their countenances meet mine not like home-faces, I can assure you most sincerely. Then when tempted to feel sad, I think of the blazing fire and the cheerful meal and the chair empty now I am gone. I can hear the cheerful voices and the merry laugh, and a desolate feeling comes home to my heart, to think I am alone. But my good angel only waits to see the tears coming and then whispers, "Only this year! only twenty-two weeks more, and then home again you will be to stay." To you, all busy and excited, I suppose the time flies faster; but to me slowly, very slowly, so that I can see his chariot wheels when they roll along, and himself is often visible. But I will no longer imagine, for your brain is full of *Arabian Nights'* fancies, and it will not do to pour fuel on your already kindled imagination. . .

I suppose you have written a few and received a quantity of valentines this week. Every night have I looked, and yet in vain, for one of Cupid's messengers. Many of the girls have received very beautiful ones; and I have not quite done hoping for one. Surely my friend *Thomas* has not lost all his former affection for me! I entreat you to tell him I am pining for a valentine. I am sure I shall not very soon forget last Valentine week, nor any the sooner the fun I had at that time. . . Monday afternoon Mistress Lyon arose in the hall, and forbade our sending "any of those foolish notes called valentines."

But those who were here last year, knowing her opinions, were sufficiently cunning to write and give them into the care of D. during the vacation; so that about 150 were despatched on Valentine morn, before orders should be put down to the contrary effect. Hearing of this act, Miss Whitman, by and with the advice and consent of the other teachers, with frowning brow, sallied over to the Post Office to ascertain, if possible, the number of the valentines, and worse still, the names of the offenders. Nothing has yet been heard as to the amount of her information, but as D. is a good hand to help the girls, and no one has yet received sentence, we begin to think her mission unsuccessful. I have not written one, nor do I intend to.

Your injunction to pile on the wood has not been unheeded, for we have been obliged to obey it to keep from freezing up. . . We cannot have much more cold weather, I am sure, for spring is near. . . Professor Smith preached here last Sabbath, and such sermons I never heard in my life. We were all charmed with him, and dreaded to have him close. . .

Your affectionate sister
EMILY

To THE SAME
(South Hadley, late May, 1848)

Monday Morn

My dear Austin,

I received a letter from home on Saturday by Mr. G——
S——, and father wrote in it that he intended to send for cousin Emily and myself on Saturday of this week to spend the Sabbath at home. I went to Miss Whitman, after receiving the letter, and asked her if we could go if you decided to come for us. She seemed stunned by my request,

and could not find utterance to an answer for sometime. At length she said, "Did you not know it was contrary to the rules of the Seminary to ask to be absent on the Sabbath?" I told her I did not. She then took a Catalogue from her table, and showed me the law in full at the last part of it. She closed by saying that we could not go, and I returned to my room without farther ado. So you see I shall be deprived of the pleasure of a visit home, and you that of seeing me, if I may have the presumption to call it a pleasure! The teachers are not willing to let the girls go home this term as it is the last one, and as I have only nine weeks more to spend here, we had better be contented to obey the commands. We shall only be the more glad to see one another after a longer absence, that will be all. I was highly edified with your imaginative note to me, and think your flights of fancy indeed wonderful at your age! When are you coming to see me—it would be very pleasant to us to receive a visit from your highness if you can be absent from home long enough for such a purpose. . .

To Mrs. Strong

Mount Holyoke Female Seminary
May 16, 1848

My dear A.,

You must forgive me, indeed you must, that I have so long delayed to write you, and I doubt not you will when I give you all my reasons for so doing. You know it is customary for the first page to be occupied with apologies, and I must not depart from the beaten track for one of my own imagining. . . I had not been very well all winter, but had not written home about it, lest the folks should take me home. During the week following examinations, a friend from Amherst came over and spent a week with me, and when that friend returned home, father and mother were duly notified of the state of my health. Have you so treacherous a friend?

Not knowing that I was to be reported at home, you can imagine my amazement and consternation when Saturday of the same week Austin arrived in full sail, with orders from head-quarters to bring me home at all events. At first I had recourse to words, and a desperate battle with those weapons was waged for a few moments, between my *Sophomore* brother and myself. Finding words of no avail, I next resorted to tears. But woman's tears are of little avail, and I am sure mine flowed in vain. As you can imagine, Austin was victorious, and poor, defeated I was led off in triumph. You must not imbibe the idea from what I have said that I do not love home—far from it. But I could not bear to leave teachers and companions before the close of the term and go home to be dosed and receive the physician daily, and take warm drinks and be condoled with on the state of health in general by all the old ladies in town.

Haven't I given a ludicrous account of going home sick from a boarding-school? Father is quite a hand to give medicine, especially if it is not desirable to the patient, and I was dosed for about a month after my return home, without any mercy, till at last out of mere pity my cough went away, and I had quite a season of peace. Thus I remained at home until the close of the term, comforting my parents by my presence, and instilling many a lesson of wisdom into the budding intellect of my only sister. I had almost forgotten to tell you that I went on with my studies at home, and kept up with my class. Last Thursday our vacation closed, and on Friday morn, midst the weeping of friends, crowing of roosters, and singing of birds, I again took my departure from home. Five days have now passed since we returned to Holyoke, and they have passed very slowly. Thoughts of home and friends "come crowding thick and fast, like lightnings from the mountain cloud," and it seems very desolate.

Father has decided not to send me to Holyoke another year, so this is my *last term*. Can it be possible that I have been here almost a year? It startles me when I really think of the advantages I have had, and I fear I have not improved them as I ought. But many an hour has fled with its report to heaven, and what has been the tale of me? . . . How glad I am that spring has come, and how it calms my mind when wearied with study to walk out in the green fields and beside the pleasant streams in which South Hadley is rich! There are not many wild flowers near, for the girls have driven them to a distance, and we are obliged to walk quite a distance to find them, but they repay us by their sweet smiles and fragrance.

The older I grow, the more do I love spring and spring flowers. Is it so with you? While at home there were several pleasure parties of which I was a member, and in our rambles we found many and beautiful children of spring, which I will mention and see if you have found them,—the trailing arbutus, adder's tongue, yellow violets, liver-leaf, blood-root, and many other smaller flowers.

What are you reading now? I have little time to read when I am here, but while at home I had a feast in the reading line, I can assure you. Two or three of them I will mention: "Evangeline," "The Princess," "The Maiden Aunt," "The Epicurean," and "The Twins and Heart," by Tupper, complete the list. Am not I a pedant for telling you what I have been reading? Have you forgotten your visit at Amherst last summer, and what delightful times we had? I have not, and I hope you will come and make another and a longer, when I get home from Holyoke. Father wishes to have me at home a year, and he will probably send me away again, where I know not.

Ever your own affectionate
EMILIE E. DICKINSON

To MR. BOWDOIN
(On returning "Jane Eyre" with an enclosure of fragrant box leaves)

December, 1849

MR. BOWDOIN

If all these leaves were altars, and everyone a prayer that Currer Bell might be saved, and you were God—would you answer it?

To MRS. GORDON L. FORD (EMILY FOWLER FORD)

Thursday Morn

DEAR EMILY,

I can't come in this morning, because I am so cold, but you will know I am here ringing the big front door-bell, and leaving a note for you.

Oh, I want to come in, I have a great mind now to follow little Jane into your warm sitting-room; are you there, dear Emily?

No, I resist temptation and run away from the door just as fast as my feet will carry me, lest if I once come in I shall grow so happy that I shall stay there always and never go home at all. You will have read this note by the time I reach the office, and you can't think how fast I run.

Affectionately
EMILY

To Mrs. Strong

AMHERST, *Jan.* 29, 1850

VERY DEAR A.,

The folks have all gone away; they thought that they left me alone, and contrived things to amuse me should they stay long, and *I* be lonely. Lonely, indeed,—they didn't look, and they couldn't have seen if they had, who should bear me company. *Three* here, instead of *one*, wouldn't it scare them? A curious trio, part earthly and part spiritual two of us, the other, all heaven, and no earth. *God* is sitting here, looking into my very soul to see if I think right thoughts. Yet I am not afraid, for I try to be right and good; and He knows everyone of my struggles. He looks very gloriously, and everything bright seems dull beside Him; and I don't dare to look directly at Him for fear I shall die. Then *you* are here, dressed in that quiet black gown and cap,—that funny little cap I used to laugh at you about,—and you don't appear to be thinking about anything in particular,— not in one of your *breaking-disk* moods, I take it. You seem aware that I'm writing you, and are amused, I should think, at any such friendly manifestation when you are already present. *Success*, however, even in making a fool of myself, isn't to be despised; so I shall persist in writing, and you may in laughing at me,—if you are fully aware of the value of time as regards your immortal spirit. I can't say that I advise you to laugh; but if you are punished, and I warned you, that can be no business of mine. So I fold up my arms, and leave you to fate—may it deal very kindly with you! The trinity winds up with me, as you may have surmised, and I certainly wouldn't be at the fag-end but for civility to you. This self-sacrificing spirit will be the ruin of me!

I am occupied principally with a cold just now, and the dear creature *will* have so much attention that my time slips away amazingly. It has heard *so* much of New Englanders, of their kind attentions to strangers, that it's come all the way from the Alps to determine the truth of the tale. It says the half wasn't told it, and I begin to be afraid it wasn't. Only think—came all the way from that distant Switzerland to find what was the truth! Neither husband, protector, nor friend accompanied it, and so utter a state of loneliness gives friends if nothing else. You are dying of curiosity; let me arrange that pillow to make your exit easier. I stayed at home all Saturday afternoon, and treated some disagreeable people who insisted upon calling here as tolerably as I could; when evening shades began to fall, I turned upon my heel, and walked. Attracted by the gayety visible in the street, I still kept walking till a little creature pounced upon a thin shawl I wore, and commenced riding. I stopped, and begged the creature to alight, as I was fatigued already, and quite unable to assist others. It wouldn't get down, and commenced talking to itself: "Can't be New England—must have made some mistake—disappointed in my reception—don't agree with accounts. Oh, what a world of deception and fraud! Marm, will you tell me the name of this country—it's Asia Minor, isn't it? I intended to stop in New England." By this time I was so completely exhausted that I made no further effort to rid me of my load, and travelled home at a moderate jog, paying no attention whatever to it, got into the house, threw off both bonnet and shawl, and out flew my tormentor, and putting both arms around my neck, began to kiss me immoderately, and express so much love it completely bewildered me. Since then it has slept in my bed, eaten from my plate, lived with me everywhere, and will tag me through life for all I know. I think I'll wake first, and get out of bed, and leave it; but early or late, it is dressed before me, and sits on the side of the bed looking right into my face with such a comical expression it almost makes me laugh in spite of myself. I can't call it interesting, but it certainly *is* curious, has two peculiarities which would quite win your heart,—a huge pocket-handkerchief and a very red nose. The first seems so very *abundant*, it gives you the idea of independence and prosperity in business. The last brings up the "jovial bowl, my boys," and such an association's worth the having. If it *ever* gets tired of *me*, I will forward it to *you*—you would love it for *my* sake, if not for its own; it will tell you some queer stories about me,—how I sneezed so loud one night that the family thought the last trump was sounding, and climbed into the currant-bushes to get out of the way; how the rest of the people, arrayed in long night-gowns, folded their arms, and were waiting; but this is a wicked story,—it can tell some better ones. Now, my dear friend, let me tell you that these last thoughts are fictions,—vain imaginations to lead astray foolish young women. They are flowers of speech; they both make and tell deliberate falsehoods; avoid them as the snake, and turn aside as from the rattle-snake, and I don't *think* you will be harmed. Honestly, though, a snake-bite is a serious matter, and there can't be too much said or done about it. The big serpent bites the deepest; and we get so accustomed to its bites that we don't mind about them. "Verily I say unto you, fear *him*." Won't you read some work upon snakes?—I have a real anxiety for you. *I* love those little green ones that slide around by your shoes in the grass, and make it rustle with their elbows; they are rather my favorites on the whole; but I wouldn't influence *you* for the world. There is an air of misanthropy about the striped snake that will commend itself at once to your taste,—there is no monotony about it—but we will more of this again. Something besides severe colds and serpents, and we will try to find *that* something. It can't be a garden, can it? or a strawberry-bed, which rather belongs to a garden; nor it can't be a school-house, nor an attorney-at-law. Oh, dear! I don't know what it is. Love for the absent don't *sound* like it; but try it and see how it goes.

I miss you very much indeed; think of you at night when the world's nodding, nid, nid, nodding—think of you in the daytime when the cares of the world, and its continual vexations choke up the love for friends in some of our hearts; remember your warnings sometimes—try to do as you told me sometimes—and sometimes conclude it's no use to try; then my heart says it *is*, and new trial is followed by disappointment again. I wondered, when you had gone, why we didn't talk more,—it wasn't for want of a subject; it never *could be* for *that*. Too many, perhaps,—such a crowd of people that nobody heard the speaker, and all went away discontented. You astonished me in the outset, perplexed me in the continuance, and wound up in a grand snarl I shall be all my pilgrimage unravelling. Rather a dismal prospect certainly; but "it's always the darkest the hour before day," and this earlier sunset promises an earlier rise—a sun in splendor—and glory, flying out of its purple nest. Wouldn't you love to see God's bird, when it first tries its wings? If you were here I would tell you something—several somethings— which have happened since you went away; but time and space, as usual, oppose themselves, and I put my treasures away till "we two meet again." The hope that I shall continue in love towards you, and *vice versa*, will sustain me till then. If you are thinking soon to go away, and to show your face no more, just inform me, will you? I would have the "long, lingering look," which you cast behind,—it would be an invaluable addition to my treasures, and "keep your memory green." "Lord, keep all our memories green," and help on our affection, and tie the "link that doth us bind " in a tight bow-knot that will keep it from separation, and stop us from growing old; if that is impossible, make old age pleasant to us, put its arms around us kindly, and when we go home, let that home be called heaven.

Your very sincere and *wicked* friend
EMILY E. DICKINSON

TO THE SAME

AMHERST, *May* 7, 1850

DEAR REMEMBERED,

The circumstances under which I write you this morning are at once glorious, afflicting, and beneficial,—glorious in *ends*, afflicting in *means*, and beneficial, I trust, in *both*. Twin loaves of bread have just been born into the world under my auspices,—fine children, the image of their mother; and here, my dear friend, is the *glory*.

On the lounge, asleep, lies my sick mother, suffering intensely from acute neuralgia, except at a moment like this, when kind sleep draws near, and beguiles her,—here is the *affliction*.

I need not draw the beneficial inference,—the good I myself derive, the winning the spirit of patience, the genial housekeeping influence stealing over my mind and soul,— you know all these things I would say, and will seem to suppose they are written, when indeed they are only thought.

On Sunday my mother was taken, had been perfectly well before, and could remember no possible imprudence which should have induced the disease. Everything has been done, and though we think her gradually throwing it off, she still has much suffering. I have always neglected the culinary arts, but attend to them now from necessity, and from a desire to make everything pleasant for father and Austin. Sickness makes desolation, and the day is dark and dreary; but health will come back, I hope, and light hearts and smiling faces. We are sick hardly ever at home, and don't know what to do when it comes,—wrinkle our little brows, and stamp with our little feet, and our tiny souls get angry, and command it to go away. Mrs. Brown will be glad to see it,—old ladies expect to die; "as for *us*, the young and active, with all longings 'for the strife,' *we* to perish by the roadside, weary with the 'march of life'—no, no, my dear 'Father Mortality,' get out of the way if you please; we will call if we ever want you. Good-morning, sir! ah, good-morning!"

When I am not at work, I sit by the side of mother, provide for her little wants, and try to cheer and encourage her. I ought to be glad and grateful that I *can* do anything now, but I do feel so very lonely, and so anxious to have her cured. I haven't repined but once, and you shall know all the why. At noon. . . I heard a well-known rap, and a friend I love *so* dearly came and asked me to ride in the woods, the sweet, still woods,—and I wanted to exceedingly. I told him I could not go, and he said he was disappointed, he wanted me very much. Then the tears came into my eyes, though I tried to choke them back, and he said I *could* and *should* go, and it seemed to me unjust. Oh, I struggled with great temptation, and it cost me much of denial; but I think in the end I conquered,—not a glorious victory, where you hear the rolling drum, but a kind of a helpless victory, where triumph would come of itself, faintest music, weary soldiers, nor a waving flag, nor a long, loud shout. I had read of Christ's temptations, and how they were like our own, only he didn't sin; I wondered if *one* was like mine, and whether it made him angry. I couldn't make up my mind; do you think he ever did?

I went cheerfully round my work, humming a little air till mother had gone to sleep, then cried with all my might— seemed to think I was much abused—that this wicked world was unworthy such devoted and terrible suffering—and came to my various senses in great dudgeon at life, and time, and love for affliction and anguish.

What shall we do, my darling, when trial grows more and more, when the dim, lone light expires, and it's dark, so very dark, and we wander, and know not where, and cannot get out of the forest—whose is the hand to help us, and to lead, and forever guide us; they talk of a "Jesus of Nazareth"—will you tell me if it be he? . . .

It's Friday, my dear A., and that in another week, yet my mission is unfulfilled—and you so sadly neglected, and don't know the reason why. Where do you think I've strayed, and from what new errand returned? I have come from "to and fro, and walking up and down " the same place that Satan hailed from, when God asked him where he'd been; but not to illustrate further, I tell you I have been dreaming, dreaming a *golden* dream, with eyes all the while wide open, and I guess it's almost morning; and besides, I have been at work, providing the "food that perisheth," scaring the timorous dust, and being obedient and kind. I am yet the Queen of the Court, if regalia be dust and dirt, have three loyal subjects, whom I'd rather relieve from service. Mother is still an invalid, though a partially restored one; father and Austin still clamor for food; and I, like a martyr, am feeding them. Wouldn't you love to see me in these bonds of great despair, looking around my kitchen, and praying for kind deliverance, and declaring by "Omai's beard" I never was in such plight? *My* kitchen, I think I called it—God forbid that it was, or shall be, my own—God keep me from what they call *households*, except that bright one of "faith "!

Don't be afraid of my imprecations—they never did anyone harm, and they make me feel so cool, and so very much more comfortable! . . . I presume you are loving your mother, and loving the stranger and wanderer—visiting the poor and afflicted, and reaping whole fields of blessings—save me a little sheaf, only a very little one! Remember and care for me sometimes, and scatter a fragrant flower in this wilderness life of mine by writing me, and by not forgetting, and by lingering longer in prayer, that the Father may bless one more!

Your affectionate friend

EMILY

To Mr. Bowdoin

Valentine Week (1850)

Awake, ye muses nine, sing me a strain divine,
Unwind the solemn twine, and tie my Valentine.

. . . .

Oh the earth was made *for lovers, for damsel, and hopeless swain,*
For sighing, and gentle whispering, and unity *made of* twain.
All things do go a courting, in earth or sea, or air,
God hath made nothing single but thee *in His world so fair!*
The bride *and then the* bridegroom, *the* two, *and then the* one,
Adam, and Eve, his consort, the moon and then the sun;
The life doth prove the precept, who obey shall happy be,
Who will not serve the sovereign, be hanged on fatal tree.
The high do seek the lowly, the great do seek the small,
None cannot find who seeketh, on this terrestrial ball;
The bee doth court the flower, the flower his suit receives,
And they make a merry wedding, whose guests are hundred leaves;
The wind doth woo the branches, the branches they are won,
And the father fond demandeth the maiden for his son.
The storm doth walk the seashore humming a mournful tune,
The wave with eye so pensive looketh to see the moon,
Their spirits meet together, they make them solemn vows,
No more he singeth mournful, her sadness she doth lose.
The worm doth woo the mortal, death claims a living bride,
Night unto day is married, morn unto eventide;

Earth is a merry damsel, and heaven a knight so true,
And Earth is quite coquettish, and beseemeth in vain to sue.
Now to the application, to the reading of the roll,
To bringing thee to justice, and marshalling thy soul:
Thou art a human *solo, a being cold, and lone,*
Wilt have no kind companion, thou reapest what thou hast sown.
Hast never silent hours, and minutes all too long,
And a deal of sad reflection, and wailing instead of song?
There's Sarah, *and* Eliza, *and* Emeline *so fair,*
And Harriet *and* Sabra, *and she with curling hair.*
Thine eyes are sadly blinded, but yet thou mayest see
Six *true and comely maidens sitting upon the tree;*
Approach that tree with caution, then up it boldly climb,
And seize the one thou lovest, nor care for space, or time.
Then bear her to the greenwood, and build for her a bower,
And give her what she asketh, jewel, or bird, or flower—
And bring the fife, and trumpet, and beat upon the drum—
And bid the world Goodmorrow, and go to glory home!

(A valentine written by Emily in 1852 somehow found
its way into "The Republican." It was to
Mr. William Howland.)

(1852)

Sic transit gloria mundi,
How doth the busy bee—
Dum vivimus vivamus,
I stay mine enemy.

Oh, veni, vidi, vici,
Oh, caput, cap-a-pie,
And oh, memento mori
When I am far from thee.

Hurrah for Peter Parley,
Hurrah for Daniel Boone,
Three cheers, sir, for the gentlemen
Who first observed the moon.

Peter put up the sunshine,
Pattie arrange the stars,
Tell Luna tea is waiting,
And call your brother Mars.

Put down the apple, Adam,
And come away with me;
So shall thou have a pippin
From off my father's tree.

I climb the hill of science,
I "view the landscape o'er,"
Such transcendental prospect
I ne'er beheld before.

Unto the Legislature
My country bids me go.
I'll take my india-rubbers,
In case the wind should blow.

During my education,
It was announced to me
That gravitation, stumbling,
Fell from an apple-tree.

The earth upon its axis
Was once supposed to turn,
By way of a gymnastic
In honor to the sun.

It was the brave Columbus,
A-sailing on the tide,
Who notified the nations
Of where I would reside.

Mortality is fatal,
Gentility is fine,
Rascality heroic,
Insolvency sublime.

Our fathers being weary
Lay down on Bunker Hill,
And though full many a morning,
Yet they are sleeping still.

The trumpet, sir, shall wake them,
In dream I see them rise,
Each with a solemn musket
A-marching to the skies.

A coward will remain, sir,
Until the fight is done,
But an immortal hero
Will take his hat and run.

Goodbye, sir, I am going—
My country calleth me.
Allow me, sir, at parting
To wipe my weeping e'e.

In token of our friendship
Accept this Bonnie Doon,
And when the hand that plucked it
Has passed beyond the moon,

The memory of my ashes
Will consolation be.
Then farewell, Tuscarora,
And farewell, sir, to thee.

To her brother Austin
(Amherst, early in 1851)

Sunday Evening

It might not come amiss, dear Austin, to have a tiding or two concerning our state and feelings, particularly when we remember that "Jamie has gone awa'."

Our state is pretty comfortable, and our feelings are somewhat solemn, which we account for satisfactorily by calling to mind the fact that it is the Sabbath day.

Whether a certain passenger in a certain yesterday's stage has any sombre effect on our once merry household or the reverse, "I dinna choose to tell," but be the case as it may, we are rather a crestfallen company, to make the best of us, and what with the sighing wind, the sobbing rain, and the whining of Nature generally, we can hardly contain ourselves, and I only hope and trust that your—this evening's—lot is cast in far more cheery places than the ones you leave behind.

We are enjoying this evening what is called a "northeast storm"—a little north of east in case you are pretty definite. Father thinks it's "amazin' raw," and I'm half disposed to think that he's in the right about it, though I keep pretty dark and don't say much about it! Vinnie is at the instrument, humming a pensive air concerning a young lady who thought she was "almost there." Vinnie seems much grieved, and I really suppose *I* ought to betake myself to weeping; I'm pretty sure that I *shall* if she don't abate her singing.

Father's just got home from meeting and Mr. Boltwood's, found the last quite comfortable and the first not quite so well. . . There has been not much stirring since when you went away—I should venture to say prudently that matters had come to a stand—unless something new "turns up," I cannot see anything to prevent a quiet season. Father takes care of the doors and mother of the windows, and Vinnie and I are secure against all outward attacks. If we can get our hearts "under," I don't have much to fear—I've got all but three feelings down, if I can only keep them! . . .

I shall think of you tomorrow with four and twenty Irish boys all in a row. I miss you very much—I put on my bonnet tonight, opened the gate very desperately, and for a little while the suspense was terrible—I think I was held in check by some invisible agent, for I returned to the house without having done any harm!

If I hadn't been afraid that you would "poke fun" at my feelings, I had written a sincere letter, but since "the world is hollow, and dollie's stuffed with sawdust," I really do not think we had better expose our feelings. . .

To the same
(Amherst, 1851)

Sunday Evening

I received your letter, Austin, permit me to thank you for it
and to request some more as soon as it's convenient—permit
me to accord with your discreet opinion concerning Swedish
Jennie, and to commend the heart brave enough to express
it—combating the opinion of two civilized worlds and New
York into the bargain must need considerable daring—indeed,
it had never occurred to me that amidst the hallelujahs one
tongue would dare be dumb, and much less, I assure you, that
this dissenting one should be my romantic brother! For I had
looked for delight and a very high style of rapture in such a
youth as you. . .

We have all been rather piqued at Jennie's singing so
well, and this first calumnious whisper pleases us so well,
we rejoice that we didn't come—our visit is yet before us. . .
You haven't told us yet as you promised about your home—
what kind of people they are—whether you find them
pleasant—whether those timid gentlemen have yet "found
tongues to say." Do you find the life and living anymore
annoying than you at first expected—do you light upon any
friends to help the time away—have you whipped anymore
bad boys—all these are solemn questions, pray give them
proper heed!

Two weeks of your time are gone; I can't help wondering
sometimes if you would love to see us, and come to this
still home. . . A Senior levee was held at Professor and
Mrs. Haven's on Tuesday of last week—Vinnie played pretty
well. There's another at the President's this next Friday
evening. *Clarum et venerabile* Seniors!

To the same
(Amherst, March, 1851)

Sunday Afternoon

. . . It's a glorious afternoon—the sky is blue and warm—the
wind blows just enough to keep the clouds sailing, and the

sunshine—oh *such* sunshine! It isn't like gold, for gold is dim beside it; it isn't like anything which you or I have seen! It seems to me "Ik Marvel" was born on such a day; I only wish you were here. Such days were made on purpose for you and me; then what in the world are you gone for? Oh, dear, I do not know, but this I do know, that if wishing would bring you home, you were here today. Is it pleasant in Boston? *Of course* it isn't, though. I might have known more than to make such an inquiry. No doubt the streets are muddy, and the sky some dingy hue, and I can think just how everything bangs and rattles, and goes rumbling along through stones and plank and clay! I don't feel as if I could have you there, possibly, another day. I'm afraid you'll turn into a bank, or a Pearl Street counting-room, if you have not already assumed some monstrous shape, living in such a place.

Let me see—April; three weeks until April—the very first of April—well, perhaps that will do, only be sure of the week, the *whole* week, and nothing but the week. If they make new arrangements, give my respects to them, and tell them old arrangements are good enough for you, and you will have them; then if they raise the wind, why, let it blow—there's nothing more excellent than a breeze now and then!

What a time we shall have Fast day, after we get home from meeting—why, it makes me dance to think of it; and Austin, if I dance so many days beforehand, what will become of me when the hour really arrives? I don't know, I'm sure; and I don't care, much, for that or for anything else but get you home. . . Much love from mother and Vinnie; we are now pretty well, and our hearts are set on April, the *very first* of April!

EMILIE

To THE SAME
(Amherst, late March, 1851)

Thursday Night

DEAR AUSTIN,
. . . I have read *Ellen Middleton*. I needn't tell you I like it, nor need I tell you more, for you know already.

I thank you more and more for all the pleasures you give me—I can give you nothing, Austin, but a warm and grateful heart that is yours now and always. Love from all.

EMILIE

Only think, you are coming Saturday! I don't know why it is that it's always *Sunday* immediately you get home. I will arrange it differently. If it wasn't twelve o'clock I would stay longer.

TO THE SAME
(Amherst, June 16, 1851)

Sunday Evening

. . . I'm glad you are so well pleased, I'm glad you are not delighted. I would not that foreign places should wear the smile of home. We are quite alarmed for the *boys*—hope you won't kill or pack away any of 'em—so near Dr. Webster's bones 'tis not strange you have had temptations! . . . The country's still just now, and the severities alluded to will have a salutary influence in waking the people up. Speaking of *getting up*, how early are metropolitans expected to wake up, especially young men— more especially school-masters? I miss my "department" mornings. I lay it quite to heart that I've no one to wake up. *Your* room looks lonely enough, I do not love to go in there; whenever I pass through I find I 'gin to whistle, as we read that little boys are wont to do in the graveyard. I am going to set out crickets as soon as I find time, that they by their shrill singing shall help disperse the gloom; will they grow if I transplant them?

You importune me for news; I am very sorry to say "Vanity of vanities" there's no such thing as news—it is almost time for the cholera, and then things will take a start! . . . All of the folks send love.

Your affectionate
EMILIE

Sunday Afternoon

I have just come in from church very hot and faded. . . Our church grows interesting—Zion lifts her head—I overhear remarks signifying Jerusalem,—I do not feel at liberty to say anymore today!

. . . I wanted to write you Friday, the night of Jennie Lind, but reaching home past midnight, and my room sometime after, encountering several perils starting and on the way, among which a kicking horse, an inexperienced driver, a number of Jove's thunderbolts, and a very terrible rain, are worthy to have record. All of us went—just four—add an absent individual and that will make full five. The concert commenced at eight, but knowing the world was *hollow* we thought we'd start at six, and come up with everybody that meant to come up with us; we had proceeded some steps when one of the beasts showed symptoms; and just by the blacksmith's shop exercises commenced, consisting of kicking and plunging on the part of the horse, and whips and moral suasion from the gentleman who drove—the horse refused to proceed, and your respected family with much chagrin dismounted, advanced to the hotel, and for a season halted; another horse procured, we were politely invited to take our seats, and proceed, which we refused to do till the animal was warranted. About half through our journey thunder was said to be heard, and a suspicious cloud came travelling up the sky. What words express our horror when rain began to fall, in drops, sheets, cataracts—what fancy conceive of drippings and of drenchings which we met on the way; how the stage and its mourning captives drew up at Warner's Hotel; how all of us alighted, and were conducted in,—how the rain did not abate,—how we walked in silence to the old Edwards church* and took our seats in the same—how Jennie came out like a child and sang and sang again—how bouquets fell in showers,

---

* Evidently a slip of the pen, as Jenny Lind sang in the old First Church at Northampton on that occasion.

and the roof was rent with applause—how it thundered outside, and inside with the thunder of God and of men— judge ye which was the loudest; how we all loved Jennie Lind, but not accustomed oft to her manner of singing didn't fancy *that* so well as we did *her*. No doubt it was very fine, but take some notes from her *Echo*, the bird sounds from the *Bird Song*, and some of her curious trills, and I'd rather have a Yankee.

Herself and not her music was what we seemed to love— she has an air of exile in her mild blue eyes, and a something sweet and touching in her native accent which charms her many friends. *Give me my thatched cottage* as she sang she grew so earnest she seemed half lost in song, and for a transient time I fancied she *had* found it and would be seen "na mair"; and then her foreign accent made her again a wanderer—we will talk about her sometime when you come. Father sat all the evening looking *mad*, and yet so much amused you would have *died* a-laughing. . . It wasn't sarcasm exactly, nor it wasn't disdain, it was infinitely funnier than either of those virtues, as if old Abraham had come to see the show, and thought it was all very well, but a little excess of *monkey*! She took $4,000 for tickets at Northampton aside from all expenses. . .

About our coming to Boston—we think we shall probably come—we want to see our friends, yourself and Aunt L.'s family. We don't care a fig for the Museum, the stillness, or Jennie Lind. . . Love from us all.

Your affectionate sister
EMILY

To THE SAME
(Late July, 1851)

Sunday Evening

. . . Oh how I wish I could see your world and its little kingdoms, and I wish I could see the king—Stranger! he was my brother! I fancy little boys of several little sizes, some of them clothed in blue cloth, some of them clad in gray—I seat them round on benches in the school-room of my mind—then I set them all to shaking—on peril of their lives that they move their lips or whisper; then I clothe you with authority and empower you to punish, and to enforce the law, I call you "Rabbi, Master," and the picture is complete! It would seem very funny, say for Vinnie and me to come round as Committee—we should enjoy the terrors of fifty little boys, and any specimens of discipline in your way would be a rare treat for us. I should love to know how you managed—whether government as a science is laid down and executed, or whether you *cuff* and *thrash* as the occasion dictates; whether you use *pure* law as in the case of commanding, or whether you enforce it by means of sticks and stones as in the case of agents. I suppose you have authority bounded but by their lives. . . I should think you'd be tired of school and teaching and such hot weather. I really wish you were here, and the Endicott school where you found it. Whenever we go to ride in our beautiful family carriage we think if "wishes were horses" we four "beggars would ride." We shall enjoy brimful everything now but half full, and to have you home once more will be like living again.

We are having a pleasant summer—without one of the five it is yet a lonely one. Vinnie says sometimes—Didn't we have a brother—it seems to me we did, his name was Austin—we call but he answers not again—echo, Where is Austin? laughing, "Where *is* Austin?" . . . I wish they need not exhibit just for once in the year, and give you up on Saturday instead of the next week Wednesday; but keep your courage up and show forth those Emerald Isles till school committees and mayors are blinded with the dazzling! Wouldn't I love to be there! . . .

Our apples are ripening fast. I am fully convinced that with your approbation they will not only pick themselves, but arrange one another in baskets and present themselves to be eaten.

Love from all
EMILIE

To the same
(August, 1851)

Sunday Afternoon

At my old stand again, dear Austin, and happy as a queen to know that while I speak those whom I love are listening, and I am happier still if I shall make them happy.

I have just finished reading your letter which was brought in since church. I like it grandly—very—because it is so long, and also it's *so* funny—we have all been laughing till the old house rung again at your delineation of men, women, and things. I feel quite like retiring in presence of one so grand, and casting my small lot among small birds and fishes; you say you don't comprehend me, you want a simpler style—gratitude indeed for all my fine philosophy! I strove to be exalted, thinking I might reach *you*, and while I pant and struggle and climb the nearest cloud, you walk out very leisurely in your slippers from Empyrean, and without the slightest notice, request me to get down! As simple as you please, the simplest sort of simple—I'll be a little ninny, a little pussy catty, a little Red Riding Hood; I'll wear a bee in my bonnet, and a rose-bud in my hair, and what remains to do you shall be told hereafter.

Your letters are richest treats, send them always just such warm days—they are worth a score of fans and many refrigerators—the only difficulty they are so *queer*, and laughing such hot weather is anything but amusing. A little more of earnest, and a little less of jest until we are out of August, and then you may joke as freely as the father of rogues himself, and we will banish care, and daily die a-laughing!

It is very hot here now; I don't believe it's any hotter in Boston than it is here. . . Vinnie suggests that she may sometimes occur to mind when you would like more collars made. I told her I wouldn't tell you—I haven't, however, decided whether I will or not.

I often put on five knives and forks, and another tumbler, forgetting for the moment that "we are not all here." It occurs to me, however, and I remove the extra, and brush a tear away in memory of my brother.

We miss you now and always. When God bestows but three, and one of those is withdrawn, the others are left alone. . . Father is as uneasy when you are gone away as if you catch a trout and put him in Sahara. When you first went away he came home very frequently—walked gravely towards the barn, and returned looking very stately—then strode away down street as if the foe was coming; *now* he is more resigned—contents himself by fancying that "we shall hear today," and then when we do not hear, he wags his head profound, and thinks without a doubt there will be news "tomorrow." "Once one is two," once one will be two—ah, I have it here!

I wish you could have some cherries—if there was anyway we would send you a basket of them—they are very large and delicious, and are just ripening now. Little Austin Grout comes everyday to pick them, and mother takes great comfort in calling him by name, from vague association with her departed boy. Austin, to tell the truth, it is very still and lonely—I do wish you were here. . . The railroad is "a-workin'." My love to all my friends. I am on my way downstairs to put the tea-kettle boiling—writing and taking tea cannot sympathize. If you forget me now, your right hand *shall* its cunning.

EMILIE

TO THE SAME

September, 1851

. . . Vinnie and I came safely, and met with no mishap—the bouquet was not withered nor was the bottle cracked. It was fortunate for the freight car that Vinnie and I were there, ours being the only baggage passing along the line. The folks looked very funny who travelled with us that day—they were dim and faded, like folks passed away—the conductor seemed so grand with about half a dozen tickets which he dispersed and demanded in a very small space of time—I judged that the minority were travelling that day, and couldn't hardly help smiling at our ticket friend, however sorry I was at the small amount of people passing along his way. He looked as if he wanted to make an apology for not having more travellers to keep him company.

The route and the cars seemed strangely—there were no boys with fruit, there were no boys with pamphlets; one fearful little fellow ventured into the car with what appeared to be publications and tracts; he offered them to no one, and

no one inquired for them, and he seemed greatly relieved
that no one wanted to buy them. . . Mother sends much love,
and Vinnie.

Your lonely sister
EMILY

To THE SAME
(Amherst, Autumn, 1851)

Saturday Morn

DEAR AUSTIN,

I've been trying to think this morning how many weeks
it was since you went away—I fail in calculations; it seems
so long to me since you went back to school that I set down
days for years, and weeks for a score of years—not reckoning
time by minutes, I don't know what to think of such great
discrepancies between the actual hours and those which
"seem to be." It may seem long to you since you returned
to Boston—how I wish you would stay and never go back
again. . .

P.S.— . . . Mother sends her love and your waistcoat,
thinking you'll like the one, and quite likely need the other.

To THE SAME

Oct. 2

. . . You say we mustn't trouble to send you any fruit, also
your clothes must give us no uneasiness. I don't ever want to
have you say anymore such things. They make me feel like
crying. If you'd only teased us for it, and declared that you
would have it, I shouldn't have cared so much that we could
find no way to send you any, but you resign so cheerfully your
birthright of purple grapes, and do not so much as murmur
at the departing peaches, that I hardly can taste the one or
drink the juice of the other. They are so beautiful, Austin,—
we have such an abundance "while you perish with hunger."

I do hope someone will make up a mind to go before
our peaches are quite gone. The world is full of people

travelling everywhere, until it occurs to you that you will send an errand, and then by "hook or crook" you can't find any traveller who, for money or love, can be induced to go and carry the opprobrious package. It's a very selfish age, that is all I can say about it. Mr. Storekeeper S—— has been "almost persuaded" to go, but I believe he has put it off "till a more convenient season," so to show my disapprobation I sha'n't buy anymore gloves at Mr. S——'s store! Don't you think it will seem very cutting to see me pass by his goods and purchase at Mr. K——'s? I don't think I shall retract should he regret his course and decide to go tomorrow, because it is the principle of disappointing people which I disapprove! . . .

The peaches are very large—one side a rosy cheek, and the other a golden, and that peculiar coat of velvet and of down which makes a peach so beautiful. The grapes, too, are fine, juicy, and *such* a purple—I fancy the robes of kings are not a tint more royal. The vine looks like a kingdom, with ripe round grapes for kings, and hungry mouths for subjects—the first instance on record of subjects devouring kings! You *shall* have some grapes, dear Austin, if I have to come on foot in order to bring them to you.

The apples are very fine—it isn't quite time to pick them—the cider is almost done—we shall have some I guess by Saturday, at any rate Sunday noon. The vegetables are not gathered, but will be before very long. The horse is doing nicely; he travels "like a bird" to use a favorite phrase of your delighted mother's. You ask about the leaves—shall I say they are falling? They had begun to fall before Vinnie and I came home, and we walked up the steps through little brown ones rustling. . .

Vinnie tells me she has detailed the news—she reserved the deaths for me, thinking I might fall short of my usual letter somewhere. In accordance with her wishes I acquaint you with the decease of your aged friend Deacon—. He had no disease that we know of, but gradually went out. . . Monday evening we were all startled by a violent church-bell ringing, and thinking of nothing but fire, rushed out in the street to see. The sky was a beautiful red, bordering on a crimson, and rays of a gold pink color were constantly shooting off from a kind of sun in the centre. People were alarmed at this beautiful phenomenon, supposing that fires somewhere were coloring the sky. The exhibition lasted for nearly fifteen minutes, and the streets were full of people wondering and admiring. Father happened to see it among the very first, and rang the bell himself to call attention to it. You will have a full account from the pen of Mr. Trumbull, who, I have not a doubt, was seen with a long lead pencil a-noting down the sky at the time of its highest glory. . . You will be here now so soon—we are impatient for it—we want to see you, Austin, how much I cannot say here.

Your affectionate
EMILY

To the same
(Amherst, early October, 1851)

Friday Morning

DEAR AUSTIN,

. . . I would not spend much strength upon those little school-boys—you will need it all for something better and braver after you get away. It would rejoice my heart if on some pleasant morning you'd turn the school-room key on Irish boys, nurse and all, and walk away to freedom and the sunshine here at home. Father says all Boston wouldn't be a temptation to you another year—I wish it would not tempt you to stay another day. Oh, Austin, it is wrong to tantalize you so while you are braving all things in trying to fulfill duty. Duty is black and brown—home is bright and shining, "and the spirit and the bride say come, and let him that " wandereth come, for "behold all things are ready." We are having such lovely weather—the air is as sweet and still—now and then a gay leaf falling—the crickets sing all day long—high in a crimson tree a belated bird is singing—a thousand little painters are tingeing hill and dale. I admit now, Austin, that autumn is *most* beautiful, and spring is but the least, yet they "differ as stars" in their distinctive glories. How happy if you were here to share these pleasures with us—the fruit should be more sweet, and the dying day more golden—merrier the falling nut if with you we gathered it and hid it down deep in the abyss of basket; but you complain not, wherefore do we?

Tuesday evening we had a beautiful time reading and talking of the good times of last summer, and we anticipated—boasted ourselves of tomorrow—of the future we created, and all of us went to ride in an air-bubble for a carriage. We cherish all the past, we glide a-down the present, awake yet dreaming; but the future of ours together—there the bird sings loudest, and the sun shines always there. . .

I had a dissertation from E. C. a day or two ago—don't know which was the author, Plato or Socrates—rather think Jove had a finger in it. . . They all send their love. Vinnie sends hers. How soon you will be here! Days, flee away—"lest with a whip of scorpions I overtake your lingering." I am in a hurry—this pen is too slow for me—"it hath done what it could."

Your affectionate
EMILY

To THE SAME
(Amherst, before "Cattle Show," 1851)

Friday Morning

. . . The breakfast is so warm, and pussy is here a-singing, and the tea-kettle sings too, as if to see which was loudest, and I am so afraid lest kitty should be beaten—yet a shadow falls upon my morning picture—where is the youth so bold, the bravest of our fold—a seat is empty here—spectres sit in your chair, and now and then nudge father with their long, bony elbows. I wish you were here, dear Austin; the dust falls on the bureau in your deserted room, and gay, frivolous spiders spin away in the comers. I don't go there after dark whenever I can help it, for the twilight seems to pause there, and I am half afraid; and if ever I have to go, I hurry with all my might, and never look behind me, for I know who I should see.

Before next Tuesday—oh, before the coming stage, will I not brighten and brush it, and open the long-closed blinds, and with a sweeping broom will I not bring each spider down from its home so high, and tell it it may come back again when master has gone—and oh, I will bid it to be a tardy spider, to tarry on the way; and I will think my eye is fuller than sometimes, though *why* I cannot tell, when it shall rap on the window and come to live again. I am so happy when I know how soon you are coming that I put away my sewing and go out in the yard to think. I have tried to delay the frosts, I have coaxed the fading flowers, I thought I *could* detain a few of the crimson leaves until you had smiled upon them; but their companions call them, and they cannot stay away.

You will find the blue hills, Austin, with the autumnal shadows silently sleeping on them, and there will be a glory lingering round the day, so you'll know autumn has been here; and the setting sun will tell you, if you don't get home till evening. . . I thank you for such a long letter, and yet if I might choose, the next should be a longer. I think a letter just about three days long would make me happier than any other kind of one, if you please,—dated at Boston, but thanks be to our Father you may conclude it here. Everything has changed since my other letter,—the doors are shut this morning, and all the kitchen wall is covered with chilly flies who are trying to warm themselves,—poor things, they do not understand that there are no summer mornings remaining to them and me, and they have a bewildered air which is really very droll, didn't one feel sorry for them. You would say 'twas a gloomy morning if you were sitting here,—the frost has been severe, and the few lingering leaves seem anxious to be going, and wrap their faded cloaks more closely about them as if to shield them from the chilly northeast wind. The earth looks like some poor old lady who by dint of pains has bloomed e'en till now, yet in a forgetful moment a few silver hairs from out her cap come stealing, and she tucks them back so hastily and thinks nobody sees. The cows are going to pasture, and little boys with their hands in their pockets are whistling to try to keep warm. Don't think that the sky will frown so the day when you come home! She will smile and look happy, and be full of sunshine then, and even should she frown upon her child returning, there is another sky, ever serene and fair, and there is another sunshine, though it be darkness there; never mind faded forests, Austin, never mind silent fields—*here* is a little forest, whose leaf is ever green; here is a brighter garden, where not a frost has been; in its unfading flowers I hear the bright bee hum; prithee, my brother, into *my* garden come!

Your very affectionate sister

To the same
(November, 1851)

Thursday Evening

Dear Austin,

Something seems to whisper "He is thinking of home this evening," perhaps because it rains, perhaps because it's evening and the orchestra of winds perform their strange, sad music. I wouldn't wonder if home were thinking of him; and it seems so natural for one to think of the other, perhaps it is no superstition or omen of this evening,—no omen "at all, at all," as Mrs. Mack would say.

Father is staying at home this evening it is so inclement— Vinnie diverts his mind with little snatches of music; and mother mends a garment to make it snugger for you—and what do you think *I* do among this family circle? I am thinking of you with all my might, and it just occurs to me to note a few of my thoughts for your own inspection. "Keeping a diary" is not familiar to me as to your sister Vinnie, but her own bright example is quite a comfort to me, so I'll try.

I waked up this morning thinking for all the world I had had a letter from you—just as the seal was breaking, father rapped at my door. I was sadly disappointed not to go on and read; but when the four black horses came trotting into town, and their load was none the heavier by a tiding for me—I was not disappointed then, it was harder to me than had I been disappointed. . . I found I had made no provision for any such time as that. . . The weather has been unpleasant ever since you went away—Monday morning we waked up in the midst of a furious snow-storm—the snow was the depth of an inch; oh, it looked so wintry! By-and-by the sun came out, but the wind blew violently and it grew so cold that we gathered all the quinces, put up the stove in the sitting-room, and bade the world goodbye. Kind clouds came over at evening; still the sinking thermometer gave terrible signs of what would be on the morning. At last the morning came, laden with mild south winds, and the winds have brought the rain, so here we are. . . Your very hasty letter just at your return rejoiced us—that you were "better—happier—heartier." What made you think of such beautiful words to tell us how you were, and how cheerful you were feeling? It did us a world of good. How little the scribe thinks of the value of his line—how many eager eyes will search its every meaning, how much swifter the strokes of "the little mystic clock, no human eye hath seen, which ticketh on and ticketh on, from morning until e'en." If it were not that I could write you, you could not go away; therefore pen and ink are very excellent things.

We had new brown bread for tea—when it came smoking on and we sat around the table, how I did wish a slice could be reserved for you! You shall have as many loaves as we have eaten slices if you will but come home. This suggests Thanksgiving, you will soon be here; then I can't help thinking of how, when we rejoice, so many hearts are breaking next Thanksgiving day. What will you say, Austin, if I tell you that Jennie Grout and merry Martha Kingman will spend the day above? They are not here—"While we delayed to let them forth, angels beyond stayed for them." . . .

Your affectionate
Emily

To the same
(Amherst, November 17, 1851)

Sunday Afternoon

Dear Austin,

We have just got home from meeting—it is very windy and cold—the hills from our kitchen window are just crusted with snow, which with their blue mantillas makes them seem so beautiful. You sat just here last Sunday, where I am sitting now; and our voices were nimbler than our pens can be, if they try never so hardly. I should be quite sad today, thinking about last Sunday, didn't another Sabbath smile at me so pleasantly, promising me on its word to present you here again when "six days' work is done."

Father and mother sit in state in the sitting-room perusing such papers, only, as they are well assured, have nothing carnal in them; Vinnie is eating an apple which makes me think of gold, and accompanying it with her favorite *Observer*, which, if you recollect, deprives us many a time of her sisterly society. Pussy hasn't returned from the afternoon assembly, so you have us all just as we are at present. We were very glad indeed to hear from you so soon, glad that a cheerful fire met you at the door. I *do* well remember how chilly the west wind blew, and how everything shook and rattled before I went to sleep, and I often thought of you in the midnight car, and hoped you were not lonely. . . We are thinking most of Thanksgiving than anything else just now—how full will be the circle, less then by none—how the things will smoke—how the board will groan with the thousand savory viands—how when the day is done, lo, the evening cometh, laden with merrie laugh and happy conversation, and then the sleep and the dream each of a knight or "Ladie"—how I love to see them, a beautiful company coming down the hill which men call the Future, with their hearts full of joy and their hands of gladness. Thanksgiving indeed to a family united once more together before they go away. . . Don't mind the days—some of them are long ones, but who cares for length when breadth is in store for him? Or who minds the cross who knows he'll have a crown? I wish I could imbue you with all the strength and courage which can be given men—I wish I could assure you of the constant remembrance of those you leave at home—I wish—but oh! how vainly—that I could bring you back again and never more to stray. You are tired now, dear Austin, with my incessant din, but I can't help saying any of these things.

The very warmest love from Vinnie and everyone of us. I am never ready to go.

Reluctant
EMILY

To the same
(December, 1851)

DEAR AUSTIN,

... I was so glad to get your letter. I had been making calls all Saturday afternoon, and came home very tired, and a little disconsolate, so your letter was more than welcome... Oh Austin, you don't know how we all wished for you yesterday. We had such a splendid sermon from Professor Park—I never heard anything like it, and don't expect to again, till we stand at the great white throne, and "he reads from the Book, the Lamb's Book." The students and chapel people all came to our church, and it was very full, and still, so still the buzzing of a fly would have boomed like a cannon. And when it was all over, and that wonderful man sat down, people stared at each other, and looked as wan and wild as if they had seen a spirit, and wondered they had not died. How I wish you had heard him—I thought of it all the time...

Affectionately
EMILIE

To the same
(Amherst, January, 1852)

Monday Morning

Did you think I was tardy, Austin? For two Sunday afternoons it has been so cold and cloudy that I didn't feel in my very happiest mood, and so I did not write until next Monday morning, determining in my heart never to write to you in any but cheerful spirits.

Even this morning, Austin, I am not in merry case, for it snows slowly and solemnly, and hardly an outdoor thing can be seen a-stirring—now and then a man goes by with a large cloak wrapped around him, and shivering at that; and now and then a stray kitten out on some urgent errand creeps through the flakes and crawls so fast as *may* crawl half frozen away. I am glad for the sake of your body that you are not here this morning, for it is a trying time for fingers and toes—

for the heart's sake I would verily have you here. You know there are winter mornings when the cold without only adds to the warm within, and the more it snows and the harder it blows brighter the fires blaze, and chirps more merrily the "cricket on the hearth." It is hardly cheery enough for such a scene this morning, and yet methinks it would be if you were only here. The future full of sleigh-rides would chase the gloom from our minds which only deepens and darkens with every flake that falls.

Black Fanny would "toe the mark" if you should be here tomorrow; but as the prospects are, I presume Black Fanny's hoofs will not attempt to fly. Do you have any snow in Boston? Enough for a ride, I hope, for the sake of "Auld Lang Syne." Perhaps the "ladie" of curls would not object to a drive. . . We miss you more and more, we do not become accustomed to separation from you. I almost wish sometimes we needn't miss you so much, since duty claims a year of you entirely to herself; and then again I think that it is pleasant to miss you if you must go away, and I would not have it otherwise, even if I could. In every pleasure and pain you come up to our minds so wishfully—we know you'd enjoy our joy, and if you were with us, Austin, we could bear little trials more cheerfully. . . When I know of anything funny I am just as apt to cry, far more so than to laugh, for I know who loves jokes best, and who is not here to enjoy them. We don't have many jokes, though, now, it is pretty much all sobriety; and we do not have much poetry, father having made up his mind that it's pretty much all real life. Father's real life and mine sometimes come into collision but as yet escape unhurt. . . I am so glad you are well and in such happy spirits—both happy and well is a great comfort to us when you are far away.

Emilie

To the same
(February 6, 1852)

Friday Morning
. . . Since we have written you the grand railroad decision is made, and there is great rejoicing throughout this town

and the neighboring; that is, Sunderland, Montague, and Belchertown. Everybody is wide awake, everything is stirring, the streets are full of people walking cheeringly, and you should really be here to partake of the jubilee. The event was celebrated by D. Warner and cannon; and the silent satisfaction in the hearts of all is its crowning attestation.

Father is really sober from excessive satisfaction, and bears his honors with a most becoming air. Nobody believes it yet, it seems like a fairy tale, a most miraculous event in the lives of us all. The men begin working next week; only think of it, Austin; why, I verily believe we shall fall down and worship the first "son of Erin" that comes, and the first sod he turns will be preserved as an emblem of the struggle and victory of our heroic fathers. Such old fellows as Col. S. and his wife fold their arms complacently and say, "Well, I declare, we have got it after all." Got it, *you* good-for-nothings! and so we have, in spite of sneers and pities and insults from all around; and we will keep it too, in spite of earth and heaven! How I wish you were here—it is really too bad, Austin, at such a time as now. I miss your big hurrahs, and the famous stir you make upon all such occasions; but it is a comfort to know that you are here—that your whole soul is here, and though apparently absent, yet present in the highest and the truest sense. . . Take good care of yourself, Austin, and think much of us all, for we do so of you.

EMILIE

To the same
(March 24, 1852)

Wednesday Morn

You wouldn't think it was spring, Austin, if you were at home this morning, for we had a great snowstorm yesterday, and things are all white this morning. It sounds funny enough to hear birds singing and sleigh-bells at a time. But it won't last long, so you needn't think 'twill be winter at the time when you come home.

I waited a day or two, thinking I might hear from you, but you will be looking for me, and wondering where I am, so

I sha'n't wait any longer. We're rejoiced that you're coming home—the first thing we said to father when he got out of the stage was to ask if you were coming. I was sure you would all the while, for father said "of course you would," he should "consent to no other arrangement," and as you say, Austin, "what father says he means." How very soon it will be now—why, when I really think of it, how near and how happy it is! My heart grows light so fast that I could mount a grasshopper and gallop around the world, and not fatigue him any! The sugar weather holds on, and I do believe it will stay until you come. . . "Mrs. S." is very feeble; "can't bear allopathic treatment, can't have homœopathic, don't want hydropathic," oh, what a pickle she is in! Shouldn't think she would deign to live, it is so decidedly vulgar! They have not yet concluded where to move—Mrs. W. will perhaps obtain board in the celestial city, but I'm sure I can't imagine what will become of the rest. . . Much love from us all.

EMILIE

To the same
(May 10, 1852)

Monday Morning, 5 o'c.

DEAR AUSTIN,

. . . Vinnie will tell you all the news, so I will take a little place to describe a thunder-shower which occurred yesterday afternoon,—the very first of the season. Father and Vinnie were at meeting, mother asleep in her room, and I at work by my window on a "Lyceum lecture." The air was really scorching, the sun red and hot, and you know just how the birds sing before a thunder-storm, a sort of hurried and agitated song—pretty soon it began to thunder, and the great "cream-colored heads" peeped out of their windows. Then came the wind and rain, and I hurried around the house to shut all the doors and windows. I wish you had seen it come, so cool and so refreshing—and everything glistening from it as with a golden dew—I thought of you all the time. This morning is fair and delightful. You will awake in dust, and with it the ceaseless din of the untiring city. Wouldn't you change your dwelling for my palace in the dew? Goodbye for now. I shall see you so soon.

E.

To the same
(Amherst, July 23, 1852)

Sunday Night

. . . You'd better not come home; I say the law will have you, a pupil of the law o'ertaken by the law, and brought to condign punishment,—scene for angels and men, or rather for archangels, who being a little higher would seem to have a 'vantage so far as view's concerned. "*Are* you pretty comfortable, though,"—and are you deaf and dumb and gone to the asylum where such afflicted persons learn to hold their tongues?

The next time you aren't going to write me, I'd thank you to let me know—this kind of *protracted* insult is what no man can bear. Fight with me like a man—let me have fair shot, and you are *caput mortuum et cap-a-pie*, and that ends the business! If you really think I so deserve this silence, tell me why—how—I'll be a thorough scamp or else I won't be any, just which you prefer.

T—— of S——'s class went to Boston yesterday; it was in my heart to send an apple by him for your private use, but father overheard some of my intentions, and said they were "rather small "—whether this remark was intended for the apple, or for my noble self I did not think to ask him; I rather think he intended to give us both a cut—however, he may not!

You are coming home on Wednesday, as perhaps you know, and I am very happy in prospect of your coming and hope you want to see us as much as we do you. Mother makes nicer pies with reference to your coming, I arrange my thoughts in a convenient shape, Vinnie grows only perter and more pert day by day.

The horse is looking finely—better than in his life—by which you may think him dead unless I add *before*. The carriage stands in state all covered in the chaise-house—we have one foundling hen into whose young mind I seek to instil the fact that "Massa is a-comin!"

The garden is amazing—we have beets and beans, have had splendid potatoes for three weeks now. Old Amos weeds and hoes and has an oversight of all thoughtless vegetables. The apples are fine and large in spite of my impression that father called them "small."

Yesterday there was a fire. At about three in the afternoon Mr. Kimberly's barn was discovered to be on fire; the wind was blowing a gale directly from the west, and having had no rain, the roofs (were) as dry as stubble. Mr. Palmer's house was charred—the little house of father's—and Mr. Kimberly's also. The engine was broken, and it seemed for a little while as if the whole street must go; the Kimberlys' barn was burnt down, and the house much charred and injured, though not at all destroyed—Mr. Palmer's barn took fire, and Deacon Leland's also, but were extinguished with only part burned roofs. We all feel very thankful at such a narrow escape. Father says there was never such imminent danger, and such miraculous escape. Father and Mr. Frink took charge of the fire—or rather of the *water*, since fire usually takes care of itself. The men all worked like heroes, and after the fire was out father gave commands to have them march to Howe's where an entertainment was provided for them. After the whole was over they gave "three cheers for Edward Dickinson," and three more for the insurance company. On the whole, it is very wonderful that we didn't all burn up, and we ought to hold our tongues and be very thankful. If there *must* be a fire, I'm sorry it couldn't wait until you had got home, because you seem to enjoy such things so very much.

There is nothing of moment now which I can find to tell you, except a case of measles in Hartford. . . Goodbye, Sir. Fare you well. My benison to your school.

To the same
(Amherst, Spring, 1853)

Tuesday Noon

Dear Austin,

. . . How soon now you are coming, and how happy we are in the thought of seeing you! I can't realize that you will come, it is so still and lonely it doesn't seem possible it can be otherwise; but we shall see, when the nails hang full of coats again, and the chairs hang full of hats, and I can count the slippers under the chair. Oh, Austin, how we miss them all, and more than them, somebody who used to hang them there, and get many a hint ungentle to carry them away. Those times seem far off now, a great way, as things we did when children. I wish we were children now—I wish we were always children, how to grow up I don't know. . . Cousin J. has made us an Æolian harp which plays beautifully whenever there is a breeze.

Austin, you mustn't care if your letters do not get here just when you think they will—they are always new to us, and delightful always, and the more you send us the happier we shall be. We all send our love to you, and think much and say much of seeing you again—keep well till you come, and if knowing that we all love you makes you happier, then, Austin, you may sing the whole day long!

Affectionately
EMILIE

To THE SAME
(Amherst, March 18, 1853)

Friday Morning

DEAR AUSTIN,

I presume you remember a story that Vinnie tells of a breach of promise case where the correspondence between the parties consisted of a reply from the girl to one she had never received but was daily expecting. Well, *I* am writing an answer to the letter I haven't had, so you will see the force of the accompanying anecdote. I have been looking for you ever since despatching my last, but this is a fickle world, and it's a great source of complacency that 'twill all be burned up by and by. I should be pleased with a line when you've published your work to father, if it's perfectly convenient!

Your letters are very funny indeed—about the only jokes we have, now you are gone, and I hope you will send us one as often as you can. Father takes great delight in your remarks to him—puts on his spectacles and reads them o'er and o'er as if it was a blessing to have an only son. He reads all the letters you write, as soon as he gets them, at the post-office, no matter to whom addressed; then he makes me read them aloud at the supper table again, and when he gets home in the evening, he cracks a few walnuts, puts his spectacles on, and with your last in his hand, sits down to enjoy the evening. . . I believe at this moment, Austin, that there's nobody living for whom father has such respect as for you. But my paper is getting low, and I must hasten to tell you that we are very happy to hear good news from you, that we hope you'll have pleasant times and learn a great deal while you're gone, and come back to us greater and happier for the life lived at Cambridge. We miss you more and more. I wish that we could see you, but letters come the next—write them often, and tell us everything.

Affectionately
EMILIE

To THE SAME
(June 14, 1853)

. . . We have been free from company by the "Amherst and Belchertown Railroad " since J. went home, though we live in constant fear of someother visitation. "Oh, would some power the giftie gie" folks to see themselves as we see them.—*Burns*.

I have read the poems, Austin, and am going to read them again. They please me very much, but I must read them again before I know just what I think of "Alexander Smith." They are not very coherent, but there's a good deal of exquisite frenzy, and some wonderful figures as ever I met in my life. We will talk about it again. The grove looks nicely, Austin, and we think must certainly grow. We love to go there—it is a charming place. Everything is singing now, and everything is beautiful that *can* be in its life. . . The time for the New London trip has not been fixed upon. I sincerely wish it may wait until you get home from Cambridge if you would like to go.

The cars continue thriving—a good many passengers seem to arrive from somewhere, though nobody knows from where.

Father expects his new buggy to arrive by the cars everyday now, and that will help a little. I expect all our grandfathers and all their country cousins will come here to spend Commencement, and don't doubt the stock will rise several percent that week. If we children could obtain board for the week in some "vast wilderness," I think we should have good times. . .

To the same
(June 20,1853)

Monday Morning

My dear Austin,

. . . The New London day passed off grandly, so all the people said. It was pretty hot and dusty, but nobody cared for that. Father was, as usual, chief marshal of the day, and went marching around with New London at his heels like some old Roman general upon a triumph day. Mrs. H. got a capital dinner, and was very much praised. Carriages flew like sparks, hither and thither and yon, and they all said 'twas fine. I "spose" it was. I sat in Professor Tyler's woods and saw the train move off, and then came home again for fear somebody would see me, or ask me how I did. Dr. Holland was here, and called to see us—was very pleasant indeed, inquired for you, and asked mother if Vinnie and I might come and see them in Springfield. . . We all send you our love.

Emilie

To the same
(Postmarked, July 2, 1853)

Friday Afternoon

Dear Austin,

. . . Some of the letters you've sent us we have received, and thank you for affectionately. Some we have not received, but thank you for the memory, of which the emblem perished. Where all those letters go, yours and ours, somebody surely knows, but we do not. There's a new postmaster today, but we don't know who's to blame. You never wrote me a letter, Austin, which I liked half so well as the one father brought me. We think of your coming home with a great deal of happiness, and are glad you want to come.

Father said he never saw you looking in better health or seeming in finer spirits. He didn't say a word about the Hippodrome or the Museum, and he came home so stern that none of us dared to ask him, and besides grandmother was here, and you certainly don't think I'd allude to a Hippodrome in the presence of that lady! I'd as soon think of popping fire-crackers in the presence of Peter the Great. But you'll tell us when you get home—how soon—how soon! . . . I admire the "Poems" very much. We all send our love to you—shall write you again Sunday.

Emilie

To the same
(1853)

I have had somethings from you to which I perceive no meaning. They either were very vast, or they didn't mean anything, I don't know certainly which. What did you mean by a note you sent me day before yesterday? Father asked me what you wrote, and I gave it to him to read. He looked very much confused, and finally put on his spectacles, which didn't seem to help him much—I don't think a telescope would have assisted him. I hope you will write to me—I love to hear from you, and now Vinnie is gone I shall feel very lonely. . . Love for them all if there are those to love and think of me, and more and most for you, from

Emily

To Mrs. J. G. Holland
(About 1853)

Friday Evening

Thank you, dear Mrs. Holland—Vinnie and I will come, if you would like to have us. We should have written before, but mother has not been well, and we hardly knew whether we could leave her, but she is better now, and I write quite late this evening, that if you still desire it, Vinnie and I will come. Then, dear Mrs. Holland, if agreeable to you, we will take the Amherst train on Tuesday morning, for Springfield, and be with you at noon.

The cars leave here at nine o'clock, and I think reach Springfield at twelve. I can think just how we dined with you a year ago from now, and it makes my heart beat faster to think perhaps we'll see you so little while from now.

To live a thousand years would not make me forget the day and night we spent there, and while I write the words, I don't believe I'm coming, so sweet it seems to me. I hope we shall not tire you; with all your other cares, we fear we should not come, but you *will* not let us trouble you, will you, dear Mrs. Holland?

Father and mother ask a very warm remembrance to yourself and Dr. Holland.

We were happy the grapes and figs seemed acceptable to you, and wished there were many more. I am very sorry to hear that "Kate" has such excellent lungs. With all your other cares, it must be quite a trial to you.

It is also a source of pleasure to me that Annie goes to sleep, on account of the "interregnum" it must afford to you.

Three days and we are there—happy—very happy! Tomorrow I will sew, but I shall think of you, and Sunday sing and pray—yet I shall not forget you, and Monday's very near, and here's to me on Tuesday! Goodnight, dear Mrs. Holland—I see I'm getting wild—you will forgive me all, and not *forget* me all, though? Vinnie is fast asleep, or her love would be here—though she is, it is. Once more, if it is fair, we will come on Tuesday, and you love to have us, but if not convenient, please surely tell us so.

Affectionately
EMILIE

To Dr. and Mrs. J. G. Holland

Tuesday Evening

DEAR DR. AND MRS. HOLLAND,

Dear Minnie—it is cold tonight, but the thought of you so warm, that I sit by it as a fireside, and am never cold anymore.

I love to write to you—it gives my heart a holiday and sets the bells to ringing. If prayers had any answers to them, you were all here tonight, but I seek and I don't find, and knock and it is not opened. Wonder if God is just—presume He is, however, and 'twas only a blunder of Matthew's.

I think mine is the case, where when they ask an egg, they get a scorpion, for I keep wishing for you, keep shutting up my eyes and looking toward the sky, asking with all my might for you, and yet you do not come. I wrote to you last week, but thought you would laugh at me, and call me sentimental, so I kept my lofty letter for "Adolphus Hawkins, Esq."

If it wasn't for broad daylight, and cooking-stoves, and roosters, I'm afraid you would have occasion to smile at my letters often, but so sure as "this mortal" essays immortality, a crow from a neighboring farm-yard dissipates the illusion, and I am here again.

And what I mean is this—that I thought of you all last week, until the world grew rounder than it sometimes is, and I broke several dishes.

Monday, I solemnly resolved I would be *sensible*, so I wore thick shoes, and thought of Dr. Humphrey, and the Moral Law. One glimpse of "The Republican" makes me break things again—I read in it every night.

Who writes those funny accidents, where railroads meet each other unexpectedly, and gentlemen in factories get their heads cut off quite informally? The author, too, relates them in such a sprightly way, that they are quite attractive. Vinnie was disappointed tonight, that there were not more accidents—I read the news aloud, while Vinnie was sewing. "The Republican" seems to us like a letter from you, and we break the seal and read it eagerly. . .

Vinnie and I talked of you as we sewed, this afternoon. I said—"how far they seem from us," but Vinnie answered me "only a little way." . . . I'd love to be a bird or bee, that whether hum or sing, still might be near you.

Heaven is large—is it not? Life is short too, isn't it? Then when one is done, is there not another, and—and—then if God is willing, we are neighbors then. Vinnie and mother send their love. Mine too is here. My letter as a bee, goes laden. Please love us and remember us. Please write us very soon, and tell us how you are. . .

Affectionately
EMILIE

To the same
(Late Autumn, 1853)

Sabbath Afternoon

DEAR FRIENDS,

I thought I would write again. I write you many letters with pens which are not seen. Do you receive them?

I think of you all today, and dreamed of you last night.

When father rapped on my door to wake me this morning, I was walking with you in the most wonderful garden, and helping you pick—roses, and though we gathered with all our might, the basket was never full. And so all day I pray that I may walk with you, and gather roses again, and as night draws on, it pleases me, and I count impatiently the hours 'tween me and the darkness, and the dream of you and the roses, and the basket never full.

God grant the basket fill not, till, with hands purer and whiter, we gather flowers of gold in baskets made of pearl; higher—higher! It seems long since we heard from you—long, since how little Annie was, or anyone of you—so long since Cattle Show, when Dr. Holland was with us. Oh, it always seems a long while from our seeing you, and even when at your house, the nights seemed much more long than they're wont to do, because separated from you. I want so much to know if the friends are all well in that dear cot in Springfield—and if well whether happy, and happy—*how* happy, and why, and what bestows the joy? And then those other questions, asked again and again, whose answers are so sweet, do they love—remember us—wish sometimes we were there? Ah, friends—dear friends—perhaps my queries tire you, but I so long to know.

The minister today, not our own minister, preached about death and judgment, and what would become of those, meaning Austin and me, who behaved improperly—and somehow the sermon scared me, and father and Vinnie looked very solemn as if the whole was true, and I would not for worlds have them know that it troubled me, but I longed to come to you, and tell you all about it, and learn how to be better. He preached such an awful sermon though, that I didn't much think I should ever see you again until the Judgment Day, and then you would not speak to me, according to his story. The subject of perdition seemed to please him, somehow. It seems very solemn to me. I'll tell you all about it, when I see you again.

I wonder what you are doing today—if you have been to meeting? Today has been a fair day, very still and blue. Tonight the crimson children are playing in the West, and tomorrow will be colder. How sweet if I could see you, and talk of all these things! Please write us very soon. The days with you last September seem a great way off, and to meet you again delightful. I am sure it won't be long before we sit together.

Then will I not repine, knowing that bird of mine, though flown—leameth beyond the sea, melody new for me, and will return.

Affectionately
EMILY

(This little poem was enclosed in the foregoing letter)

Truth is as old as God,
His twin identity—
And will endure as long as He,
A co-eternity,
And perish on the day
That He is borne away
From mansion of the universe,
A lifeless Deity.

To the same
(Enclosing some leaves, 1854)

January 2d

May it come *today?*

Then New Year the sweetest, and long life the merriest, and the Heaven highest—by and by!

EMILIE

To her brother Austin
(March 17, 1854)

. . . Since you went back to Cambridge the weather has been wonderful,—the thermometer every noon between 60 and 70 above zero, and the air full of birds.

Today has not seemed like a day. It has been most unearthly,—so mild, so bright, so still, the windows open, and fires uncomfortable.

Since supper it lightens frequently. In the south you can see the lightning—in the north the northern lights. Now a furious wind blows just from the north and west, and winter comes back again. . .

There is to be a party at Professor Haven's tomorrow night, for married people merely. Celibacy excludes me and my sister. Father and mother are invited. Mother will go. . . Mother and Vinnie send love. They are both getting ready for Washington. Take care of yourself.

EMILIE

To Mrs. J. G. Holland
(Spring, 1854)

PHILADELPHIA

DEAR MRS. HOLLAND AND MINNIE, and Dr. Holland too—I have stolen away from company to write a note to you; and to say that I love you still.

I am not at home—I have been away just five weeks today, and shall not go quite yet back to Massachusetts. Vinnie is with me here, and we have wandered together into many new ways.

We were three weeks in Washington, while father was there, and have been two in Philadelphia. We have had many pleasant times, and seen much that is fair, and heard much that is wonderful—many sweet ladies and noble gentlemen have taken us by the hand and smiled upon us pleasantly—and the sun shines brighter for our way thus far.

I will not tell you what I saw—the elegance, the grandeur; you will not care to know the value of the diamonds my Lord and Lady wore, but if you haven't been to the sweet Mount Vernon, then I *will* tell you how on one soft spring day we glided down the Potomac in a painted boat, and jumped upon the shore—how hand in hand we stole along up a tangled pathway till we reached the tomb of General George Washington, how we paused beside it, and no one spoke a word, then hand in hand, walked on again, not less wise or sad for that marble story; how we went within the door— raised the latch he lifted when he last went home—thank the Ones in Light that he's since passed in through a brighter wicket! Oh, I could spend a long day, if it did not weary you, telling of Mount Vernon—and I will sometime if we live and meet again, and God grant we shall!

I wonder if you have all forgotten us, we have stayed away so long. I hope you haven't—I tried to write so hard before I went from home, but the moments were so busy, and then they *flew* so. I was sure when days *did* come in which I was less busy, I should seek your forgiveness, and it did not occur to me that you might not forgive me. Am I too late today? Even if you are angry, I shall keep praying you, till from very weariness, you will take me in. It seems to me many a day since we were in Springfield, and Minnie and the *dumb-bells* seem as vague—as vague; and sometimes I wonder if I ever dreamed—then if I'm dreaming now, then if I *always* dreamed, and there is not a world, and not these darling friends, for whom I would not count my life too great a sacrifice. Thank God there is a world, and that the friends we love dwell forever and ever in a house above. I fear I grow incongruous, but to meet my friends does delight me so that I quite forget time and sense and so forth.

Now, my precious friends, if you won't forget me until I get home, and become more sensible, I will write again, and more properly. Why didn't I ask before, if you were well and happy?

Forgetful
EMILIE

TO HER BROTHER AUSTIN
(Amherst, May, 1854)

Saturday Mom

DEAR AUSTIN,

A week ago we were all here—today we are not all here—yet the bee hums just as merrily, and all the busy things work on as if the same. They do not miss you, child, but there is a humming-bee whose song is not so merry, and there are busy ones who pause to drop a tear. Let us thank God, today, Austin, that we can love our friends, our brothers and our sisters, and weep when they are gone, and smile at their return. It is indeed a joy which we are blest to know.

Today is very beautiful—just as bright, just as blue, just as green and as white and as crimson as the cherry-trees full in bloom, and the half-opening peach-blossoms, and the grass just waving, and sky and hill and cloud can make it, if they try. How I wish you were here, Austin; you thought last Saturday beautiful, yet to this golden day 'twas but one single gem to whole handfuls of jewels. You will ride today, I hope, or take a long walk somewhere, and recollect us all,—Vinnie and me and father and mother and home. Yes, Austin, everyone of us, for we all think of you, and bring you to recollection many times each day—not bring you to recollection, for we never put you away, but keep recollecting on. . .

You must think of us tonight while Mr. Dwight takes tea here, and we will think of you far away down in Cambridge.

Don't mind the can, Austin, if it is rather dry, don't mind the daily road though it is rather dusty, but remember the brooks and the hills, and remember while you're but one, we are but four at home!

EMILIE

To Dr. J. G. Holland
(November, 1854)

Saturday Eve

I come in flakes, dear Dr. Holland, for verily it snows, and as descending swans, here a pinion and there a pinion, and anon a plume, come the bright inhabitants of the white home.

I know they fall in Springfield; perhaps you see them now—and therefore I look out again, to see if you are looking.

How pleasant it seemed to hear your voice—so said Vinnie and I, as we as individuals, and then collectively, read your brief note. Why didn't you speak to us before? We thought you had forgotten us—we concluded that one of the bright things had gone forever more. That is a sober feeling, and it mustn't come too often in such a world as this. A violet came up next day, and blossomed in our garden, and were it not for these same flakes, I would go in the dark and get it, so to send to you. Thank Him who is in Heaven, Katie Holland lives! Kiss her on every cheek for me—I really can't remember how many the bairn has—and give my warmest recollection to Mrs. Holland and Minnie, whom to love, this Saturday night, is no trifling thing. I'm very happy that you are happy—and that you cheat the angels of another one.

I would the many households clad in dark attire had succeeded so. You must all be happy and strong and well. I love to have the lamps shine on your evening table. I love to have the sun shine on your daily walks.

The "new house"! God bless it! You will leave the "maiden and married life of Mary Powell" behind.

Love and remember
EMILIE

To her brother's wife
(1854)

DEAR SUE:

Adventure most unto itself
The Soul condemned to be;
Attended by a Single Hound—
Its own Identity.

EMILY

To the same
(1854)

DEAR SUE:

The Soul that hath a Guest,
Doth seldom go abroad.
Diviner Crowd at home
Obliterate the need,
And courtesy forbid
A Host's departure, when
Upon Himself be visiting
The Emperor of Men!

EMILY

To the same
(1854)

DEAR SUE:

The right to perish might be thought
An undisputed right,
Attempt it, and the Universe upon the opposite
Will concentrate its officers—
You cannot even die,
But Nature and Mankind must pause
To pay you scrutiny.

EMILY

To the same
(1854)

SUE:

There is another Loneliness
That many die without.
Not want or friend occasions it.
Or circumstances or lot.

But nature sometimes, sometimes thought.
And whoso it befall
Is richer than could be divulged
By mortal numeral.

EMILY

To the same
(1854)

SUE:

The missing All prevented me
From missing minor things.
If nothing larger than a World's
Departure from a hinge,
Or Sun's extinction be observed,
'Twas not so large that I
Could lift my forehead from my work
For curiosity.

EMILY

To the same
(1855)

SISTER SUE:

The difference between despair
And fear, is like the one
Between the instant of a wreck.
And when the wreck has been.

The mind is smooth,—no motion—
Contented as the eye
Upon the forehead of a Bust,
That knows it cannot see.

EMILY

To the same
(1855)

DEAR SUE:

There is a solitude of space,
A solitude of sea,
A solitude of death, but these
Society shall be,
Compared with that profounder site.
That polar privacy,

A Soul admitted to Itself:
Finite Infinity.

EMILY

TO THE SAME
(1855)

SUE:

Two lengths has everyday.
Its absolute extent—
And area superior
By hope or heaven lent.
Eternity will be
Velocity, or pause,
At fundamental signals
From fundamental laws.
To die, is not to go—
On doom's consummate chart
No territory new is staked,
Remain thou as thou art.

EMILY

TO THE SAME
(1855)

SUE:

Safe Despair it is that raves,
Agony is frugal,
Puts itself severe away
For its own perusal.

Garrisoned no Soul can be
In the front of Trouble,
Love is one, not aggregate,
Nor is Dying double.

EMILY

To the same
(1855)

Dear Sue:

The Face we choose to miss.
Be it but for a day—
As absent as a hundred years
When it has rode away.

Emily

To the same
(1855)

Sue:

Of so divine a loss
We enter but the gain,
Indemnity for loneliness
That such a bliss has been.

Emily

To Mrs. J. G. Holland
(1855)

Your voice is sweet, dear Mrs. Holland. I wish I heard it oftener. One of the mortal musics Jupiter denies, and when indeed its gentle measures fall upon my ear, I stop the birds to listen. Perhaps you think I have no bird—and this is rhetoric—pray, Mr. Whately, what is that upon the cherry tree? Church is done, and the winds blow, and Vinnie is in that pallid land the simple call "sleep." They will be wiser by and by. We shall all be wiser! While I sit in the snows, the summer day on which you came and the bees and the south wind, seem fabulous as heaven seems to a sinful world—and I keep remembering it till it assumes a spectral air, and nods and winks at me, and then all of you turn to phantoms and vanish slow away.

To the same
(Spring, 1856?)

. . . February passed like a skate and I know March. Here is the "light" the stranger said "was not on sea or land." Myself could arrest it, but will not chagrin him.

. . . Cousin Peter told me the Doctor would address Commencement—trusting it insure you both for papa's *fête* I endowed Peter. We do not always know the source of the smile that flows to us. . .

My flowers are near and foreign, and I have but to cross the floor to stand in the Spice Isles.

The wind blows gay today and the jays bark like blue terriers.

I tell you what I see—the landscape of the spirit requires a lung, but no tongue. I hold you few I love, till my heart is red as February and purple as March.

Hand for the Doctor.

EMILY

To the same
(Late Summer, 1856)

Sabbath Night

Don't tell, dear Mrs. Holland, but wicked as I am, I read my Bible sometimes, and in it as I read today, I found a verse like this, where friends should "go no more out"; and there were "no tears," and I wished as I sat down tonight that we were *there*—not *here*—and that wonderful world had commenced, which makes such promises, and rather than to write you, I were by your side, and the "hundred and forty and four thousand" were chatting pleasantly, yet not disturbing us. And I'm half tempted to take my seat in that Paradise of which the good man writes, and begin forever and ever *now*, so wondrous does it seem. My only sketch, profile, of Heaven is a large, blue sky, bluer and larger than the *biggest* I have seen in June, and in it are my friends—all of them—everyone of them—those who are with me now, and those who were "parted " as we walked, and "snatched up to Heaven."

If roses had not faded, and frosts had never come, and one had not fallen here and there whom I could not waken, there were no need of other Heaven than the one below—and if God had been here this summer, and seen the things that *I* have seen—I guess that He would think His Paradise superfluous. Don't tell Him, for the world, though, for after all He's said about it, I should like to see what He *was* building for us, with no hammer, and no stone, and no journeyman either. Dear Mrs. Holland, I love, tonight—love you and Dr. Holland, and "time and sense"—and fading things, and things that do *not* fade.

I'm so glad you are not a blossom, for those in my garden fade, and then a "reaper whose name is Death" has come to get a few to help him make a bouquet for himself, so I'm glad you are not a rose—and I'm glad you are not a bee, for where they go when summer's done, only the thyme knows, and even were you a robin, when the west winds came, you would coolly wink at me, and away, some morning!

As "little Mrs. Holland," then, I think I love you most, and trust that tiny lady will dwell below while we dwell, and when with many a wonder we seek the new Land, *her* wistful face, *with* ours, shall look the last upon the hills, and first upon—well, *Home!*

Pardon my sanity, Mrs. Holland, in a world *insane*, and love me if you will, for I had rather *be* loved than to be called a king in earth, or a lord in Heaven.

Thank you for your sweet note—the clergy are very well. Will bring such fragments from them as shall seem me good. I kiss my paper here for you and Dr. Holland—would it were cheeks instead.

Dearly
EMILIE

P.S. The bobolinks have gone.

To the same
(1857?)

Dear Sister,

After you went, a low wind warbled through the house like a spacious bird, making it high but lonely. When you had gone the love came. I supposed it would. The supper of the heart is when the guest has gone.

Shame is so intrinsic in a strong affection we must all experience Adam's reticence. I suppose the street that the lover travels is thenceforth divine, incapable of turnpike aims.

That you be with me annuls fear and I await Commencement with merry resignation. Smaller than David you clothe me with extreme Goliath.

Friday I tasted life. It was a vast morsel. A circus passed the house—still I feel the red in my mind though the drums are out.

The book you mention, I have not met. Thank you for tenderness.

The lawn is full of south and the odors tangle, and I hear today for the first the river in the tree.

You mentioned spring's delaying—I blamed her for the opposite. I would eat evanescence slowly.

Vinnie is deeply afflicted in the death of her dappled cat, though I convince her it is immortal which assists her some. Mother resumes lettuce, involving my transgression—suggestive of yourself, however, which endears disgrace.

"House" is being "cleaned." I prefer pestilence. That is more classic and less fell.

Yours was my first arbutus. It was a rosy boast.

I will send you the first witch hazel.

A woman died last week, young and in hope but a little while—at the end of our garden. I thought since of the power of Death, not upon affection, but its mortal signal. It is to us the Nile.

You refer to the unpermitted delight to be with those we love. I suppose that to be the license not granted of God.

Count not that far that can be had,
Though sunset lie between—

> *Nor that adjacent, that beside,*
> *Is further than the sun.*

Love for your embodiment of it.

EMILY

To MR. SAMUEL BOWLES
(Late August, 1858?)

AMHERST

DEAR MR. BOWLES,

I got the little pamphlet. I think you sent it to me, though unfamiliar with your hand—I may mistake.

Thank you, if I am right. Thank you, if not, since here I find bright pretext to ask you how you are tonight, and for the health of four more, elder and minor Mary, Sallie and Sam, tenderly to inquire.

I hope your cups are full.

I hope your vintage is untouched. In such a porcelain life one likes to be *sure* that all is well lest one stumble upon one's hopes in a pile of broken crockery.

My friends are my estate. Forgive me then the avarice to hoard them! They tell me those were poor early have different views of gold. I don't know how that is.

God is not so wary as we, else He would give us no friends, lest we forget Him! The charms of the heaven in the bush are superseded, I fear, by the heaven in the hand, occasionally.

Summer stopped since you were here. Nobody noticed her—that is, no men and women. Doubtless, the fields are rent by petite anguish, and "mourners go about" the woods. But this is not for us. Business enough indeed, our stately resurrection! A special courtesy, I judge, from what the clergy say! To the "natural man" bumblebees would seem an improvement, and a spicing of birds, but far be it from me to impugn such majestic tastes!

Our pastor says we are a "worm." How is that reconciled? "Vain, sinful worm" is possibly of another species.

Do you think we shall "see God"? Think of Abraham strolling with Him in genial promenade!

The men are mowing the second hay. The cocks are smaller than the first, and spicier. I would distil a cup, and bear to all my friends, drinking to her no more astir, by beck, or burn, or moor!

Goodnight, Mr. Bowles. This is what they say who come back in the morning; also the closing paragraph on repealed lips. Confidence in daybreak modifies dusk.

Blessings for Mrs. Bowles, and kisses for the bairns' lips. We want to see you, Mr. Bowles, but spare you the rehearsal of "familiar truths."

Goodnight
EMILY

To Mrs. Samuel Bowles
(Winter, 1858?)

Monday Eve

DEAR MRS. BOWLES,

You send sweet messages. Remembrance is more sweet than robins in May orchards.

I love to trust that round bright fires, some, braver than I, take my pilgrim name. How are papa, mamma, and the little people? . . .

It storms in Amherst five days—it snows, and then it rains, and then soft fogs like veils hang on all the houses, and then the days turn topaz, like a lady's pin.

Thank you for bright bouquet, and afterwards verbena. I made a plant of a little bough of yellow heliotrope which the bouquet bore me, and call it Mary Bowles. It is many days since the summer day when you came with Mr. Bowles, and before another summer day it will be many days. My garden is a little knoll with faces under it, and only the pines sing tunes, now the birds are absent. I cannot walk to the distant friends on nights piercing as these, so I put both hands on the window-pane, and try to think how birds fly, and imitate, and fail, like Mr. "Rasselas." I could make a balloon of a dandelion, but the fields are gone, and only "Professor Lowe" remains to weep with me. If I built my house I should like to call you. I talk of all these things with Carlo, and his eyes grow meaning, and his shaggy feet keep a slower pace. Are you safe tonight? I hope you may be glad. I ask God on my knee to send you much prosperity, few winter days, and long suns. I have a childish hope to gather all I love together and sit down beside and smile. . .

Will you come to Amherst? The streets are very cold now, but we will make you warm. But if you never came, perhaps you could write a letter, saying how much you would like to, if it were "God's will." I give goodnight, and daily love to you and Mr. Bowles.

EMILIE

To the Same
(1859)

AMHERST

I should like to thank dear Mrs. Bowles for the little book, except my cheek is red with shame because I write so often. Even the "lilies of the field" have their dignities.

Why did you bind it in green and gold? The *immortal* colors. I take it for an emblem. I never read before what Mr. Parker wrote.

I heard that he was "poison." Then I like poison very well. Austin stayed from service yesterday afternoon, and I. . . found him reading my Christmas gift. . . I wish the "faith of the fathers" didn't wear brogans, and carry blue umbrellas. I give you all "New Year!" I think you kept gay Christmas, from the friend's account, and can only sigh with one not present at "John Gilpin," "and when he next doth ride a race," etc. You picked your berries from my holly. Grasping Mrs. Bowles!

Today is very cold, yet have I much bouquet upon the window-pane of moss and fern. I call them saints' flowers, because they do not romp as other flowers do, but stand so still and white.

The snow is very tall, . . . which makes the trees so low that they tumble my hair, when I cross the bridge.

I think there will be no spring this year, the flowers are gone so far. Let us have spring in our heart, and never mind the orchises! . . . Please have my love, mother's, and Vinnie's.

Carlo sends a brown kiss, and pussy a gray and white one, to each of the children.

Please, now I write so often, make lamplighter of me, then I shall not have lived in vain.

Dear Mrs. Bowles, dear Mr. Bowles, dear Sally—Sam and Mamie, now all shut your eyes, while I do benediction!

Lovingly
EMILY

To Mrs. Kate Scott Anthon

AMHERST (1859)

. . . Sweet at my door this March night another candidate. Go home! We don't like Katies here! Stay! My heart votes for you, and what am I, indeed, to dispute her ballot!

What are your qualifications? Dare you dwell in the East where we dwell? Are you afraid of the sun? When you hear the new violet sucking her way among the sods, shall you be resolute? All we are strangers, dear, the world is not acquainted with us, because we are not acquainted with her; and pilgrims. Do you hesitate? And soldiers, oft—some of us victors, but those I do not see tonight, owing to the smoke. We are hungry, and thirsty, sometimes, we are barefoot and cold—will you still come?

Then, bright I record you—Kate, gathered in March! It is a small bouquet, dear, but what it lacks in size it gains in fadelessness. Many can boast a hollyhock, but few can bear a rose! And should new flower smile at limited associates, pray her remember were there many, they were not worn upon the breast, but tilled in the pasture. So I rise wearing her—so I sleep holding,—sleep at last with her fast in my hand, and wake bearing my flower.

EMILIE

To the same

There are two ripenings, one of sight,
Whose forces spheric wind,
Until the velvet product

Drops spicy to the ground.
A homelier maturing,
A process in the burr
That teeth of frosts alone disclose
On far October air.

EMILIE

To Mrs. J. G. Holland
(1859)

God bless you, dear Mrs. Holland! I read it in the paper.

I'm so glad it's a little boy, since now the little sisters have someone to draw them on the sled—and if a grand old lady you should live to be, there's something sweet, they say, in a son's arm.

I pray for the tenants of that holy chamber, the wrestler, and the wrestled for. I pray for distant father's heart, swollen, happy heart!

Saviour keep them all!

EMILY

To her cousin Miss Louise Norcross
(January, 1859)

Since it snows this morning, dear L——, too fast for interruption, put your brown curls in a basket, and come and sit with me.

I am sewing for Vinnie, and Vinnie is flying through the flakes to buy herself a little hood. It's quite a fairy morning, and I often lay down my needle, and "build a castle in the air" which seriously impedes the sewing project. What if I pause a little longer, and write a note to you! Who will be the wiser? I have known little of you, since the October morning when our families went out driving, and you and I in the dining-room decided to be distinguished. It's a great thing to be "great," L——, and you and I might tug for a life, and never accomplish it, but no one can stop our looking on, and you know some cannot sing, but the orchard is full of birds, and we all can listen. What if we learn, ourselves, someday!

Who indeed knows?—— said you had many little cares; I hope they do not fatigue you. I would not like to think of L—— as weary, now and then. Sometimes *I* get tired, and I would rather none I love would understand the word. . .

Do you still attend Fanny Kemble? "Aaron Burr" and father think her an "animal," but I fear zoölogy has few such instances. I have heard many notedly *bad* readers, and a fine one would be almost a fairy surprise. When will you come again, L——? For you remember, dear, you are one of the ones from whom I do not run away! I keep an ottoman in my heart exclusively for you. My love for your father and F——.

EMILY

TO THE SAME
(March, 1859)

The little "apple of my eye" is not dearer than L——; she knows I remember her,—why waste an instant in defence of an absurdity? My birds fly far off, nobody knows where they go to, but you see I know they are coming back, and other people don't, that makes the difference.

I've had a curious winter, very swift, sometimes sober, for I haven't felt well, much, and March amazes me! I didn't think of it, that's all! Your "hay" don't look so dim as it did at one time. I hayed a little for the horse two Sundays ago, and mother thought it was summer, and set one plant outdoors which she brought from the deluge, but it snowed since, and we have fine sleighing, now, on *one* side of the road, and wheeling on the other, a kind of variegated turnpike quite picturesque to see!

You are to have Vinnie, it seems, and I to tear my hair, or engage in any other vocation that seems fitted to me. Well, the earth is round, so if Vinnie rolls your side sometimes, 'tisn't strange; I wish I were there too, but the geraniums felt so I couldn't think of leaving them, and one minute carnation pink cried, till I shut her up—see box!

Now, my love, robins, for both of you, and when you and Vinnie sing at sunrise on the apple boughs, just cast your eye to my twig.

POOR PLOVER

To the same
(Early Summer, 1859)

Dear L——,

You did not acknowledge my vegetable; perhaps you are not familiar with it. I was reared in the garden, you know. It was to be eaten with mustard! Bush eighty feet high, just under chamber window—much used at this season when other vegetables are gone. You should snuff the hay if you were here today, infantile as yet, homely, as cubs are prone to be, but giving brawny promise of hay-cocks by and by. "Methinks I see you," as school-girls say, perched upon a cock with the "latest work," and confused visions of bumblebees tugging at your hat. Not so far off, cousin, as it used to be, that vision and the hat. It makes me feel so hurried, I run and brush my hair so to be all ready.

I enjoy much with a precious fly, during sister's absence, not one of your blue monsters, but a timid creature, that hops from pane to pane of her white house, so very cheerfully, and hums and thrums, a sort of speck piano. Tell Vinnie I'll kill him the day she comes, for I sha'n't need him anymore, and she don't mind flies!

Tell F—— and papa to come with the sweet-williams.

Tell Vinnie I counted three peony noses, red as Sammie Matthews's, just out of the ground, and get her to make the accompanying face.

By-Bye
Emily

To Dr. and Mrs. J. G. Holland
(Autumn, 1859)

Dear Hollands,

Belong to me! We have no fires yet, and the evenings grow cold. Tomorrow, stoves are set. How many barefoot shiver I trust their Father knows who saw not fit to give them shoes.

Vinnie is sick tonight, which gives the world a russet tinge, usually so red. It is only a headache, but when the head aches next to you, it becomes important. When she is well, time leaps. When she is ill, he lags, or stops entirely.

Sisters are brittle things. God was penurious with me, which makes me shrewd with Him.

One is a dainty sum! One bird, one cage, one flight; one song in those far woods, as yet suspected by faith only!

This is September, and you were coming in September. Come! Our parting is too long. There has been frost enough. We must have summer now, and "whole legions" of daisies.

The gentian is a greedy flower, and overtakes us all. Indeed, this world is short, and I wish, until I tremble, to touch the ones I love before the hills are red—are gray—are white—are "born again"! If we knew how deep the crocus lay, we never should let her go. Still, crocuses stud many mounds whose gardeners till in anguish some tiny, vanished bulb.

We saw you that Saturday afternoon, but heedlessly forgot to ask where you were going, so did not know, and could not write. Vinnie saw Minnie flying by, one afternoon at Palmer. She supposed you were all there on your way from the sea, and untied her fancy! To say that her fancy wheedled her is superfluous.

We talk of you together, then diverge on life, then hide in you again, as a safe fold. Don't leave us long, dear friends! You know we're children still, and children fear the dark.

Are you well at home? Do you work now? Has it altered much since I was there? Are the children women, and the women thinking it will soon be afternoon? We will help each other bear our unique burdens.

Is Minnie with you now? Take her our love, if she is. Do her eyes grieve her now? Tell her she may have half ours.

Mother's favorite sister is sick, and mother will have to bid her goodnight. It brings mists to us all;—the aunt whom Vinnie visits, with whom she spent, I fear, her last inland Christmas. Does God take care of those at sea? My aunt is such a timid woman!

Will you write to us? I bring you all their loves—*many*. They tire me.

EMILIE

To Mrs. Kate Scott Anthon
(1860)

The prettiest of pleas, dear, but with a lynx like me quite unavailable. Finding is slow, facilities for losing so frequent, in a world like this, I hold with extreme caution. A prudence so astute may seem unnecessary, but plenty moves those most, dear, who h you write to us ave been in want, and Saviour tells us, Kate, the poor are always with us. Were you ever poor? I have been a beggar, and rich tonight, as by God's leave I believe I am, the "lazzaroni's" faces haunt, pursue me still!

You do not yet "dislimn," Kate. Distinctly sweet your face stands in its phantom niche—I touch your hand—my cheek your cheek—I stroke your vanished hair. Why did you enter, sister, since you must depart? Had not its heart been torn enough but you must send your shred?

Oh, our condor Kate! Come from your crags again! Oh, dew upon the bloom fall yet again a summer's night! Of such have been the frauds which have vanquished faces, sown plant of flesh the churchyard plats, and occasioned angels.

There is a subject, dear, on which we never touch. Ignorance of its pageantries does not deter me. I too went out to meet the dust early in the morning. I too in daisy mounds possess hid treasure, therefore I guard you more. You did not tell me you had once been a "millionaire." Did my sister think that opulence could be mistaken? Some trinket will remain, some babbling plate or jewel.

I write you from the summer. The murmuring leaves fill up the chinks through which the winter red shone when Kate was here, and F—— was here, and frogs sincerer than our own splash in their Maker's pools. It's but a little past, dear, and yet how far from here it seems, fled with the snow! So through the snow go many loving feet parted by "Alps." How brief, from vineyards and the sun!

Parents and Vinnie request love to be given girl.

EMILIE

To Mrs. Holland
(1860)

How is your little Byron? Hope he gains his foot without
losing his genius. Have heard it ably argued that the poet's
genius lay in his foot—as the bee's prong and his song are
concomitant. Are you stronger than these? To assault so
minute a creature seems to me malign, unworthy of Nature—
but the frost is no respecter of persons.

To her sister Lavinia
(April, 1860)

Vinnie,

I can't believe it, when your letters come, saying what
Aunt L—— said "just before she died." Blessed Aunt L——
now; all the world goes out, and I see nothing but her room,
and angels bearing her into those great countries in the blue
sky of which we don't know anything.

Then I sob and cry till I can hardly see my way 'round the
house again; and then sit still and wonder if she sees us now,
if she sees *me*, who said that she "loved Emily." Oh! Vinnie,
it is dark and strange to think of summer afterward! How she
loved the summer! The birds keep singing just the same. Oh!
The thoughtless birds!

Poor little L——! Poor F——! You must comfort
them!

If you were with me, Vinnie, we could talk about her
together.

And I thought she would live! I wanted her to live so, I
thought she could not die! To think how still she lay while
I was making the little loaf, and fastening her flowers! Did
you get my letter in time to tell her how happy I would be to
do what she requested? Mr. Brady is coming tomorrow
to bring arbutus for her. Dear little aunt! Will she look
down?

You must tell me all you can think about her. Did she
carry my little bouquet? So many broken-hearted people have
got to hear the birds sing, and see all the little flowers grow,

just the same as if the sun hadn't stopped shining forever! . . .
How I wish I could comfort you! How I wish you could
comfort me, who weep at what I did not see and never can
believe. I will try and share you a little longer, but it is so
long, Vinnie.

We didn't think, that morning when I wept that you left
me, and you, for other things, that we should weep more
bitterly before we saw each other.

Well, she is safer now than "we know or even think."

Tired little aunt, sleeping ne'er so peaceful! Tuneful little
aunt, singing, as we trust, hymns than which the robins have
no sweeter ones.

Goodnight, broken hearts, L——, and F——, and Uncle
L——. Vinnie, remember

SISTER

To Miss Louisa Norcross
(Autumn, 1860)

Bravo, L——, the cape is a beauty, and what shall I render
unto F——, for all her benefits? I will take my books and
go into a corner and give thanks! Do you think I am going
"upon the boards" that I wish so smart attire? Such are my
designs, though. I beg you not to disclose them! May I not
secure L—— for drama, and F—— for comedy? You are a
brace of darlings, and it would give me joy to see you both,
in any capacity. . . Will treasure all till I see you. Never fear
that I shall forget! In event of my decease, I will still exclaim
"Dr. Thompson," and he will reply "Miss Montague." My
little L—— pined for the hay in her last communication. Not
to be saucy, dear, we sha'n't have anymore before the first of
March, Dick having hid it all in the barn in a most malicious
manner; but he has not brought the sunset in, so there is still
an inducement to my little girls. We have a sky or two, well
worth consideration, and trees so fashionable they make us
all *passée.*

I often remember you both, last week. I thought that
flown mamma could not, as was her wont, shield from crowd,
and strangers, and was glad Eliza was there. I knew she

would guard my children, as she has often guarded me, from publicity, and help to fill the deep place never to be full. Dear cousins, I know you both better than I did, and love you both better, and always I have a chair for you in the smallest parlor in the world, to wit, my heart.

This world is just a little place, just the red in the sky, before the sun rises, so let us keep fast hold of hands, that when the birds begin, none of us be missing.

"Burnham" must think F—— a scholastic female. I wouldn't be in her place! If she feels delicate about it, she can tell him the books are for a friend in the East Indies.

Won't F—— give my respects to the "Bell and Everett party" if she passes that organization on her way to school? I hear they wish to make me Lieutenant-Governor's daughter. Were they cats I would pull their tails, but as they are only patriots, I must forego the bliss. . .

Love to papa.

EMILY

To her cousins
(Winter, 1860–61)

Dear Friends,

L——'s note to Miss W—— only stopped to dine. It went out with a beautiful name on its face in the evening mail. "Is there nothing else," as the clerk says? So pleased to enact a trifle for my little sister. It is little sisters you are, as dear F—— says in the hallowed note. Could mamma read it, it would blur her light even in Paradise.

It was pretty to lend us the letters from the new friends. It gets us acquainted. We will preserve them carefully. . . I regret I am not a scholar in the Friday class. I believe the love of God may be taught not to seem like bears. Happy the reprobates under that loving influence.

I have one new bird and several trees of old ones. A snow slide from the roof, dispelled mother's "sweetbrier." You will of course feel for her, as you were named for him! There are as yet no streets, though the sun is riper, and these small bells have rung so long I think it "tea-time" always.

To the same
(Spring, 1861)

. . . Send a sundown for L——, please, and a crocus for
F——. Shadow had no stem, so they could not pick him.

To Dr. and Mrs. J. G. Holland
(1861)

Friday

DEAR FRIENDS,

I write to you. I receive no letter.

I say "they dignify my trust." I do not disbelieve. I go again.
Cardinals wouldn't do it. Cockneys wouldn't do it, but I *can't*
stop to strut, in a world where bells toll. I hear through visitor
in town, that "Mrs. Holland is not strong." The little peacock
in me, tells me not to inquire again. Then I remember my tiny
friend—how brief she is—how dear she is, and the peacock
quite dies away. Now, you need not speak, for perhaps you are
weary, and "Herod" requires all your thought, but if you are
well—let Annie draw me a little picture of an erect flower; if
you are *ill*, she can hang the flower a little on one side!

Then, I shall understand, and you need not stop to
write me a letter. Perhaps you laugh at me! Perhaps the
whole United States are laughing at me too! *I* can't stop for
that! *My* business is to love. I found a bird, this morning,
down—down—on a little bush at the foot of the garden, and
wherefore sing, I said, since nobody *hears*?

One sob in the throat, one flutter of bosom—"*My*
business is to *sing*"—and away she rose! How do I know
but cherubim, once, themselves, as patient, listened, and
applauded her unnoticed hymn?

EMILY

To Mrs. Samuel Bowles

DEAR MARY,

Can you leave your flower long enough just to look at
mine?

Which is the prettiest? I shall tell you myself, someday. I used to come to comfort you, but now to tell you how glad I am, and how glad we all are. . . You must not stay in New York anymore—you must come back now, and bring the blanket to Massachusetts where we can all look. What a responsible shepherd! Four lambs in one flock! Shall you be glad to see us, or shall we seem old- fashioned, by the face in the crib?

Tell him I've got a pussy for him, with a spotted gown; and a dog with ringlets.

We have very cold days since you went away, and I think you hear the wind blow far as the Brevoort House, it comes from so far, and crawls so. Don't let it blow baby away. Will you call him Robert for me? He is the bravest man alive, but *his* boy has no mamma. That makes us all weep, don't it?

Goodnight, Mary.
EMILY

BABY

Teach him, when he makes the names.
Such an one to say
On his babbling, berry lips
As should sound to me—
Were my ear as near his nest
As my thought, today—
As should sound—"forbid us not"—
Some like "Emily."

TO THE SAME
(August, 1861)

MARY,

I do not know of you, a long while. I remember you— several times. I wish I knew if you kept me? The doubt, like the mosquito, buzzes round my faith. We are all human, Mary, until we are divine, and to some of us, that is far off, and to some as near as the lady ringing at the door; perhaps *that's* what alarms. I say I will go myself—I cross the river, and climb the fence—now I am at the gate, Mary—now I am in the hall—now I am looking your heart in the eye!

Did it wait for me—did it go with the company? Cruel company, who have the stocks, and farms, and creeds—and *it* has just its heart! I hope you are glad, Mary; no pebble in the brook today—no film on noon.

I can think how you look; you can't think how I look; I've got more freckles, since you saw me, playing with the school-boys; then I pare the "Juneating" to make the pie, and get my fingers "tanned."

Summer went very fast—she got as far as the woman from the hill, who brings the blueberry, and that is a long way. I shall have no winter this year, on account of the soldiers. Since I cannot weave blankets or boots, I thought it best to omit the season. Shall present a "memorial" to God when the maples turn. Can I rely on your "name"?

How is your garden, Mary? Are the pinks true, and the sweet williams faithful? I've got a geranium like a sultana, and when the humming-birds come down, geranium and I shut our eyes, and go far away.

Ask "Mamie" if I shall catch her a butterfly with a vest like a Turk? I will, if she will build him a house in her "morning-glory."

Vinnie would send her love, but she put on a white frock, and went to meet tomorrow—a few minutes ago; mother would send her love, but she is in the "eave spout," sweeping up a leaf that blew in last November; I brought my own, myself, to you and Mr. Bowles.

Please remember me, because I remember you—always. . .

Don't cry, dear Mary. Let us do that for you, because you are too tired now. We don't know how dark it is, but if you are at sea, perhaps when we say that we are there, you won't be as afraid.

The waves are very big, but everyone that covers you, covers us, too.

Dear Mary, you can't see us, but we are close at your side. May we comfort you?

Lovingly
EMILY

To Mr. Samuel Bowles
(Autumn, 1861)

Friend, Sir,

I did not see you. I am very sorry. Shall I keep the wine till you come again, or send it in by Dick? It is now behind the door in the library, also an unclaimed flower. I did not know you were going so soon. Oh! my tardy feet.

Will you not come again?

Friends are gems, infrequent. Potosi is a care, sir. I guard it reverently, for I could not afford to be poor now, after affluence. I hope the hearts in Springfield are not so heavy as they were. God bless the hearts in Springfield.

I am happy you have a horse. I hope you will get stalwart, and come and see us many years.

I have but two acquaintance, the "quick and the dead"— and would like more.

I write you frequently, and am much ashamed. My voice is not quite loud enough to cross so many fields, which will, if you please, apologize for my pencil.

Will you take my love to Mrs. Bowdes, whom I remember everyday?

Emilie

Vinnie hallos from the world of night-caps, "don't forget her love."

To Mrs. Kate Scott Anthon
(1861?)

Katie,

Last year at this time I did not miss you, but positions shifted, until I hold your black in strong hallowed remembrance, and trust my colors are to you tints slightly beloved.

You cease, indeed, to talk, which is a custom prevalent among things parted and torn, but shall I class this, dear, among elect exceptions, and bear you just as usual unto the kind Lord?

We dignify our faith when we can cross the ocean with it, though most prefer ships.

How do you do this year? . . . How many years, I wonder, will sow the moss upon them, before we bind again, a little altered, it may be, elder a little it *will* be, and yet the same, as suns which shine between our lives and loss, and violets—not last year's, but having the mother's eyes.

Do you find plenty of food at home? Famine is unpleasant.

It is too late for frogs—or what pleases me better, dear, not quite early enough! The pools were full of you for a brief period, but that brief period blew away, leaving me with many stems, and but a few foliage! Gentlemen here have a way of plucking the tops of the trees, and putting the fields in their cellars annually, which in point of taste is execrable, and would they please omit, I should have fine vegetation and foliage all the year round, and never a winter month. Insanity to the sane seems so unnecessary—but I am only one, and they are "four and forty," which little affair of numbers leaves me impotent. Aside from this, dear Katie, inducements to visit Amherst are as they were—I am pleasantly located in the deep sea, but love will row you out, if her hands are strong, and don't wait till I land, for I'm going ashore on the other side.

EMILIE

To Louisa and Fannie Norcross
(1861)

. . . —— fed greedily upon "Harper's Magazine's" while here. Suppose he is restricted to Martin Luther's works at home. It is a criminal thing to be a boy in a godly village, but maybe he will be forgiven.

. . . The seeing pain one can't relieve makes a demon of one. If angels have the heart beneath their silver jackets, I think such things could make them weep, but Heaven is so cold! It will never look kind to me that God, who causes all, denies such little wishes. It could not hurt His glory, unless it were a lonesome kind. I 'most conclude it is.

. . . Thank you for the daisy. With nature in my ruche I shall not miss the spring. What would become of us, dear, but for love to reprieve our blunders?

. . . I'm afraid that home is 'most done, but do not say I fear so. Perhaps God will be better. They're happy, you know. That makes it doubtful. Heaven hunts round for those that find itself below, and then it snatches.

. . . Think Emily lost her wits—but she found 'em, likely. Don't part with wits long in this neighborhood.

. . . Your letters are all real, just the tangled road children walked before you, some of them to the end, and others but a little way, even as far as the fork in the road. That Mrs. Browning fainted, we need not read "Aurora Leigh" to know, when she lived with her English aunt; and George Sand "must make no noise in her grandmother's bedroom." Poor children! Women, now, queens, now! And one in the Eden of God. I guess they both forget that now, so who knows but we, little stars from the same night, stop twinkling at last? Take heart, little sister, twilight is but the short bridge, and the moon stands at the end. If we can only get to her! Yet, if she sees us fainting, she will put out her yellow hands. . .

To Louisa Norcross
(December, 1861)

Dear Peacock,

I received your feather with profound emotion. It has already surmounted a work, and crossed the Delaware. Doubtless you are moulting à la canary bird—hope you will not suffer from the reduction of plumage these December days. The latitude is quite stiff for a few nights, and gentlemen and ladies who go barefoot in our large cities must find the climate uncomfortable. A land of frosts and zeros is not precisely the land for me; hope you find it congenial. I believe it is several hundred years since I met you and F——, yet I am pleased to say, you do not become dim; I think you rather brighten as the hours fly. I should love to see you dearly, girls; perhaps I may, before south winds, but

I feel rather confused today, and the future looks "higglety-piggglety."

You seem to take a smiling view of my finery. If you knew how solemn it was to me, you might be induced to curtail your jests. My sphere is doubtless calicoes, nevertheless I thought it meet to sport a little wool. The mirth it has occasioned will deter me from further exhibitions! Won't you tell "the public" that at present I wear a brown dress with a cape if possible browner, and carry a parasol of the same! We have at present one cat, and twenty-four hens, who do nothing so vulgar as lay an egg, which checks the ice-cream tendency.

I miss the grasshoppers much, but suppose it is all for the best. I should become too much attached to a trotting world.

My garden is all covered up by snow; picked gilliflower Tuesday, now gilliflowers are asleep. The hills take off their purple frocks, and dress in long white nightgowns.

There is something fine and something sad in the year's toilet. . .

We often talk of you and your father these new winter days. Write, dear, when you feel like it.

Lovingly
EMILY

TO THE SAME
(December 29, 1861)

. . . Your letter didn't surprise me, L——; I brushed away the sleet from eyes familiar with it—looked again to be sure I read it right—and then took up my work hemming strings for mother's gown. I think I hemmed them faster for knowing you weren't coming, my fingers had nothing else to do. . . Odd, that I, who say "no" so much, cannot bear it from others. Odd, that I, who run from so many, cannot brook that one turn from me. Come when you will, L——, the hearts are never shut here. I don't remember "May." Is that the one that stands next April? And is that the month for the river-pink?

Mrs. Adams had news of the death of her boy today, from a wound at Annapolis. Telegram signed by Frazer Stearns. You remember him. Another one died in October—from fever caught in the camp. Mrs. Adams herself has not risen from bed since then. "Happy new year" step softly over such doors as these! "Dead! Both her boys! One of them shot by the sea in the East, and one of them shot in the West by the sea." . . . Christ be merciful! Frazer Stearns is just leaving Annapolis. His father has gone to see him today. I hope that ruddy face won't be brought home frozen. Poor little widow's boy, riding tonight in the mad wind, back to the village burying-ground where he never dreamed of sleeping! Ah! the dreamless sleep! . . .

To Mr. Samuel Bowles
(January, 1862)

Dear Friend,

Are you willing? I am so far from land. To offer you the cup, it might some Sabbath come *my* turn. Of wine how solemn-full!

Did you get the doubloons—did you vote upon "Robert"? You said you would come in February. Only three weeks more to wait at the gate!

While you are sick, we—are homesick. Do you look out tonight? The moon rides like a girl through a topaz town. I don't think we shall ever be merry again—you are ill so long. When did the dark happen?

I skipped a page tonight, because I come so often, now, I might have tired you.

That page is fullest, though.

Vinnie sends her love. I think father and mother care a great deal for you, and hope you may be well. When you tire with pain, to know that eyes would cloud, in Amherst—might that comfort, *some*?

Emily

We never forget Mary.

To the same

DEAR MR. BOWLES,
Thank you.

> *Faith is a fine invention*
> *When gentlemen can see!*
> *But microscopes are prudent*
> *In an emergency!*

You spoke of the "East." I have thought about it this winter.
Don't you think you and I should be shrewder to take the mountain road?

That bareheaded life, under the grass, worries one like a wasp.

The rose is for Mary.

EMILY

To the same

> *The zeros taught us phosphorus—*
> *We learned to like the fire*
> *By playing glaciers when a boy,*
> *And tinder guessed by power*
>
> *Of opposite to balance odd.*
> *If white, a red must be!*
> *Paralysis, our primer dumb*
> *Unto vitality.*

I couldn't let Austin's note go, without a word.

EMILY

To FANNIE NORCROSS
(February, 1862)

DEAR F——,
I fear you are getting as driven as Vinnie. We consider her standard for superhuman effort erroneously applied. Dear

L—— remembers the basket Vinnie "never got to." But we must blame with lenience. Poor Vinnie has been very sick, and so have we all, and I feared one day our little brothers would see us no more, but God was not so hard. Now health looks so beautiful, the tritest "How do you do" is living with meaning. No doubt you "heard a bird," but which route did he take? Hasn't reached here yet. Are you sure it wasn't a "down brakes"? Best of ears will blunder! Unless he come by the first of April, I sha'n't countenance him. We have had fatal weather—thermometer two below zero all day, without a word of apology. Summer was always dear, but such a kiss as she'll get from me if I ever see her again, will make her cry, I know. . .

To Louisa and Fannie Norcross
(April, 1862)

Dear Children,

You have done more for me—'tis least that I can do, to tell you of brave Frazer—"killed at Newbern," darlings. His big heart shot away by a "Minie ball."

I had read of those—I didn't think that Frazer would carry one to Eden with him. Just as he fell, in his soldier's cap, with his sword at his side, Frazer rode through Amherst. Classmates to the right of him, and classmates to the left of him, to guard his narrow face! He fell by the side of Professor Clark, his superior officer—lived ten minutes in a soldier's arms, asked twice for water—murmured just, "My God!" and passed! Sanderson, his classmate, made a box of boards in the night, put the brave boy in, covered with a blanket, rowed six miles to reach the boat,—so poor Frazer came. They tell that Colonel Clark cried like a little child when he missed his pet, and could hardly resume his post. They loved each other very much. Nobody here could look on Frazer—not even his father. The doctors would not allow it.

The bed on which he came was enclosed in a large casket shut entirely, and covered from head to foot with the sweetest flowers. He went to sleep from the village church. Crowds came to tell him goodnight, choirs sang to him, pastors told how brave he was—early-soldier heart. And the family bowed their heads, as the reeds the wind shakes.

So our part in Frazer is done, but you must come next summer, and we will mind ourselves of this young crusader— too brave that he could fear to die. We will play his tunes— maybe he can hear them; we will try to comfort his broken- hearted Ella, who, as the clergyman said, "gave him peculiar confidence." . . . Austin is stunned completely. Let us love better, children, it's most that's left to do.

Love from
EMILY

. . . Sorrow seems more general than it did, and not the estate of a few persons, since the war began; and if the anguish of others helped one with one's own, now would be many medicines.

'Tis dangerous to value, for only the precious can alarm. I noticed that Robert Browning had made another poem, and was astonished—till I remembered that I, myself, in my smaller way, sang off charnel steps. Everyday life feels mightier, and what we have the power to be, more stupendous.

To MR. SAMUEL BOWLES

(March, 1862)

Perhaps you thought I didn't care—because I stayed out, yesterday. I *did* care, Mr. Bowles. I pray for your sweet health to Allah every morning, but something troubled me, and I knew you needed light and air, so I didn't come. Nor have I the conceit that you *noticed* me—but I couldn't bear that you, or Mary, so gentle to me, should think me forgetful.

It's little at the most, we can do for ours, and we must do *that* flying, or our things are flown!

Dear friend, I wish you were well.

It grieves me till I cannot speak, that you are suffering. Won't you come back? Can't I bring you something? My little balm might be o'erlooked by wiser eyes, you know. Have you tried the breeze that swings the sign, or the hoof of the dandelion? *I* own 'em—wait for mine! This is all I have to say. Kinsmen need say nothing, but "Swiveller" may be sure of the

Love for Mary
"Marchioness"

To the same

Dear Friend,

. . . Austin is disappointed—he expected to see you today. He is sure you won't go to sea without first speaking to him. I presume if Emily and Vinnie knew of his writing, they would entreat him to ask you not.

Austin is chilled by Frazer's murder. He says his brain keeps saying over "Frazer is killed"—"Frazer is killed," just as father told it to him. Two or three words of lead, that dropped so deep they keep weighing. Tell Austin how to get over them!

He is very sorry you are not better. He cares for you when at the office, and afterwards, too, at home; and sometimes wakes at night, with a worry for you he didn't finish quite by day. He would not like it that I betrayed him, so you'll never tell. . .

Mary sent beautiful flowers. Did she tell you?

To the same
(Spring, 1862)

Dear Friend,

The hearts in Amherst ache tonight—you could not know how hard. They thought they could not wait, last night, until the engine sang a pleasant tune that time, because that you were coming. The flowers waited, in the vase, and love got peevish, watching. A railroad person rang, to bring an evening paper—Vinnie tipped pussy over, in haste to let you in, and I, for joy and dignity, held tight in my chair. My hope put out a petal.

You would come, today,—but. . . we don't believe it, now; "Mr. Bowles not coming!" Wouldn't you, tomorrow, and this but be a bad dream, gone by next morning?

Please do not take our *spring* away, since you blot summer out! We cannot count our tears for this, because they drop so fast. . .

Dear friend, we meant to make *you* brave, but moaned before we thought. . . If you'll be sure and get well, we'll try to bear it. If we could only care the less, it would be so much easier. Your letter troubled my throat. It gave that little scalding we could not know the reason for till we grew far up.

I must do my goodnight in crayon I meant to in red.

Love for Mary
EMILY

After Mr. Bowles had sailed for Europe, Emily sent this quaintly consoling note to Springfield.

To Mrs. SAMUEL BOWLES
(Early summer, 1862)

DEAR MARY,

When the best is gone, I know that other things are not of consequence. The heart wants what it wants, or else it does not care.

You wonder why I write so. Because I cannot help. I like to have you know some care—so when your life gets faint for its other life, you can lean on us. We won't break, Mary. We look very small, but the reed can carry weight.

Not to see what we love is very terrible, and talking doesn't ease it, and nothing does but just itself. The eyes and hair we chose are all there are—to us. Isn't it so, Mary?

I often wonder how the love of Christ is done when that below holds so.

I hope the little "Robert" coos away the pain. Perhaps your flowers help, some. . .

The frogs sing sweet today—they have such pretty, lazy times—how nice to be a frog! . . .

Mother sends her love to you—she has a sprained foot, and can go but little in the house, and not abroad at all.

Don't dishearten, Mary, we'll keep thinking of you. Kisses for all.

EMILY

To Mr. Samuel Bowles
(June, 1862)

DEAR FRIEND,

You go away—and where you go we cannot come—but then the months have names—and each one comes but once a year—and though it seems they never could, they sometimes do, go by.

We hope you are more well than when you lived in America, and that those foreign people are kind, and true, to you. We hope you recollect each life you left behind, even ours, the least.

We wish we knew how Amherst looked, in your memory. Smaller than it did, maybe, and yet things swell, by leaving, if big in themselves.

We hope you will not alter, but be the same we grieved for when the *China* sailed.

If you should like to hear the news, we did not die here—we did not change. We have the guests we did, except yourself—and the roses hang on the same stems as before you went. Vinnie trains the honeysuckle, and the robins steal the string for nests—quite, quite as they used to.

I have the errand from my heart—I might forget to tell it. Would you please to come home? The long life's years are scant, and fly away, the Bible says, like a told story—and sparing is a solemn thing, somehow, it seems to me—and I grope fast, with my fingers, for all out of my sight I own, to get it nearer.

I had one letter from Mary. I think she tries to be patient—but you wouldn't want her to succeed, would you, Mr. Bowles?

It's fragrant news, to know they pine, when we are out of sight.

It is 'most Commencement. The little cousin from Boston has come, and the hearts in Pelham have an added thrill.

We shall miss you, most, dear friend, who annually smiled with us, at the gravities. I question if even Dr. Vaill have his wonted applause.

Should anybody, where you go, talk of Mrs. Browning, you must hear for us, and if you touch her grave, put one hand on the head, for me—her unmentioned mourner.

Father and mother, and Vinnie and Carlo, send their love to you, and warm wish for your health—and I am taking lessons in prayer, so to coax God to keep you safe. Goodnight, dear friend. You sleep so far, how can I know you hear?

EMILY

TO THE SAME

DEAR FRIEND,

I cannot see you. You will not less believe me. That you return to us alive is better than a summer, and more to hear your voice below than news of any bird.

EMILY

TO THE SAME
(August, 1862)

DEAR MR. BOWLES,

Vinnie is trading with a tin peddler—buying water-pots for me to sprinkle geraniums with when you get home next winter, and she has gone to the war.

Summer isn't so long as it was, when we stood looking at it before you went away; and when I finish August, we'll hop the autumn very soon, and then 'twill be yourself.

I don't know how many will be glad to see you,—because I never saw your whole friends, but I have heard that in large cities noted persons chose you—though how glad those I know will be, is easier told.

I tell you, Mr. Bowles, it is a suffering to have a sea—no care how blue—between your soul and you.

The hills you used to love when you were in Northampton, miss their old lover, could they speak; and the puzzled look deepens in Carlo's forehead as the days go by and you never come.

I've learned to read the steamer place in newspapers now. It's 'most like shaking hands with you, or more like your ringing at the door.

We reckon your coming by the fruit. "When the grape gets by, and the pippin and the chestnut—when the days are a little short by the clock, and a little long by the want—when the sky has new red gowns and a purple bonnet—then we say you will come. I am glad that kind of time goes by.

It is easier to look behind at a pain, than to see it coming.

A soldier called, a morning ago, and asked for a nosegay to take to battle. I suppose he thought we kept an aquarium.

How sweet it must be to one to come home, whose home is in so many houses, and every heart a "best room." I mean you, Mr. Bowles. . . Have not the clovers names to the bees?

EMILY

To the same

Before he comes
We weigh the time,
'Tis heavy, and 'tis light.
When he departs
An emptiness
Is the superior freight.

EMILY

To the same

While asters
On the hill
Their everlasting fashions set.
And covenant gentians frill!

EMILY

To the same
(Late autumn, 1862)

So glad we are, a stranger'd deem
'Twas sorry that we were;
For where the holiday should be
There publishes a tear;
Nor how ourselves be justified.
Since grief and joy are done
So similar, an optizan
Could not decide between.

To the same
(Early winter, 1862)

Dear Friend,

Had we the art like you, to endow so many, by just recovering our health, 'twould give us tender pride, nor could we keep the news, but carry it to you, who seem to us to own it most.

So few that live have life, it seems of quick importance not one of those escape by death. And since you gave us fear, congratulate us for ourselves—you give us safer peace.

How extraordinary that life's large population contain so few of power to us—and those a vivid species who leave no mode, like Tyrian dye.

Remembering these minorities, permit our gratitude for you. We ask that you be cautious, for many sakes, excelling ours. To recapitulate the stars were useless as supreme. Yourself is yours, dear friend, but ceded, is it not, to here and there a minor life? Do not defraud these, for gold may be bought, and purple may be bought, but the sale of the spirit never did occur.

Do not yet work. No public so exorbitant of any as its friend, and we can wait your health. Besides, there is an idleness more tonic than toil.

The loss of sickness—was it loss?
Or that ethereal gain

You earned by measuring the grave,
Then measuring the sun.

Be sure, dear friend, for want you have estates of lives.

EMILY

TO THE SAME
(With flowers)

If she had been the mistletoe,
And I had been the rose,
How gay upon your table
My velvet life to close!

Since I am of the Druid,
And she is of the dew,
I'll deck tradition's buttonhole.
And send the rose to you.

E.

TO COLONEL T. W. HIGGINSON
(April 16, 1862)

MR. HIGGINSON,

Are you too deeply occupied to say if my verse is alive?

The mind is so near itself it cannot see distinctly, and I have none to ask.

Should you think it breathed, and had you the leisure to tell me, I should feel quick gratitude.

If I make the mistake, that you dared to tell me would give me sincerer honor toward you.

I enclose my name, asking you, if you please, sir, to tell me what is true?

That you will not betray me it is needless to ask, since honor is its own pawn.

To the same
(April 26, 1862)

Mr. Higginson,

Your kindness claimed earlier gratitude, but I was ill, and write today from my pillow.

Thank you for the surgery; it was not so painful as I supposed. I bring you others, as you ask, though they might not differ. While my thought is undressed, I can make the distinction; but when I put them in the gown, they look alike and numb.

You asked how old I was? I made no verse, but one or two, until this winter, sir.

I had a terror since September, I could tell to none; and so I sing, as the boy does of the burying ground, because I am afraid.

You inquire my books. For poets, I have Keats, and Mr. and Mrs. Browning. For prose, Mr. Ruskin, Sir Thomas Browne, and the "Revelations." I went to school, but in your manner of the phrase had no education. When a little girl, I had a friend who taught me Immortality; but venturing too near, himself, he never returned. Soon after my tutor died, and for several years my lexicon was my only companion. Then I found one more, but he was not contented I be his scholar, so he left the land.

You ask of my companions. Hills, sir, and the sundown, and a dog large as myself, that my father bought me. They are better than beings because they know, but do not tell; and the noise in the pool at noon excels my piano.

I have a brother and sister; my mother does not care for thought, and father, too busy with his briefs to notice what we do. He buys me many books, but begs me not to read them, because he fears they joggle the mind. They are religious, except me, and address an eclipse, every morning, whom they call their "Father."

But I fear my story fatigues you. I would like to learn. Could you tell me how to grow, or is it unconveyed, like melody or witchcraft?

You speak of Mr. Whitman. I never read his book, but was told that it was disgraceful.

I read Miss Prescott's "Circumstance," but it followed me in the dark, so I avoided her.

Two editors of journals came to my father's house this winter, and asked me for my mind, and when I asked them "why" they said I was penurious, and they would use it for the world.

I could not weigh myself, myself. My size felt small to me. I read your chapters in the "Atlantic," and experienced honor for you. I was sure you would not reject a confiding question.

Is this, sir, what you asked me to tell you?

Your friend
E. DICKINSON

TO THE SAME
(June 8, 1862)

DEAR FRIEND,

Your letter gave no drunkenness, because I tasted rum before. Domingo comes but once; yet I have had few pleasures so deep as your opinion, and if I tried to thank you, my tears would block my tongue.

My dying tutor told me that he would like to live till I had been a poet, but Death was much of mob as I could master, then. And when, far afterward, a sudden light on orchards, or a new fashion in the wind troubled my attention, I felt a palsy, here, the verses just relieve.

Your second letter surprised me, and for a moment, swung. I had not supposed it. Your first gave no dishonor, because the true are not ashamed. I thanked you for your justice, but could not drop the bells whose jingling cooled my tramp. Perhaps the balm seemed better, because you bled me first. I smile when you suggest that I delay "to publish," that being foreign to my thought as firmament to fin.

If fame belonged to me, I could not escape her; if she did not, the longest day would pass me on the chase, and the approbation of my dog would forsake me then. My barefoot rank is better.

You think my gait "spasmodic." I am in danger, sir. You think me "uncontrolled." I have no tribunal.

Would you have time to be the "friend" you should think

I need? I have a little shape: it would not crowd your desk, nor make much racket as the mouse that dents your galleries.

If I might bring you what I do—not so frequent to trouble you—and ask you if I told it clear, 'twould be control to me. The sailor cannot see the north, but knows the needle can. The "hand you stretch me in the dark" I put mine in, and turn away. I have no Saxon now:

> *As if I asked a common alms,*
> *And in my wondering hand*
> *A stranger pressed a kingdom.*
> *And I, bewildered, stand;*
> *As if I asked the Orient*
> *Had it for me a morn,*
> *And it should lift its purple dikes*
> *And shatter me with dawn!*

But, will you be my preceptor, Mr. Higginson?

To the same
(In reply to a request for a likeness of her)
(July, 1862)

Could you believe me without? I had no portrait, now, but am small, like the wren; and my hair is bold, like the chestnut burr; and my eyes, like the sherry in the glass that the guest leaves. Would this do just as well?

It often alarms father. He says death might occur, and he has moulds of all the rest, but has no mould of me; but I noticed the quick wore off those things in a few days, and forestall the dishonor. You will think no caprice of me.

You said "dark." I know the butterfly, and the lizard, and the orchis. Are not those *your* countrymen?

I am happy to be your scholar, and will deserve the kindness I cannot repay.

If you truly consent, I recite now. Will you tell me my fault, frankly, as to yourself, for I had rather wince than die. Men do not call the surgeon to commend the bone, but to set it, sir, and fracture within is more critical. And for this, preceptor, I shall bring you obedience, the blossom from my garden, and every gratitude I know.

Perhaps you smile at me. I could not stop for that. My business is circumference. An ignorance, not of customs, but if caught with the dawn, or the sunset see me, myself the only kangaroo among the beauty, sir, if you please, it afflicts me, and I thought that instruction would take it away.

Because you have much business, beside the growth of me, you will appoint, yourself, how often I shall come without your inconvenience.

And if at anytime you regret you received me, or I prove a different fabric to that you supposed, you must banish me.

When I state myself, as the representative of the verse, it does not mean me, but a supposed person.

You are true about the "perfection." Today makes yesterday mean.

You spoke of "Pippa Passes." I never heard anybody speak of "Pippa Passes" before. You see my posture is benighted.

To thank you baffles me. Are you perfectly powerful? Had I a pleasure you had not, I could delight to bring it.

YOUR SCHOLAR

TO THE SAME

DEAR FRIEND,

Are these more orderly? I thank you for the truth.

I had no monarch in my life, and cannot rule myself; and when I try to organize, my little force explodes and leaves me bare and charred.

I think you called me "wayward." Will you help me improve?

I suppose the pride that stops the breath, in the core of woods, is not of ourself.

You say I confess the little mistake, and omit the large. Because I can see orthography; but the ignorance out of sight is my preceptor's charge.

Of "shunning men and women,"—they talk of hallowed things, aloud, and embarrass my dog. He and I don't object to them, if they'll exist their side. I think Carlo would please you. He is dumb, and brave. I think you would like the chestnut-tree I met in my walk. It hit my notice suddenly, and I thought the skies were in blossom.

Then there's a noiseless noise in the orchard that I let persons hear.

You told me in one letter you could not come to see me "now," and I made no answer; not because I had none, but did not think myself the price that you should come so far.

I do not ask so large a pleasure, lest you might deny me.

You say, "Beyond your knowledge." You would not jest with me, because I believe you; but, preceptor, you cannot mean it?

All men say "What" to me, but I thought it a fashion.

When much in the woods, as a little girl, I was told that the snake would bite me, that I might pick a poisonous flower, or goblins kidnap me; but I went along and met no one but angels, who were far shyer of me than I could be of them, so I haven't that confidence in fraud which many exercise.

I shall observe your precept, though I don't understand it, always.

I marked a line in one verse, because I met it after I made it, and never consciously touch a paint mixed by another person. I do not let go it, because it is mine.

Have you the portrait of Mrs. Browning? Persons sent me three. If you had none, will you have mine?

YOUR SCHOLAR

TO MR. SAMUEL BOWLES
(1862)

DEAR MR. BOWLES,

I can't thank you anymore. You are thoughtful so many times you grieve me always; *now* the old words are numb, and there aren't any new ones.

Brooks are useless in freshet time. When you come to Amherst—please God it were today—I will tell you about the picture—if I *can*, I will.

Speech *is a prank of Parliament,*
Tears *a trick of the nerve,—*
But the heart with the heaviest freight on
Doesn't always swerve.

EMILY

TO THE SAME

Perhaps you think me stooping!
I'm not ashamed of that!
Christ stooped until he touched the grave!
Do those at sacrament
Commemorate dishonor—
Or love, annealed of love,
Until it bend as low as death
Re-royalized above?

The juggler's hat her country is.
The mountain gorse the bee's.

I stole them from a bee.
Because—thee!
Sweet plea—
He pardoned me!

EMILY

TO MR. AND MRS. SAMUEL BOWLES
(Summer, 1863)

DEAR FRIENDS,

I am sorry you came, because you went away.

Hereafter, I will pick no rose, lest it fade or prick me.
I would like to have you dwell here.

Though it is almost nine o'clock, the skies are gay and
yellow, and there's a purple craft or so, in which a friend
could sail. Tonight looks like "Jerusalem"! . . . I hope we may
all behave so as to reach Jerusalem.

How are your hearts today? Ours are pretty well. I hope
your tour was bright, and gladdened Mrs. Bowles.

Perhaps the retrospect will call you back some morning.

You shall find us all at the gate if you come in a hundred years, just as we stood that day. If it become of "jasper" previously, you will not object, so that we lean there still, looking after you.

I rode with Austin this morning. He showed me mountains that touched the sky, and brooks that sang like bobolinks. Was he not very kind? I will give them to you, for they are mine, and "all things are mine," excepting "Cephas and Apollos," for whom I have no taste. Vinnie's love brims mine.

Take

EMILIE

To Mrs. Samuel Bowles

DEAR MRS. BOWLES,

Since I have no sweet flower to send you, I enclose my heart. A little one, sunburnt, half broken sometimes, yet close as the spaniel to its friends. Your flowers come from heaven, to which, if I should ever go, I will pluck you palms.

My words are far away when I attempt to thank you, so take the silver tear instead, from my full eye.

You have often remembered me.

I have little dominion. Are there not wiser than I, who, with curious treasure, could requite your gift?

Angels fill the hand that loaded

EMILY'S

Nature and God, I neither knew,
Yet both, so well knew me
They startled, like executors
Of an identity.

Yet neither told, that I could learn;
My secret as secure
As Herschel's private interest,
Or Mercury's affair.

To Mr. Samuel Bowles
(1863)

Dear Friend,

You remember the little "meeting" we held for you last spring? We met again, Saturday.

'Twas May when we "adjourned," but then adjourns are all. The meetings were alike, Mr. Bowles.

The topic did not tire us, so we chose no new. We voted to remember you so long as both should live, including immortality; to count you as ourselves, except sometimes more tenderly, as now, when you are ill, and we, the haler of the two—and so I bring the bond we sign so many times, for you to read when chaos comes, or treason, or decay, still witnessing for morning. . . We hope our joy to see you gave of its own degree to you. We pray for your new health, the prayer that goes not down when they shut the church. We offer you our cups—stintless, as to the bee,—the lily, her new liquors.

Would you like summer? Taste of ours.
Spices? Buy here!
Ill! We have berries, for the parching!
Weary! Furloughs of down!
Perplexed! Estates of violet trouble ne'er looked on!
Captive! We bring reprieve of roses!
Fainting! Flasks of air!
Even for Death, a fairy medicine.
But, which is it, sir?

Emily

To the same

I'll send the feather from my hat!
Who knows but at the sight of that
My sovereign will relent?
As trinket, worn by faded child,
Confronting eyes long comforted
Blisters the adamant!

Emily

To Colonel T. W. Higginson
(Sent to him in camp, during the Civil War,
postmarked South Carolina)
(1863)

AMHERST

Dear Friend,

I did not deem that planetary forces annulled, but suffered
an exchange of territory, or world.

I should have liked to see you before you became
improbable. War feels to me an oblique place. Should there
be other summers, would you perhaps come?

I found you were gone, by accident, as I find systems
are, or seasons of the year, and obtain no cause, but suppose
it a treason of progress that dissolves as it goes. Carlo still
remained, and I told him

> *Best gains must have the losses' test,*
> *To constitute them gains.*

My shaggy ally assented.

Perhaps death gave me awe for friends, striking sharp
and early, for I held them since in a brittle love, of more
alarm than peace. I trust you may pass the limit of war; and
though not reared to prayer, when service is had in church
for our arms, I include yourself. . . I was thinking today,
as I noticed, that the "supernatural" was only the natural
disclosed.

> *Not "Revelation" 'tis that waits,*
> *But our unfurnished eyes.*

But I fear I detain you. Should you, before this reaches
you, experience Immortality, who will inform me of the
exchange? Could you, with honor, avoid death, I entreat you,
sir. It would bereave

YOUR GNOME

I trust the "Procession of Flowers" was not a premonition.

To Louisa and Fannie Norcross
(May, 1863)

. . . The nights turned hot, when Vinnie had gone, and I must keep no window raised for fear of prowling "booger," and I must shut my door for fear front door slide open on me at the "dead of night," and I must keep "gas" burning to light the danger up, so I could distinguish it—these gave me a snarl in the brain which don't unravel yet, and that old nail in my breast pricked me; these, dear, were my cause. Truth is so best of all I wanted you to know. Vinnie will tell of her visit. . .

About Commencement, children, I can have no doubt, if you should fail me then, my little life would fail of itself. Could you only lie in your little bed and smile at me, that would be support. Tell the doctor I am inexorable, besides I shall heal you quicker than he. You need the balsam word. And who is to cut the cake, ask F——, and chirp to those trustees? Tell me, dears, by the coming mail, that you will not fail me. . .

Jennie Hitchcock's mother was buried yesterday, so there is one orphan more, and her father is very sick besides. My father and mother went to the service, and mother said while the minister prayed, a hen with her chickens came up, and tried to fly into the window. I suppose the dead lady used to feed them, and they wanted to bid her goodbye.

> *Life is death we're lengthy at,*
> *Death the hinge to life.*

Love from all
EMILY

To the same
(Autumn, 1863)

Wednesday

DEAR CHILDREN,

Nothing has happened but loneliness, perhaps too daily to relate. Carlo is consistent, has asked for nothing to eat or drink, since you went away. Mother thinks him a model dog, and conjectures what he might have been, had not Vinnie "demoralized" him. Margaret objects to furnace heat on account of bone decrepitudes, so I dwell in my bonnet and suffer comfortably. . .

Miss Kingman called last evening to inspect your garden; I gave her a lanthorn, and she went out, and thanks you very much. No one has called so far, but one old lady to look at a house. I directed her to the cemetery to spare expense of moving.

I got down before father this morning, and spent a few moments profitably with the South Sea rose. Father detecting me, advised wiser employment, and read at devotions the chapter of the gentleman with one talent. I think he thought my conscience would adjust the gender.

EMILY

To the same
(Autumn, 1863)

. . . I should be wild with joy to see my little lovers. The writing them is not so sweet as their two faces that seem so small way off, and yet have been two weeks from me—two wishful, wandering weeks. Now, I begin to doubt if they ever came.

I bid the stiff "goodnight" and the square "goodmorning" to the lingering guest, I finish mamma's sack, all but the overcasting—that fatal sack, you recollect. I pick up tufts of mignonette, and sweet alyssum for winter, dim as winter seems these red, and gold, and ribbon days.

I am sure I feel as Noah did, docile, but somewhat sceptic, under the satinet.

No frost at our house yet. Thermometer frost, I mean.

L—— goes to Sunderland, Wednesday, for a minute or two; leaves here at half-past six—what a fitting hour—and will breakfast the night before; such a smart atmosphere! The trees stand right up straight when they hear her boots, and will bear crockery wares instead of fruit, I fear. She hasn't starched the geraniums yet, but will have ample time, unless she leaves before April. Emily is very mean, and her children in dark mustn't remember what she says about damsel.

Grateful for little notes, and shall ask for longer when my birds locate. Would it were here. Three sisters are prettier than one. . . Tabby is a continual shrine, and her jaunty ribbons put me in mind of fingers far out at sea. F——'s admonition made me laugh and cry too. In the hugest haste, and the engine waiting.

EMILY

To the same
(After the death of their father, January, 1864)

What shall I tell these darlings except that my father and mother are half their father and mother, and my home half theirs, whenever, and for as long as, they will. And sometimes a dearer thought than that creeps into my mind, but it is not for tonight. Wasn't dear papa so tired always after mamma went, and wasn't it almost sweet to think of the two together these new winter nights? The grief is our side, darlings, and the glad is theirs. Vinnie and I sit down tonight, while mother tells what makes us cry, though we know it is well and easy with uncle and papa, and only our part hurts. Mother tells how gently he looked on all who looked at him—how he held his bouquet sweet, as he were a guest in a friend's parlor and must still do honor. The meek, mild gentleman who thought no harm, but peace toward all.

Vinnie intended to go, but the day was cold, and she wanted to keep Uncle L—— as she talked with him, always, instead of this new way. She thought too, for the crowd, she could not see you, children, and she would be another one to give others care. Mother said Mr. V——, yes, dears, even Mr. V——, at whom we sometimes smile, talked about "Lorin' and Laviny" and his friendship towards them, to your father's guests. We won't smile at him anymore now, will we? Perhaps he'll live to tell some gentleness of us, who made merry of him.

But never mind that now. When you have strength, tell us how it is, and what we may do for you, of comfort, or of service. Be sure you crowd all others out, precious little cousins. Goodnight. Let Emily sing for you because she cannot pray:

> *It is not dying hurts us so,—*
> *'Tis living hurts us more;*
> *But dying is a different way,*
> *A kind, behind the door,—*
> *The southern custom of the bird*
> *That soon as frosts are due*
> *Adopts a better latitude.*
> *We are the birds that stay,*
> *The shiverers round farmers' doors.*
> *For whose reluctant crumb*
> *We stipulate, till pitying snows*
> *Persuade our feathers home.*

EMILY

To Mr. Samuel Bowles

> *Her breast is fit for pearls,*
> *But I was not a diver.*
> *Her brow is fit for thrones,*
> *But I had not a crest.*
> *Her heart is fit for rest—*
> *I, a sparrow, build there*
> *Sweet of twigs and twine,*
> *My perennial nest.*

To the same
(1864?)

DEAR FRIEND,

How hard to thank you—but the large heart requites itself. Please to need me. I wanted to ask you to receive Mr. Browning from me, but you denied my Brontë—so I did not dare.

Is it too late now? I should like so much to remind you how kind you had been to me.

You could choose—as you did before—if it would not be obnoxious—except where you "measured by your heart," you should measure this time by mine. I wonder which would be biggest!

Austin told, Saturday morning, that you were not so well. 'Twas sundown, all day, Saturday—and Sunday such a long bridge no news of you could cross!

Teach us to miss you less because the fear to miss you more haunts us all the time. We didn't care so much, once. I wish it was then, now, but you kept tightening, so it can't be stirred today. You didn't mean to be worse, did you? Wasn't it a mistake?

Won't you decide soon to be the strong man we first knew? 'Twould lighten things so much—and yet that man was not so dear—I guess you'd better not.

We pray for you, every night. A homely shrine our knee, but Madonna looks at the heart first.

Dear friend—don't discourage!

Affectionately
EMILY

To the same

No wilderness can be
Where this *attendeth thee—*
No desert noon,
No fear of frost to come
Haunt the perennial bloom,
But certain June!

EMILY

To the same

If recollecting were forgetting
Then I remember not.
And if forgetting, recollecting,
How near I had forgot!
And if to miss were merry,

And if to mourn were gay,
How very blithe the fingers
That gathered this, today!

EMILIE

TO THE SAME

"They have not chosen me," he said,
"But I have chosen them."
Brave, broken-hearted statement
Uttered in Bethlehem!

I *could not have told it,*
But since Jesus dared,
Sovereign! know a daisy
Thy dishonor shared.

EMILY

TO THE SAME

Saturday

Mother never asked a favor of Mr. Bowles before—that he
accept from her the little barrel of apples.

"Sweet apples," she exhorts me, with an occasional
Baldwin for Mary and the squirrels.

EMILY

TO THE SAME

Just once—oh! least request!
Could adamant refuse
So small a grace,
So scanty put,
Such agonizing terms?

Would not a God of flint
Be conscious of a sigh,
As down his heaven dropt remote,
"Just once, sweet Deity?"

To her sister Lavinia
(1864)

Dear Vinnie,

Many write that they do not write because that they have too much to say, I that I have enough. Do you remember the whippoorwill that sang one night on the orchard fence, and then drove to the south, and we never heard of him afterward?

He will go home, and I shall go home, perhaps in the same train. It is a very sober thing to keep my summer in strange towns—what, I have not told, but I have found friends in the wilderness. You know Elijah did, and to see the "ravens" mending my stockings would break a heart long hard.

Fanny and Lou are solid gold, and Mrs. B—— and her daughter very kind, and the doctor enthusiastic about my getting well. I feel no gayness yet—I suppose I had been discouraged so long.

You remember the prisoner of Chillon did not know liberty when it came, and asked to go back to jail.

C—— and A—— came to see me and brought beautiful flowers. Do you know what made them remember me? Give them my love and gratitude.

They told me about the day at Pelham, you, dressed in daisies, and Mr. McD——. I couldn't see you, Vinnie. I am glad of all the roses you find, while your primrose is gone. How kind Mr. C—— grew. Was Mr. D—— dear?

Emily wants to be well—if anyone alive wants to get well more, I would let him, first.

Give my love to father and mother and Austin. Tell Margaret I remember her, and hope Richard is well. . . How I wish I could rest all those who are tired for me.

Emily

To the same
(1865)

Dear Vinnie,

The hood is far under way, and the girls think it a
beauty. . . I hope the chimneys are done, and the hemlocks
set, and the two teeth filled in the front yard. How
astonishing it will be to me! . . .

The pink lily you gave Lou has had five flowers since I
came, and has more buds. The girls think it my influence.
Lou wishes she knew father's view of Jeff Davis' capture—
thinks no one but him can do it justice. She wishes to send
a photograph of the arrest to Austin, including the skirt and
spurs, but fears he will think her trifling with him. I advised
her not to be rash.

How glad I should be to see you all, but it won't be long,
Vinnie. You will be willing, won't you, for a little while? It
has rained and been very hot, and mosquitoes, as in August.
I hope the flowers are well. The tea-rose I gave Aunt L——
has a flower now. Is the lettuce ripe? Persons wear no bonnets
here. Fanny has a blade of straw with handle of ribbon.

Affectionately
Emily

To the same

. . . Father told me you were going. I wept for the little
plants, but rejoiced for you. Had I loved them as well as I
did, I could have begged you to stay with them, but they are
foreigners now, and all, a foreigner. I have been sick so long
I do not know the sun. I hope they may be alive, for home
would be strange except them, now the world is dead.

A—— N—— lives here since Saturday, and two new
people more, a person and his wife, so I do little but fly, yet
always find a nest. I shall go home in two weeks. You will get
me at Palmer?

Love for E—— and Mr. D——.

Sister

To the same

. . . The Doctor will let me go Monday of Thanksgiving week. He wants to see me Sunday, so I cannot before. . . Love for the Middletown pearls. Shall write E—— after Tuesday, when I go to the Doctor. Thank her for sweet note.

The drums keep on for the still man—but Emily must stop.

Love of Fanny and Lou.

SISTER

To Mrs. Gertrude Vanderbilt
(On her recovery from being accidentally shot)

To this world she returned,
But with a tingle of that;
A compound manner,
As a sod
Espoused a violet
That chiefer to the skies
Than to himself allied,
Dwelt, hesitating,
Half of dust,
And half of day, the bride.

EMILY

EMILY'S GOODBYE

We'll pass without a parting,
So to spare
Certificate of absence,
Deeming where
I left her I could find her
If I tried.
This way I keep from missing
Those who died.

EMILY

To Mrs. J. G. Holland
(1864)

. . . I winced at her loss, because I was in the habit of her, and even a new rolling-pin has an embarrassing element, but to all except anguish, the mind soon adjusts.

It is also November. The noons are more laconic and the sundowns sterner, and Gibraltar lights make the village foreign. November always seemed to me the Norway of the year. —— is still with the sister who put her child in an ice nest last Monday forenoon. The redoubtable God! I notice where Death has been introduced, he frequently calls, making it desirable to forestall his advances.

It is hard to be told by the papers that a friend is failing, not even know where the water lies. Incidentally, only, that he comes to land. Is there no voice for these? Where is Love today?

Tell the dear Doctor we mention him with a foreign accent, party already to transactions spacious and untold. Nor have we omitted to breathe shorter for our little sister. Sharper than dying is the death for the dying's sake.

News of these would comfort, when convenient or possible.

EMILY

To the same

DEAR SISTER,

It was incredibly sweet that Austin had seen you, and had stood in the dear house which had lost its friend. To see one who had seen you was a strange assurance. It helped dispel the fear that you departed too, for notwithstanding the loved notes and the lovely gift, there lurked a dread that you had gone or would seek to go. "Where the treasure is," there is the prospective.

Austin spoke very warmly and strongly of you, and we all felt firmer, and drew a vocal portrait of Kate at Vinnie's request, so vivid that we saw her. . .

Not all die early, dying young,
Maturity of fate

Is consummated equally
In ages or a night.
A hoary boy I've known to drop
Whole-statured, by the side
Of junior of fourscore—'twas act,
Not period, that died.

Will someone lay this little flower on Mrs. Holland's pillow?

EMILIE

SENT TO THE HOLLANDS AT VARIOUS TIMES

Away from home are some and I,
An emigrant to be
In a metropolis of homes
Is common possibility.
The habit of a foreign sky
We, difficult, acquire,
As children who remain in face,
The more their feet retire.

Though my destiny be fustian
Hers be damask fine—
Though she wear a silver apron,
I, a less divine,

Still, my little gypsy being,
I would far prefer,
Still my little sunburnt bosom,
To her rosier.

For when frosts their punctual fingers
On her forehead lay,
You and I and Doctor Holland
Bloom eternally,

Roses of a steadfast summer
In a steadfast land,

Where no autumn lifts her pencil,
And no reapers stand.

To Colonel T. W. Higginson
(Summer, 1864)

Dear Friend,

Are you in danger? I did not know that you were hurt. Will you tell me more? Mr. Hawthorne died.

I was ill since September, and since April in Boston for a physician's care. He does not let me go, yet I work in my prison, and make guests for myself.

Carlo did not come, because that he would die in jail; and the mountains I could not hold now, so I brought but the gods.

I wish to see you more than before I failed. Will you tell me your health? I am surprised and anxious since receiving your note.

The only news I know
Is bulletins all day
From Immortality.

Can you render my pencil? The physician has taken away my pen. I enclose the address from a letter, lest my figures fail.

Knowledge of your recovery would excel my own.

E. Dickinson

To Louisa and Fannie Norcross
(1864)

Be sure you don't doubt about the sparrow.

Poor —— and ——, in their genteel, antique way, express their sympathy, mixing admiring anecdotes of your father and mother's youth, when they, God help them, were not so sere. Besides these others, children, shall we tell them who else cherishes, everyday the same, the bright one and the black one too? Could it be Emily?

Would it interest the children to know that crocuses come up, in the garden off the dining-room, and a fuchsia, that pussy partook, mistaking it for strawberries? And that we have primroses, like the little pattern sent in last winter's note, and heliotrope by the aprons full—the mountain colored one—and a jasmine bud, you know the little odor like Lubin—and gilliflowers, magenta, and few mignonette, and sweet alyssum bountiful, and carnation buds?

Will it please them to know that the ice-house is filled, to make their tumblers cool next summer, and once in a while a cream?

And that father has built a new road round the pile of trees between our house and Mr. S——'s, where they can take the soldier's shirt to make, or a sweet poem, and no man find them but the fly, and he such a little man?

Love, dears, from us all, and won't you tell us how you are?

We seem to hear so little.

EMILY

TO THE SAME
(January, 1865)

. . . I am glad my little girl is at peace. Peace is a deep place. Some, too faint to push, are assisted by angels.

I have more to say to you all than March has to the maples, but then I cannot write in bed. I read a few words since I came home—John Talbot's parting with his son, and Margaret's with Suffolk. I read them in the garret, and the rafters wept.

Remember me to your company, their Bedouin guest.

Everyday in the desert, Ishmael counts his tents. New heart makes new health, dear.

Happiness is haleness. I dreamed last night I heard bees fight for pond-lily stamens, and waked with a fly in my room.

Shall you be strong enough to lift me by the first of April? I won't be half as heavy as I was before. I will be good and chase my spools.

I shall think of my little Eve going away from Eden.
Bring me a jacinth for every finger, and an onyx shoe.

EMILY

To Louisa Norcross
(February, 1865)

All that my eyes will let me shall be said for L——, dear little
solid gold girl. I am glad to the foot of my heart that you will
go to M——. It will make you warm. Touches "from home,"
tell Gungl, are better than "sounds."

You persuade me to speak of my eyes, which I shunned
doing, because I wanted you to rest. I could not bear a single
sigh should tarnish your vacation, but, lest through me one
bird delay a change of latitude, I will tell you, dear.

The eyes are as with you, sometimes easy, sometimes sad.
I think they are not worse, nor do I think them better than
when I came home.

The snow-light offends them, and the house is bright;
notwithstanding, they hope some. For the first few weeks I
did nothing but comfort my plants, till now their small green
cheeks are covered with smiles. . . Go, little girl, to M——.
Life is so fast it will run away, notwithstanding our sweetest
whoa.

Already they love you. Be but the maid you are to me, and
they will love you more.

Carry your heart and your curls, and nothing more but
your fingers. Mr. D—— will ask for these every candlelight.
How I miss ten robins that never flew from the rosewood
nest!

To the same

Dear L——,

This is my letter—an ill and peevish thing, but when my
eyes get well I'll send you thoughts like daisies, and sentences
could hold the bees. . .

To the same
(1865)

DEAR SISTER,

Brother has visited, and the night is falling, so I must close with a little hymn.

I had hoped to express more. Love more I never can, sweet D—— or yourself.

> *This was in the white of the year,*
> *That was in the green.*
> *Drifts were as difficult then to think,*
> *As daisies now to be seen.*
> *Looking back is best that is left,*
> *Or if it be before,*
> *Retrospection is prospect's half,*
> *Sometimes almost more.*

EMILY

To Colonel T. W. Higginson
(1865)

AMHERST

DEAR FRIEND,

You were so generous to me, that if possible I offended you, I could not too deeply apologize.

To doubt my high behavior is a new pain. I could be honorable no more, till I asked you about it. I know not what to deem myself—yesterday "your scholar," but might I be the one you tonight forgave, 'tis a better honor. Mine is but just the thief's request.

Please, sir, hear
"BARABBAS"

To Mr. Samuel Bowles
(With a bit of pine)

> *A feather from the whippoorwill*
> *That everlasting sings!*

> *Whose galleries are sunrise,*
> *Whose opera the springs,*
> *Whose emerald nest the ages spin*
> *Of mellow, murmuring thread,*
> *Whose beryl egg, what school-boys hunt*
> *In "recess" overhead!*

EMILY

We part with the river at the flood through a timid custom, though with the same waters we have often played.

EMILY

To the same
(1865?)

DEAR FRIEND,

Vinnie accidentally mentions that you hesitated between the "Theophilus" and the "Junius."

Would you confer so sweet a favor as to accept that too, when you come again?

I went to the room as soon as you left, to confirm your presence, recalling the Psalmist's sonnet to God beginning

> *I have no life but this—*
> *To lead it here.*
> *Nor any death but lest*
> *Dispelled from there.*
> *Nor tie to earths to come,*
> *Nor action new,*
> *Except through this extent—*
> *The love of you.*

It is strange that the most intangible thing is the most adhesive.

Your "rascal"

I washed the adjective.

To Louisa Norcross
(1866)

. . . Oh, L——, why were the children sent too faint to stand alone? . . . Every hour is anxious now, and heaven protect the lamb who shared her fleece with a timider, even Emily.

To Colonel T. W. Higginson

The possibility to pass
Without a moment's bell
Into conjecture's presence,
Is like a face of steel
That suddenly looks into ours
With a metallic grin;
The cordiality of Death
Who drills his welcome in.

To the same
(1868)

AMHERST

Dear Friend,

Whom my dog understood could not elude others.

I should be so glad to see you, but think it an apparitional pleasure, not to be fulfilled. I am uncertain of Boston.

I had promised to visit my physician for a few days in May, but father objects because he is in the habit of me.

Is it more far to Amherst?

You will find a minute host, but a spacious welcome. . .

If I still entreat you to teach me, are you much displeased? I will be patient, constant, never reject your knife, and should my slowness goad you, you knew before myself that

Except the smaller size
No lives are round.
These hurry to a sphere
And show and end.

The larger slower grow
And later hang;
The summers of Hesperides
Are long.

To Louisa and Fannie Norcross
(1868)

DEAR CHILDREN,

The little notes shall go as fast as steam can take them.

Our hearts already went. Would we could mail our faces for your dear encouragement.

Remember

The longest day that God appoints
Will finish with the sun.
Anguish can travel to its stake,
And then it must return.

I am in bed today—a curious place for me, and cannot write as well as if I was firmer, but love as well, and long more. Tell us all the load. Amherst's little basket is never so full but it holds more. That's a basket's cause. Not a flake assaults my birds but it freezes me. Comfort, little creatures—whatever befall us, this world is but this world. Think of that great courageous place we have never seen!

Write at once, please, I am so full of grief and surprise and physical weakness. I cannot speak until I know.

Lovingly
EMILY

To Colonel T. W. Higginson
(1868)

AMHERST

DEAR FRIEND,

A letter always feels to me like Immortality because it is the mind alone without corporeal friend. Indebted in our talk to attitude and accent, there seems a spectral power in thought that walks alone. I would like to thank you for your great kindness, but never try to lift the words which I cannot hold.

Should you come to Amherst, I might then succeed, though gratitude is the timid wealth of those who have nothing. I am sure that you speak the truth, because the noble do, but your letters always surprise me.

My life has been too simple and stern to embarrass any. "Seen of angels," scarcely my responsibility.

It is difficult not to be fictitious in so fair a place, but tests' severe repairs are permitted all.

When a little girl I remember hearing that remarkable passage and preferring the "power," not knowing at the time that "kingdom" and "glory" were included.

You noticed my dwelling alone. To an emigrant, country is idle except it be his own. You speak kindly of seeing me; could it please your convenience to come so far as Amherst, I should be very glad, but I do not cross my father's ground to any house or town.

Of our greatest acts we are ignorant. You were not aware that you saved my life. To thank you in person has been since then one of my few requests. . . You will excuse each that I say, because no one taught me.

To Mr. Samuel Bowles
(1868?)

I should think you would have few letters, for your own are so noble that they make men afraid. And sweet as your approbation is, it is had in fear, lest your depth convict us.

You compel us each to remember that when water ceases to rise, it has commenced falling. That is the law of flood.

The last day that I saw you was the newest and oldest of my life.

Resurrection can come but once, first, to the same house. Thank you for leading us by it.

Come always, dear friend, but refrain from going. You spoke of not liking to be forgotten. Could you, though you would?

Treason never knew you.

EMILY

To the same
(1869?)

DEAR FRIEND,

You have the most triumphant face out of Paradise, probably because you are there constantly, instead of ultimately.

Ourselves we do inter with sweet derision the channel of the dust; who once achieves, invalidates the balm of that religion, that doubts as fervently as it believes.

EMILY

To Louisa and Fannie Norcross
(Spring, 1870)

DEAR CHILDREN,

I think the bluebirds do their work exactly like me. They dart around just so, with little dodging feet, and look so agitated. I really feel for them, they seem to be so tried.

The mud is very deep—up to the wagons' stomachs— arbutus making pink clothes, and everything alive.

Even the hens are touched with the things of Bourbon, and make republicans like me feel strangely out of scene.

Mother went rambling, and came in with a burdock on her shawl, so we know that the snow has perished from the earth. Noah would have liked mother.

I am glad you are with Eliza. It is next to shade to know that those we love are cool on a parched day. . .

To the same

Maggie is ironing, and a cotton and linen and ruffle heat makes the pussy's cheeks red. It is lonely without the birds today, for it rains badly, and the little poets have no umbrellas. . .

. . . Fly from Emily's window for L——. Botanical name unknown.

(Enclosing a pressed insect.)

To the same
(September, 1870)

Little Sisters,

I wish you were with me, not precisely here, but in those sweet mansions the mind likes to suppose. Do they exist or nay? We believe they may, but do they, how know we? "The light that never was on sea or land" might just as soon be had for the knocking.

F——'s rustic note was as sweet as fern; L——'s token also tenderly estimated. Maggie and I are fighting which shall give L—— the "plant," though it is quite a pleasant war. . . A—— went this morning, after a happy egg and toast provided by Maggie, whom he promised to leave his sole heir.

The "pussum" is found. "Two dollars reward" would return John Franklin. . .

Love for Aunt O——. Tell her I think to instruct flowers will be her labor in heaven. . .

Nearly October, sisters! No one can keep a sumach and keep a secret too. That was my "pipe" F—— found in the woods.

Affectionately
Modoc

To the same
(1870)

Untiring Little Sisters,

What will I ever do for you, yet have done the most, for love is that one perfect labor nought can supersede. I suppose the pain is still there, for pain that is worthy does not go so soon. The small can crush the great, however, only temporarily. In a few days we examine, muster our forces, and cast it away. Put it out of your hearts, children. Faith is too fair to taint it so. There are those in the morgue that bewitch us with sweetness, but that which is dead must go with the ground. There is a verse in the Bible that says there are those who shall not see death. I suppose them to be the faithful. Love will not expire. There was never the instant when it was lifeless in the world, though the quicker deceit dies, the better for the truth, who is indeed our dear friend.

I am sure you will gain, even from this wormwood. The martyrs may not choose their food.

> *God made no act without a cause,*
> *Nor heart without an aim,*
> *Our inference is premature,*
> *Our premises to blame.*

. . . Sweetest of Christmas to you both, and a better year.

To the same

Dear Children,

When I think of your little faces I feel as the band does before it makes its first shout. . .

Emily

To the same
(1870)

. . . Mother drives with Tim to carry pears to settlers. Sugar pears with hips like hams, and the flesh of bonbons. Vinnie fastens flowers from the frosts. . .

Lifetime is for two, never for committee.

I saw your Mrs. H——. She looks a little tart, but Vinnie says makes excellent pies after one gets acquainted.

To the same
(Spring, 1871)

The will is always near, dear, though the feet vary. The terror of the winter has made a little creature of me, who thought myself so bold.

Father was very sick. I presumed he would die, and the sight of his lonesome face all day was harder than personal trouble. He is growing better, though physically reluctantly. I hope I am mistaken, but I think his physical life don't want to live any longer. You know he never played, and the straightest engine has its leaning hour. Vinnie was not here. Now we will turn the corner. All this while I was with you all, much of every hour, wishing we were near enough to assist each other. Would you have felt more at home, to know we were both in extremity? That would be my only regret that I had not told you.

As regards the "pine" and the "jay," it is a long tryst, but I think they are able. I have spoken with them.

Of the "thorn," dear, give it to me, for I am strongest. Never carry what I can carry, for though I think I bend, something straightens me. Go to the "wine-press," dear, and come back and say has the number altered. I descry but one. What I would I cannot say in so small a place.

Interview is acres, while the broadest letter feels a bandaged place. . .

Tell F—— we hold her tight. Tell L—— love is oldest and takes care of us, though just now in a piercing place.

Emily

To Perez Cowan
(October, 1870)

Home is the definition of God.

Emily

To Colonel T. W. Higginson
(August, 1870)

Dear Friend,

I will be at home and glad.

I think you said the 15th. The incredible never surprises us, because it is the incredible.

E. Dickinson

To the same

Truth is such a rare thing, it is delightful to tell it.

I find ecstasy in living; the mere sense of living is joy enough.

How do most people live without any thoughts? There are many people in the world,—you must have noticed them in the street,—how do they live? How do they get strength to put on their clothes in the morning?

If I read a book and it makes my whole body so cold no fire can ever warm me, I know that is poetry. If I feel physically as if the top of my head were taken off, I know that is poetry. These are the only ways I know it. Is there any other way?

To the same
(August, 1870)

Enough is so vast a sweetness, I suppose it never occurs, only pathetic counterfeits.

Fabulous to me as the men of the *Revelations* who "shall not hunger anymore." Even the possible has its insoluble particle.

After you went, I took Macbeth and turned to "Birnam Wood." Came *twice* "to Dunsinane." I thought and went about my work. . .

The vein cannot thank the artery, but her solemn indebtedness to him, even the stolidest admit, and so of me who try, whose effort leaves no sound.

You ask great questions accidentally. To answer them would be events. I trust that you are safe.

I ask you to forgive me for all the ignorance I had. I find no nomination sweet as your low opinion.

Speak, if but to blame your obedient child.

You told me of Mrs. Lowell's poems. Would you tell me where I could find them, or are they not for sight? An article of yours, too, perhaps the only one you wrote that I never knew. It was about a "Latch." Are you willing to tell me?

If I ask too much, you could please refuse. Shortness to live has made me bold.

Abroad is close tonight and I have but to lift my hands to touch the "Heights of Abraham."

Dickinson

To the same
(Winter, 1871)

To live is so startling, it leaves but little room for other occupations, though friends are, if possible, an event more fair.

I am happy you have the travel you so long desire, and chastened that my master met neither accident nor Death.

Our own possessions, though our own, 'tis well to hoard anew, remembering the dimensions of possibility. I often saw your name in illustrious mention, and envied an occasion so abstinent to me. Thank you for having been to Amherst. Could you come again that would be far better, though the finest wish is the futile one.

When I saw you last, it was mighty summer—now the grass is glass, and the meadow stucco, and "still waters" in the pool where the frog drinks.

These behaviors of the year hurt almost like music, shifting when it ease us most. Thank you for the "lesson."

I will study it, though hitherto,—

> *Menagerie to me*
> *My neighbor be.*

YOUR SCHOLAR

To Perez Cowan

It is long since I knew of you, Peter, and much may have happened to both; but that is the rarest book, which, opened at whatever page, equally enchants us.

I hope that you have power, and as much of peace as in our deep existence may be possible.

To multiply the harbors does not reduce the sea.

We learn, through Cousin Montague, that you have lost your sister through that sweeter loss which we call gain.

I am glad she is glad.

Her early pain had seemed to me peculiarly cruel.

Tell her how tenderly we are pleased.

Recall me too to your other sisters, who though they may have mislaid me, I can always find; and include me to your sweet wife. We are daily reminded of you by the clergyman, Mr. Jenkins, whom you strongly resemble.

Thank you for the paper. It is homelike to know where you are.

We can almost hear you announce the text, when the air is clear; and how social if you should preach us a note some Sunday in recess!

EMILY

To Louisa and Fannie Norcross
(March, 1872)

Thank you, own little girls, for the sweet remembrance—sweet specifically. Be sure it was pondered with loving thoughts not unmixed with palates.

But love, like literature, is "its exceeding great reward." . . . I am glad you heard "Little Em'ly." I would go far to hear her, except I have lost the run of the roads. . . Infinite March is here, and I "hered" a bluebird. Of course I am standing on my head!

> *Go slow, my soul, to feed thyself*
> *Upon his rare approach.*
> *Go rapid, lest competing death*
> *Prevail upon the coach.*
> *Go timid, should his testing eye*
> *Determine thee amiss,*
> *Go boldly, for thou paidst the price,*
> *Redemption for a kiss.*

Tabby is singing "Old Hundred," which, by the way, is her maiden name. Would they address and mail the note to their friend J—— W——?

Tidings of a book.
EMILY

To the same
(1872)

I like to thank you, dear, for the annual candy. Though you make no answer, I have no letter from the dead, yet daily love them more. No part of mind is permanent. This startles the happy, but it assists the sad.

This is a mighty morning. I trust that L—— is with it, on hill or pond or wheel. Too few the mornings be, too scant the nights. No lodging can be had for the delights that come to earth to stay, but no apartment find and ride away. F—— was brave and dear, and helped as much by counsel as by actual team. Whether we missed L—— we will let her guess; riddles are healthful food.

Eliza was not with us, but it was owing to the trains. We know she meant to come.

Oh! Cruel Paradise! We have a chime of bells given for brave Frazer. You'll stop and hear them, won't you?

"We conquered, but Bozzaris fell." That sentence always chokes me.

EMILY

To MacGregor Jenkins and his
sister Mrs. Squires
(1872?)

HAPPY "DID" AND MAC,

We can offer you nothing so charming as your own hearts, which we would seek to possess, had we the requisite wiles.

To her niece and Mrs. Squires
(In childhood)

DEAR BOYS,

Please never grow up, which is "far better." Please never "improve"—you are perfect now.

EMILY

LITTLE WOMEN,

Which shall it be, geraniums or tulips?

> *The butterfly upon the sky, who doesn't know its name,*
> *And hasn't any tax to pay, and hasn't any home,*
> *Is just as high as you and I, and higher, I believe—*
> *So soar away and never sigh, for that's the way to grieve.*

To Louisa and Fannie Norcross
(Early summer, 1872)

DEAR CHILDREN,

We received the news of your loving kindness through Uncle J—— last evening, and Vinnie is negotiating with neighbor Gray, who goes to a wedding in Boston next week, for the procuring of the nest. Vinnie's views of expressage do not abate with time. The crocuses are with us and several other colored friends. Cousin H—— broke her hip, and is in a polite bed, surrounded by mint juleps. I think she will hate to leave it as badly as *Marian Erie* did. Vinnie says there is a tree in Mr. Sweetser's woods that shivers. I am afraid it is cold. I am going to make it a little coat. I must make several, because it is tall as the barn, and put them on as the circus men stand on each other's shoulders. . . There is to be a "show" next week, and little Maggie's bed is to be moved to the door so she can see the tents. Folding her own like the Arabs gives her no apprehension. While I write, dear children, the colors Eliza loved quiver on the pastures, and day goes gay to the northwest, innocent as she.

EMILY

. . . Thank you for the passage. How long to live the truth is! A word is dead when it is said, some say. I say it just begins to live that day. . .

An ill heart, like a body, has its more comfortable days, and then its days of pain, its long relapse, when rallying requires more effort than to dissolve life, and death looks choiceless.

Of Miss P—— I know but this, dear. She wrote me in October, requesting me to aid the world by my chirrup more. Perhaps she stated it as my duty, I don't distinctly remember, and always burn such letters, so I cannot obtain it now. I replied declining. She did not write to me again—she might have been offended, or perhaps is extricating humanity from some hopeless ditch. . .

To Louisa Norcross
(1872, or 1873)

Thank you, dear, for the love. I am progressing timidly. Experiment has a stimulus which withers its fear.

> *This is the place they hoped before,*
> *Where I am hoping now.*
> *The seed of disappointment grew*
> *Within a capsule gay,*
> *Too distant to arrest the feet*
> *That walk this plank of balm—*
> *Before them lies escapeless sea—*
> *The way is closed they came.*

Since you so gently ask, I have had but one serious adventure—getting a nail in my foot, but Maggie pulled it out. It only kept me awake one night, and the birds insisted on sitting up, so it became an occasion instead of a misfortune. There was a circus, too, and I watched it away at half-past three that morning. They said "hoy, hoy" to their horses.

Glad you heard Rubinstein. Grieved L—— could not hear him. He makes me think of polar nights Captain Hall could tell. Going from ice to ice! What an exchange of awe!

I am troubled for L——'s eye. Poor little girl! Can I help her? She has so many times saved me. Do take her to Arlington Street.* Xerxes must go now and see to her worlds. You shall "taste," dear.

Lovingly

---

* Her physician.

To the same
(Winter, 1873)

. . . I know I love my friends—I feel it far in here where
neither blue nor black eye goes, and fingers cannot reach.
I know 'tis love for them that sets the blister in my throat,
many a time a day, when winds go sweeter than their wont,
or a different cloud puts my brain from home.

> *I cannot see my soul, but know 'tis there,*
> *Nor ever saw his house nor furniture,*
> *Who has invited me with him to dwell;*
> *But a confiding guest consult as well,*
> *What raiment honor him the most,*
> *That I be adequately dressed,*
> *For he insures to none*
> *Lest men specifical adorn*
> *Procuring him perpetual drest*
> *By dating it a sudden feast.*

Love for the glad if you know them, for the sad if they
know you.

To the same
(March, 1873)

. . . I open my window, and it fills the chamber with white
dirt. I think God must be dusting; and the wind blows so I
expect to read in "The Republican" "Cautionary signals for
Amherst," or, "No ships ventured out from Phœnix Row." . . .
Life is so rotatory that the wilderness falls to each, sometime.
It is safe to remember that. . .

To Mr. Samuel Bowles

Wednesday

Dear Mr. Bowles's note, of itself a blossom, came only tonight.
I am glad it lingered, for each was all the heart could hold.

Emily

To the same

Of your exquisite act there can be no acknowledgment, but the ignominy that grace gives.

EMILY

> *Could mortal lip divine*
> *The undeveloped freight*
> *Of a delivered syllable,*
> *'Twould crumble with the weight!*

To the same
(1873)

DEAR FRIEND,

It was so delicious to see you—a peach before the time—it makes all seasons possible, and zones a caprice.

We, who arraign the "Arabian Nights" for their understatement, escape the stale sagacity of supposing them sham.

We miss your vivid face, and the besetting accents you bring from your Numidian haunts.

Your coming welds anew that strange trinket of life which each of us wear and none of us own; and the phosphorescence of yours startles us for its permanence.

Please rest the life so many own—for gems abscond.

In your own beautiful words—for the voice is the palace of all of us,—

> *"Near, but remote."*

EMILY

To the same
(1874)

DEAR FRIEND,

The paper wanders so I cannot write my name on it, so I give you father's portrait instead.

As summer into autumn slips
And yet we sooner say
"The summer" than "the autumn," lest
We turn the sun away,

And almost count it an affront
The presence to concede
Of one however lovely, not
The one that we have loved,—

So we evade the charge of years,
One, one attempting shy
The circumvention of the shaft
Of life's declivity.

EMILY

To the same

If we die, will you come for us, as you do for father?
"Not born," yourself "to die," you must reverse us all.

Last to adhere
When summers swerve away—
Elegy of
Integrity.

To remember our own, Mr. Bowles, is all we can do. With grief it is done, so warmly and long, it can never be new.

EMILY

To Mrs. Edward Tuckerman
(January, 1874)

DEAR FRIEND,

I fear my congratulation, like repentance according to Calvin, is too late to be plausible, but might there not be an exception, were the delight or the penitence found to be durable?

EMILY

. . . Have thousands of things to say as also ten thousands but must abate now.

Lovingly
EMILY

To Louisa and Fannie Norcross
(1874)

DEAR CHILDREN,

Father is ill at home. I think it is the "Legislature" reacting on an otherwise obliging constitution. Maggie is ill at Tom's—a combination of cold and superstition of fever—of which her enemy is ill—and longing for the promised land, of which there is no surplus. "Apollyon" and the "Devil" fade in martial lustre beside Lavinia and myself. "As thy day is so shall thy" stem "be." We can all of us sympathize with the man who wanted the roan horse to ride to execution, because he said 'twas a nimble hue, and 'twould be over sooner. . .

Dear L——, shall I enclose the slips, or delay till father? Vinnie advises the latter. I usually prefer formers, latters seeming to me like Dickens's hero's dead mamma, "too some weeks off" to risk. Do you remember the "sometimes" of childhood, which invariably never occurred? . . .

Be pleased you have no cat to detain from justice. Ours have taken meats, and the wife of the "general court" is trying to lay them out, but as she has but two wheels and they have four, I would accept their chances. Kitties eat kindlings now. Vinnie thinks they are "cribbers." I wish I could make you as long a call as De Quincey made North, but that morning cannot be advanced.

EMILY

To Fannie Norcross
(1874)

. . . I was sick, little sister, and write you the first that I am able. The loveliest sermon I ever heard was the disappointment of Jesus in Judas. It was told like a mortal story of intimate young men. I suppose no surprise we can ever have will be so sick as that. The last "I never knew you" may resemble it. I would your hearts could have rested from the first severity before you received this other one, but "not as I will." I suppose the wild flowers encourage themselves in the dim woods, and the bird that is bruised limps to his house in silence, but we have human natures, and these are different. It is lovely that Mrs. W—— did not disappoint you; not that I thought it possible, but you were so much grieved. . . A finite life, little sister, is that peculiar garment that were it optional with us we might decline to wear. Tender words to L——, not most, I trust, in need of them.

Lovingly
EMILY

To the same

. . . How short it takes to go, dear, but afterward to come so many weary years—and yet 'tis done as cool as a general trifle. Affection is like bread, unnoticed till we starve, and then we dream of it, and sing of it, and paint it, when every urchin in the street has more than he can eat. We turn not older with years, but newer everyday.

Of all these things we tried to talk, but the time refused us. Longing, it may be, is the gift no other gift supplies. Do you remember what you said the night you came to me? I secure that sentence. If I should see your face no more it will be your portrait, and if I should, more vivid than your mortal face. We must be careful what we say. No bird resumes its egg.

A word left careless on a page
May consecrate an eye,
When folded in perpetual seam
The wrinkled author lie.

EMILY

To the same

. . . A tone from the old bells, perhaps, might wake the children.

> *We send the wave to find the wave,*
> *An errand so divine*
> *The messenger enamored too,*
> *Forgetting to return,*
> *We make the sage decision still*
> *Soever made in vain,*
> *The only time to dam the sea*
> *Is when the sea is gone.*

EMILY, with love.

To Louisa and Fannie Norcross

Spring is a happiness so beautiful, so unique, so unexpected, that I don't know what to do with my heart. I dare not take it, I dare not leave it—what do you advise?

Life is a spell so exquisite that everything conspires to break it.

"What do I think of 'Middlemarch'?" What do I think of glory—except that in a few instances this "mortal has already put on immortality."

George Eliot is one. The mysteries of human nature surpass the "mysteries of redemption," for the infinite we only suppose, while we see the finite. . . I launch Vinnie on Wednesday; it will require the combined efforts of Maggie, Providence and myself, for whatever advances Vinnie makes in nature and art, she has not reduced departure to a science. . .

Your loving
EMILY

To the same
(Spring, 1874)

SISTERS,

I hear robins a great way off, and wagons a great way off, and rivers a great way off, and all appear to be hurrying

somewhere undisclosed to me. Remoteness is the founder
of sweetness; could we see all we hope, or hear the whole
we fear told tranquil, like another tale, there would be
madness near. Each of us gives or takes heaven in corporeal
person, for each of us has the skill of life. I am pleased by
your sweet acquaintance. It is not recorded of any rose that
it failed of its bee, though obtained in specific instances
through scarlet experience. The career of flowers differs
from ours only in inaudibleness. I feel more reverence as I
grow for these mute creatures whose suspense or transport
may surpass my own. Pussy remembered the judgment,
and remained with Vinnie. Maggie preferred her home
to "Miggles" and "Oakhurst," so with a few spring touches,
nature remains unchanged.

> *The most triumphant bird*
> *I ever knew or met,*
> *Embarked upon a twig today,—*
> *And till dominion set*
> *I perish to behold*
> *So competent a sight—*
> *And sang for nothing scrutable*
> *But impudent delight.*
> *Retired and resumed*
> *His transitive estate;*
> *To what delicious accident*
> *Does finest glory fit!*

EMILY

To her cousins
(June, 1874)

You might not remember me, dears. I cannot recall
myself. I thought I was strongly built, but this stronger has
undermined me.

   We were eating our supper the fifteenth of June, and
Austin came in. He had a despatch in his hand, and I saw by
his face we were all lost, though I didn't know how. He said
that father was very sick, and he and Vinnie must go. The

train had already gone. While horses were dressing, news came he was dead.

Father does not live with us now—he lives in a new house. Though it was built in an hour it is better than this. He hasn't any garden because he moved after gardens were made, so we take him the best flowers, and if we only knew he knew, perhaps we could stop crying. . . The grass begins after Pat has stopped it.

I cannot write anymore, dears. Though it is many nights, my mind never comes home. Thank you each for the love, though I could not notice it. Almost the last tune that he heard was, "Rest from thy loved employ."

EMILY

To COLONEL T. W. HIGGINSON
(July, 1874)

The last afternoon that my father lived, though with no premonition, I preferred to be with him, and invented an absence for mother, Vinnie being asleep. He seemed peculiarly pleased, as I oftenest stayed with myself; and remarked, as the afternoon withdrew, he "would like it to not end."

His pleasure almost embarrassed me, and my brother coming, I suggested they walk. Next morning I woke him for the train, and saw him no more.

His heart was pure and terrible, and I think no other like it exists.

I am glad there is Immortality, but would have tested it myself, before intrusting him. Mr. Bowles was with us. With that exception, I saw none. I have wished for you, since my father died, and had you an hour unengrossed, it would be almost priceless. Thank you for each kindness. . . Your beautiful hymn, was it not prophetic? It has assisted that pause of space which I call "father."

To THE SAME
(August, 1874)

When I think of my father's lonely life and lonelier death, there is this redress—

Take all away;
The only thing worth larceny
Is left—the Immortality.

My earliest friend wrote me the week before he died, "If I
live, I will go to Amherst; if I die, I certainly will." Is your
house deeper off?

YOUR SCHOLAR

TO THE SAME

DEAR FRIEND,

I find you with dusk, for day is tired, and lays her
antediluvian cheek to the hill like a child.

Nature confides now.

I hope you are joyful frequently, these beloved days, and
the health of your friend bolder.

I remember her with my blossoms and wish they were
hers

Whose pink career may have a close
Portentous as our own, who knows?
To imitate these neighbors fleet,
In awe and innocence, were meet.

Summer is so kind I had hoped you might come. Since
my father's dying, everything sacred enlarged so it was
dim to own. When a few years old, I was taken to a
funeral which I now know was of peculiar distress, and the
clergyman asked, "Is the arm of the Lord shortened, that it
cannot save?"

He italicised the "cannot." I mistook the accent for a
doubt of Immortality, and not daring to ask, it besets me
still, though we know that the mind of the heart must
live if its clerical part do not. Would you explain it to
me? . . . It comforts an instinct if another have felt it too.
I was re-reading your "Decoration." You may have
forgotten it.

DEAR FRIEND,

Mother was paralyzed Tuesday, a year from the evening father died. I thought perhaps you would care.

YOUR SCHOLAR

A death-blow is a life-blow to some
Who, till they died, did not alive become;
Who, had they lived, had died, but when
They died, vitality begun.

To the same
(1875)

DEAR FRIEND,

The flower was jasmine. I am glad if it pleased your friend. It is next dearest to daphne, except wild-flowers—those are dearer.

I have a friend in Dresden, who thinks the love of the field a misplaced affection—and says he wilt send me a meadow that is better than summer's. If he does, I will send it to you.

I have read nothing of Tourguéneff's, but thank you for telling me—and will seek him immediately. I did not read Mr. Miller because I could not care about him.

Mrs. Hunt's poems are stronger than any written by women since Mrs. Browning, with the exception of Mrs. Lewes's; but truth like ancestors' brocades can stand alone. You speak of "Men and Women." That is a broad book.

"Bells and Pomegranates" I never saw, but have Mrs. Browning's endorsement. While Shakespeare remains, literature is firm.

An insect cannot run away with Achilles's head. Thank you for having written the "Atlantic Essays." They are a fine joy, though to possess the ingredient for congratulation renders congratulation superfluous.

Dear friend, I trust you as you ask. If I exceed permission, excuse the bleak simplicity that knew no tutor but the north. Would you but guide

DICKINSON?

To a cousin who sent a wreath for her father's grave
(December, 1874)

I am sure you must have remembered that father had
"become as little children," or you would never have
dared send him a Christmas gift, for you know how he
frowned upon Santa Claus, and all such prowling
gentlemen.

To MacGregor Jenkins
(Christmas, 1874)

. . . Atmospherically it was the most beautiful Christmas on
record. The hens came to the door with Santa Claus, the
pussies washed themselves in the open air without chilling
their tongues, and Santa Claus—sweet old gentleman—was
even gallanter than usual. Visitors from the chimney were
a new dismay, but all of them brought their hands so full
and behaved so sweetly, only a churl could have turned
them away. And then the ones at the barn were so happy!
Maggie gave the hens a check for potatoes, each of the cats
had a gilt-edged bone, and the horse had new blankets from
Boston.

Do you remember dark-eyed Mr. Dickinson who used to
shake your hand when it was so little it had hardly a stem?
He, too, had a beautiful gift of roses from a friend away. It
was a lovely Christmas. But what made you remember me?
Tell me with a kiss—or is it a secret?

EMILY

To Mrs. J. S. Cooper
(Later summer, 1874)

DEAR FRIEND,

It was my first impulse to take them to my father, whom I
cannot resist the grief to expect.

Thank you.

VINNIE'S SISTER

To the same

Should it be possible for me to speak of my father before
I behold him, I shall try to do so to you, whom he always
remembered.

EMILY

To the same
(January, 1875)

Is it too late to express my sorrow for my grieved friend?
Though the first moment of loss is eternity, other eternities
remain.

> *Though the great waters sleep*
> *That they are still the deep*
> *We cannot doubt.*
> *No vacillating God*
> *Ignited this abode*
> *To put it out.*

To Mrs. Edward Tuckerman
(March, 1875)

DEAR FRIEND,

It was so long my custom to seek you with the birds, they
would scarcely feel at home should I do otherwise, though
as home itself is far from home since my father died, why
should custom tire?

EMILY

To the same
(With yellow flowers during a torrential rain)
(May, 1875)

I send you inland buttercups as out-door flowers are still at
sea.

EMILY

To the same
(With her own rich caramels no one could ever duplicate)

Vinnie says the dear friend would like the rule. We have no statutes here, but each does as it will, which is the sweetest jurisprudence.

With it, I enclose Love's "remainder biscuit," somewhat scorched perhaps in baking, but "Love's oven is warm." Forgive the base proportions.

To Mrs. Stearns

Dear Friends,

I hope no bolder lover brought you the first pond lilies. The water is deeper than the land. The swimmer never stagnates.

I shall bring you a handful of lotus next, but do not tell the Nile.

He is a jealous brook.

Emily

To the same

"A little flower, a faded flower, the gift of one who cared for me."

Please usurp the pronoun.

Emily

To the same
(1875)

Dear Friend,

That a pansy is transitive, is its only pang.

This, precluding that, is indeed divine.

Bringing you handfuls in prospective, thank you for the love. Many an angel, with its needle, toils beneath the snow.

With tenderness for your mate

Emily

To Louisa and Fannie Norcross
(April, 1875)

I have only a buttercup to offer for the centennial, as an "embattled farmer" has but little time.

Begging you not to smile at my limited meadows, I am modestly

Yours

To the same
(Summer, 1875)

Dear Children,

I decide to give you one more package of lemon drops, as they only come once a year. It is fair that the bonbons should change hands, you have so often fed me. This is the very weather that I lived with you those amazing years that I had a father. W. D——'s wife came in last week for a day and a night, saying her heart drove her. I am glad that you loved Miss W—— on knowing her nearer. Charlotte Brontë said "Life is so constructed that the event does not, cannot, match the expectation."

The birds that father rescued are trifling in his trees. How flippant are the saved! They were even frolicking at his grave, when Vinnie went there yesterday. Nature must be too young to feel, or many years too old.

Now children, when you are cutting the loaf, a crumb, peradventure a crust, of love for the sparrows' table. . .

To the same
(August, 1876)

Dear Cousins,

Mr. S—— had spoken with pleasure of you, before you spoke of him. Good times are always mutual; that is what makes good times. I am glad it cheered you.

We have had no rain for six weeks except one thunder shower, and that so terrible that we locked the doors, and the clock stopped—which made it like Judgment day. The heat is very great, and the grass so still that the flies speck it. I fear L—— will despair. The notices of the "fall trade" in the hurrying dailies, have a whiff of coolness.

Vinnie has a new pussy the color of Branwell Brontë's hair. She thinks it a little "lower than the angels," and I concur with her. You remember my ideal cat has always a huge rat in its mouth, just going out of sight—though going out of sight in itself has a peculiar charm. It is true that the unknown is the largest need of the intellect, though for it, no one thinks to thank God. . . Mother is worn with the heat, but otherwise not altering. I dream about father every night, always a different dream, and forget what I am doing daytimes, wondering where he is. Without anybody, I keep thinking. What kind can that be?

Dr. Stearns died homelike, asked Eliza for a saucer of strawberries, which she brought him, but he had no hands. "In such an hour as ye think not" means something when you try it.

Lovingly
EMILY

To MRS. STEAMS
(Easter, 1875)

It is possible, dear friend, that the rising of the one we lost would have engrossed me to the exclusion of Christ's—but for your lovely admonition.

Sabbath morning was peculiarly dear to my father, and his unsuspecting last earthly day with his family was that heavenly one.

Vinnie and I were talking of you as we went to sleep Saturday night, which makes your beautiful gift of today almost apparitional.

Please believe how sweetly I thank you.

EMILY

To the same
(1875)

What tenements of clover
Are fitting for the bee,
What edifices azure
For butterflies and me—

What residences nimble
Arise and evanesce
Without a rhythmic rumor
Or an assaulting guess.

With love
E. Dickinson

To Colonel T. W. Higginson
(1875)

Dear Friend,

I am sorry your brother is dead. I fear he was dear
to you. I should be glad to know you were painlessly
grieved.

Of Heaven above the firmest proof
We fundamental know—
Except for its marauding hand
It had been heaven below.

Dickinson

To the same
(Early in 1876)

Dear Friend,

Are you willing to tell me what is right? Mrs. Jackson,
of Colorado, was with me a few moments this week, and
wished me to write for this.* I told her I was unwilling, and
she asked me why? I said I was incapable, and she seemed

---

* A circular of the *No Name Series* enclosed.

not to believe me and asked me not to decide for a few days. Meantime, she would write to me. She was so sweetly noble, I would regret to estrange her, and if you would be willing to give me a note saying you disapproved it and thought me unfit, she would believe you. I am sorry to flee so often to my safest friend, but hope he permits me.

To THE SAME
(Acknowledging a photograph, 1876)

DEAR FRIEND,

Except your coming I know no gift so great, and in one extent it exceeds that,—it is permanent.

Your face is more joyful when you speak, and I miss an almost arrogant look that at times haunts you, but with that exception, it is so real I could think it you.

Thank you with delight, and please to thank your friend for the lovely suggestion.

I hope she has no suffering now.

Was it Browning's flower that "ailed till evening"? I shall think of your "keeping house" at night when I close the shutter—but to be Mrs. Higginson's guest is the boon of birds.

Judge Lord was with us a few days since, and told me that the joy we most revere we profane in taking. I wish that was wrong.

Mrs. Jackson has written. It was not stories she asked of me. But may I tell her just the same that you don't prefer it? Thank you if I may, for it almost seems sordid to refuse from myself again.

My brother and sister speak of you, and covet your remembrance, and perhaps you will not reject my own to Mrs. Higginson?

> *Summer laid her supple glove*
> *In its sylvan drawer—*
> *Wheresoe'er, or was she*
> *The demand of awe?*

YOUR SCHOLAR

. . . But two had mentioned the "spring" to me—yourself and the "Revelations." "I, Jesus, have sent mine angel."

I inferred your touch in the papers on Lowell and Emerson. It is delicate that each mind is itself, like a distinct bird.

I was lonely there was an "or" in that beautiful "I would go to Amherst," though grieved for its cause. I wish your friend had my strength, for I don't care for roving—she perhaps might, though to remain with you is journey.

To abstain from "Daniel Deronda" is hard—you are very kind to be willing. . . I am glad "Immortality" pleased you. I believed it would. I suppose even God Himself could not withhold that now.

To disappear enhances,
The man that runs away
Is tinctured for an instant
With Immortality.

But yesterday a vagrant,
Today in memory lain
With superstitious value—
We tamper with again.

But "never" far as honor
Withdraws the worthless thing,
And impotent to cherish
We hasten to adorn.

Of Death the sternest function
That just as we discern
The excellence defies us—
Securest gathered then

The fruit perverse to plucking,
But leaning to the sight
With the ecstatic limit
Of unobtained delight.

To the same
(Autumn, 1876)

Dear Friend,

Thank you for permission to write Mrs. Higginson. I hope I have not fatigued her—also for thinking of my brother, who is slowly better, and rides for an hour, kind days.

I am glad if I did as you would like. The degradation to displease you, I hope I may never incur.

Often, when troubled by entreaty, that paragraph of yours has saved me—"Such being the majesty of the art you presume to practise, you can at least take time before dishonoring it," and Enobarbus said, "Leave that which leaves itself."

I shall look with joy for the "little book" because it is yours, though I seek you in vain in the magazines where you once wrote. I recently found two papers of yours that were unknown to me, and wondered anew at your withdrawing thought so sought by others.

When flowers annually died and I was a child, I used to read Dr. Hitchcock's book on the "Flowers of North America." This comforted their absence, assuring me they lived.

YOUR SCHOLAR

To the same
(1877)

Thank you, dear friend, for my "New Year," but did you not confer it? Had your scholar permission to fashion yours, it were perhaps too fair. I always ran home to awe when a child, if anything befell me. He was an awful mother, but I liked him better than none.

There remained this shelter after you left me the other day.

Of your flitting coming it is fair to think, like the bee's coupé, vanishing in music.

> *Would you with the bee return,*
> *What a firm of noon!*
> *Death obtains the rose,*

But the news of dying goes
No further than the breeze.

The ear is the last face. We hear after we see, which to tell you first is still my destiny.

Meeting a bird this morning, I began to flee. He saw it and sung.

Presuming on that lone result,
His infinite disdain,
But vanquished him with my defeat—
'Twas victory was slain.

I shall read the book.
Thank you for telling me.

To the same
(After Colonel Higginson had met with a bereavement, in 1877)

Dear Friend,

We must be less than Death to be lessened by it, for nothing is irrevocable but ourselves.

I am glad you are better. I had feared to follow you, lest you would rather be lonely, which is the will of sorrow; but the papers had spoken of you with affectionate deference, and to know you were deeply remembered might not too intrude.

To be human is more than to be divine, for when Christ was divine he was uncontented till he had been human.

I remember nothing so strong as to see you. . .

To the same
(1877)

Dear Friend,

I think of you so wholly that I cannot resist to write again, to ask if you are safe? Danger is not at first, for then we are unconscious, but in the after, slower days.

Do not try to be saved, but let redemption find you, as it certainly will. Love is its own rescue, for we, at our supremest, are but its trembling emblems.

YOUR SCHOLAR

TO THE SAME

Must I lose the friend that saved my life without inquiring why? Affection gropes through drifts of awe for his tropic door.

That every bliss we know or guess hourly befall him, is his scholar's prayer.

TO THE SAME
(January, 1878)

DEAR FRIEND,

I felt it shelter to speak to you.

My brother and sister are with Mr. Bowles, who is buried this afternoon.

The last song that I heard—that was, since the birds—was, "He leadeth me, he leadeth me; yea, though I walk"—then the voices stooped, the arch was so low.

TO THE SAME
(Summer, 1878)

DEAR FRIEND,

When you wrote you would come in November, it would please me it were November then—but the time has moved. You went with the coming of the birds—they will go with your coming, but to see you is so much sweeter than birds, I could excuse the spring.

With the bloom of the flower your friend loved, I have wished for her, but God cannot discontinue Himself.

Mr. Bowles was not willing to die.

When you have lost a friend, Master, you remember you could not begin again, because there was no world. I have thought of you often since the darkness, though we cannot assist another's night.

I have hoped you were saved.

That those have immortality with whom we talked about it, makes it no more mighty but perhaps more sudden. . .

> *How brittle are the piers*
> *On which our faith doth tread—*
> *No bridge below doth totter so,*
> *Yet none hath such a crowd.*
>
> *It is as old as God—*
> *Indeed, 'twas built by Him—.*
> *He sent His son to test the plank,*
> *And he pronounced it firm.*

I hope you have been well. I hope your rambles have been sweet, and your reveries spacious.

To have seen Stratford on Avon, and the Dresden Madonna, must be almost peace.

And perhaps you have spoken with George Eliot. Will you "tell me about it"? Will you come in November, and will November come, or is this the hope that opens and shuts, like the eye of the wax doll?

YOUR SCHOLAR

To Dr. and Mrs. J. G. Holland
(Autumn, 1876)

Saturday Eve

DEAR HOLLANDS,

Goodnight! I can't stay any longer in a world of death. Austin is ill of fever. I buried my garden last week—our man, Dick, lost a little girl through the scarlet fever. I thought perhaps that *you* were dead, and not knowing the sexton's address, interrogate the daisies. Ah! dainty—dainty Death! Ah! democratic Death! Grasping the proudest zinnia from my purple garden,—then deep to his bosom calling the serf's child!

Say, is he everywhere? Where shall I hide my things? Who is alive? The woods are dead. Is Mrs. H. alive? Annie and Katie—are they below, or received to nowhere?

I shall not tell how short time is, for I was told by lips which sealed as soon as it was said, and the open revere the shut. You were not here in summer. *Summer?* My memory flutters—had I—was there a summer? You should have seen the fields go—gay little entomology! Swift little ornithology! Dancer, and floor, and cadence quite gathered away, and I, a phantom, to you a phantom, rehearse the story! An orator of feather unto an audience of fuzz,—and pantomimic plaudits. "Quite as good as a play," indeed! Tell Mrs. Holland she is mine.

Ask her if *vice versa?* Mine is but just the thief's request— "Remember me today." Such are the bright chirographies of the "Lamb's Book." Goodnight! My ships are in!—My window overlooks the wharf! One yacht, and a man-of-war; two brigs and a schooner! "Down with the topmast! Lay her a' hold, a' hold!"

EMILIE

To Mrs. J. G. Holland
(Replying to a letter addressed to both sisters)
(1877)

SISTER,

A mutual plum is not a plum. I was too respectful to take the pulp and do not like a stone.

Send no union letters. The soul must go by Death alone, so, it must by life, if it is a soul.

If a committee—no matter.

I saw the sunrise on the Alps since I saw you. Travel why to Nature, when she dwells with us? Those who lift their hats shall see her, as devout do God.

I trust you are merry and sound. The chances are all against the dear, when we are not with them, though paws of principalities cannot affront if we are by.

Dr. Vaill called here Monday on his way to your house to get the Doctor to preach for him. Shall search "The Republican" for a brief of the sermon. Today is very homely and awkward as the homely are who have not mental beauty.

To Mrs. W. A. Stearns
(Spring, 1876)

DEAR FRIENDS,

Might these be among the fabrics which the Bible designates as beyond rubies?

Certainly they are more accessible to the fingers of your thief

EMILY

When President Steams died, this stanza came to Mrs. Stearns:

(June 8, 1876)

Love's stricken "why"
Is all that love can speak—
Built of but just a syllable
The hugest hearts that break.

EMILY

To the family of Professor Snell after his death—with flowers
(September, 1876)

I had a father once.

To Louisa and Fannie Norcross
(November, 1876)

. . . Oh that beloved witch-hazel which would not reach me till part of the stems were a gentle brown, though one loved stalk as hearty as if just placed in the mail by the woods. It looked like tinsel fringe combined with staider fringes, witch and witching too, to my joyful mind.

I never had seen it but once before, and it haunted me like childhood's Indian pipe, or ecstatic puff-balls, or that mysterious apple that sometimes comes on river-pinks; and is there not a dim suggestion of a dandelion, if her hair were ravelled and she grew on a twig instead of a tube,—though this is timidly submitted. For taking Nature's hand to lead her to me, I am softly grateful—was she willing to come? Though her reluctances are sweeter than other ones' avowals.

Trusty as the stars
Who quit their shining working
Prompt as when I lit them
In Genesis' new house,
Durable as dawn
Whose antiquated blossom
Makes a world's suspense
Perish and rejoice.

Love for the cousin sisters, and the lovely alien. . .

Lovingly
EMILY

TO MISS MARIA WHITNEY
(1877)

How well I know her not
Whom not to know has been
A bounty in prospective, now
Next door to mine the pain.

EMILY

TO THE SAME

. . . To relieve the irreparable degrades it.

Brabantio's resignation is the only one—"I here do give thee that with all my heart, which but thou hast already, with all my heart I would keep from thee."

EMILY

TO THE SAME
(1878)

DEAR FRIEND,

I am constantly more astonished that the body contains the spirit—except for over-mastering work it could not be borne.

I shall miss saying to Vinnie when we hear the Northampton bell—as in subtle states of the west we do—"Miss Whitney is going to church" though must not everywhere be church to hearts that have, or have had, a friend?

> *Could that sweet darkness where they dwell*
> *Be once disclosed to us,*
> *The clamor for their loveliness*
> *Would burst the loneliness.*

I trust you may have the dearest summer possible to loss. One sweet, sweet more, one liquid more, of that Arabian presence!

You spoke very sweetly to both of us, and your sewing and recollecting is a haunting picture, a sweet, spectral protection. Your name is taken as tenderly as the names of our birds, or the flower, for some mysterious cause, sundered from its dew. . .

In a brief memoir of Parepa, in which she was likened to a rose,—"thornless until she die," some bereaved one added. To miss him is his only stab, but that he never gave!

A word from you would be sacred.

EMILY

. . . The crucifix requires no glove.

TO THE SAME

Intrusiveness of flowers is brooked by even troubled hearts.

They enter and then knock—then chide their ruthless sweetness, and then remain forgiven.

May these molest as fondly!

EMILY

TO THE SAME

> *Than Heaven more remote,*
> *For Heaven is the root,*
> *But these the flitted seed.*
> *More flown indeed*

Than ones that never were,
Or those that hide, and are.

What madness, by their side,
A vision to provide
Of future days
They cannot praise.

My soul, to find them, come.
They cannot call, they're dumb,
Nor prove, nor woo,
But that they have abode
Is absolute as God,
And instant, too.

EMILY

To Mrs. Edward Tuckerman
(June, 1878)

Is it that words are suddenly small, or that we are suddenly large, that they cease to suffice us to thank a friend?

Perhaps it is chiefly both.

To the same
(July, 1878)

Would it be prudent to subject an apparitional interview to a grosser test?

The Bible portentously says "that which is spirit is spirit."

Go not too near a house of rose,
The depredation of a breeze
Or inundation of a dew
Alarm its walls away;
Nor try to tie the butterfly,
Nor climb the bars of ecstasy.
In insecurity to lie
Is joy's insuring quality.

E. DICKINSON

To the same
(August, 1878)

To see is perhaps never quite the sorcery that it is to surmise, though the obligation to enchantment is always binding.

It is sweet to recall that we need not retrench, as magic is our most frugal meal.

I fear you have much happiness, because you spend so much.

Would adding to it take it away, or is that a penurious question?

To cherish you is intuitive.

As we take Nature, without permission, let us covet you.

To Mrs. W. A. Stearns
(1878)

Dear Friends,

The seraphic shame generosity causes is perhaps its most heavenly result.

To make even Heaven more heavenly, is within the aim of us all.

To Mrs. Samuel Bowles
(After the death of Mr. Bowles)
(January, 1878)

I hasten to you, Mary, because no moment must be lost when a heart is breaking, for though it broke so long, each time is newer than the last, if it broke truly. To be willing that I should speak to you was so generous, dear.

Sorrow almost resents love, it is so inflamed.

I am glad if the broken words helped you. I had not hoped so much, I felt so faint in uttering them, thinking of your great pain. Love makes us "heavenly" without our trying in the least. 'Tis easier than a Saviour—it does not stay on high and call us to its distance; its low "Come unto me" begins in every place. It makes but one mistake, it tells us it is "rest"—perhaps its toil is rest, but what we have not known we shall know again, that divine "again" for which we are all breathless.

I am glad you "work." Work is a bleak redeemer, but it does redeem; it tires the flesh so that can't tease the spirit.

Dear "Mr. Sam" is very near, these midwinter days. When purples come on Pelham, in the afternoon, we say "Mr. Bowles's colors." I spoke to him once of his Gem chapter, and the beautiful eyes rose till they were out of reach of mine, in some hallowed fathom.

Not that he goes—we love him more who led us while he stayed. Beyond earth's trafficking frontier, for what he moved, he made.

Mother is timid and feeble, but we keep her with us. She thanks you for remembering her, and never forgets you. . . Your sweet "and left me all alone," consecrates your lips.

EMILY

To the same
(Spring, 1878)

Had you never spoken to any, dear, they would not upbraid you, but think of you more softly, as one who had suffered too much to speak. To forget you would be impossible, had we never seen you; for you were his for whom we moan while consciousness remains. As he was himself Eden, he is with Eden, for we cannot become what we were not.

I felt it sweet that you needed me—though but a simple shelter I will always last. I hope your boys and girls assist his dreadful absence, for sorrow does not stand so still on their flying hearts.

How fondly we hope they look like him—that his beautiful face may be abroad.

Was not his countenance on earth graphic as a spirit's? The time will be long till you see him, dear, but it will be short, for have we not each our heart to dress—heavenly as his?

He is without doubt with my father. Thank you for thinking of him, and the sweet, last respect you so faithfully paid him.

Mother is growing better, though she cannot stand, and has not power to raise her head for a glass of water. She thanks you for being sorry, and speaks of you with love. . . Your timid "for his sake," recalls that sheltering passage, "for his sake who loved us, and gave himself to die for us."

EMILY

TO THE SAME
(1879)

How lovely to remember! How tenderly they told of you! Sweet toil for smitten hands to console the smitten!

Labors as endeared may engross our lost. Buds of other days quivered in remembrance. Hearts of other days lent their solemn charm.

Life of flowers lain in flowers—what a home of dew! And the bough of ivy; was it as you said? Shall I plant it softly?

There were little feet, white as alabaster.

Dare I chill them with the soil?

Nature is our eldest mother, she will do no harm.

Let the phantom love that enrolls the sparrow shield you softer than a child.

TO MRS. J. G. HOLLAND
(Spring, 1878)

I thought that "Birnam Wood" had "come to Dunsinane." Where did you pick arbutus? In Broadway, I suppose. They say that God is everywhere, and yet we always think of Him as somewhat of a recluse. . . It is hard not to hear again that vital "Sam is coming"—though if grief is a test of a priceless life, he is compensated. He was not ambitious for redemption—that was why it is his. "To him that hath, shall be given." Were it not for the eyes, we would know of you oftener. Have they no remorse for their selfishness? "This tabernacle" is a blissful trial, but the bliss predominates.

I suppose you will play in the water at Alexandria Bay, as the baby does at the tub in the drive. . . Speak to us when your eyes can spare you, and "keep us, at home, or by the way," as the clergyman says, when he folds the church till another Sabbath.

Lovingly
EMILY

To the same
(August, 1879)

LOVED AND LITTLE SISTER,

Vinnie brought in a sweet pea today, which had a pod on the "off" side. Startled by the omen, I hasten to you.

An unexpected impediment to my reply to your dear last, was a call from my Aunt Elizabeth—"the only male relative on the female side," and though many days since, its flavor of court-martial still sets my spirit tingling.

With what dismay I read of those columns of kindred in the Bible—the Jacobites and the Jebusites and the Hittites and the Jacqueminots!

I am sure you are better, for no rheumatism in its senses would stay after the thermometer struck ninety!

We are revelling in a gorgeous drought.

The grass is painted brown, and how nature would look in other than the standard colors, we can all infer. . . I bade—— call on you, but Vinnie said you were "the other side of the globe," yet Vinnie thinks Vermont is in Asia, so I don't intend to be disheartened by trifles.

Vinnie has a new pussy that catches a mouse an hour. We call her the "minute hand." . . .

To Colonel T. W. Higginson
(In acknowledgment of his *Short Studies of American Authors*, 1879)

DEAR FRIEND,

Brabantio's gift was not more fair than yours, though I trust without his pathetic inscription, "Which but thou hast already, with all my heart I would keep from thee."

Of Poe, I know too little to think—Hawthorne appalls— entices.

Mrs. Jackson soars to your estimate lawfully as a bird, but of Howells and James one hesitates. Your relentless music dooms as it redeems.

Remorse for the brevity of a book is a rare emotion, though fair as Lowell's "sweet despair" in the "slipper hymn."

> One thing of it we borrow
> And promise to return,
> The booty and the sorrow
> Its sweetness to have known.
> One thing of it we covet—
> The power to forget,
> The anguish of the avarice
> Defrays the dross of it.

Had I tried before reading your gift to thank you, it had perhaps been possible, but I waited, and now it disables my lips.

Magic, as it electrifies, also makes decrepit. Thank you for thinking of me.

YOUR SCHOLAR

To Miss Maria Whitney

> The face in evanescence lain
> Is more distinct than ours,
> And ours, considered for its sake,
> As capsules are for flowers.

EMILY

To the same
(1879)

DEAR FRIEND,

Your touching suggestion. . . is a tender permission. . .

We cannot believe for each other—thought is too sacred a despot, but I hope that God, in whatever form, is true to our friend. . . Consciousness is the only home of which we *now* know. That sunny adverb had been enough, were it not foreclosed.

When not inconvenient to your heart, please remember

us, and let us help you carry it, if you grow tired. Though we are each unknown to ourself and each other, 'tis not what well conferred it, the dying soldier asks, it is only the water.

We knew not that we were to live,
Nor when we are to die
Our ignorance our cuirass is;
We wear mortality
As lightly as an option gown
Till asked to take it off.
By His intrusion God is known—
It is the same with life.

EMILY

To LOUISA AND FANNIE NORCROSS
(About July 4, 1879)

DEAR COUSINS,

Did you know there had been a fire here, and that but for a whim of the wind Austin and Vinnie and Emily would have all been homeless? But perhaps you saw "The Republican."

We were waked by the ticking of the bells,—the bells tick in Amherst for a fire, to tell the firemen.

I sprang to the window, and each side of the curtain saw that awful sun. The moon was shining high at the time, and the birds singing like trumpets.

Vinnie came soft as a moccasin, "Don't be afraid, Emily, it is only the fourth of July."

I did not tell that I saw it, for I thought if she felt it best to deceive, it must be that it was.

She took hold of my hand and led me into mother's room. Mother had not waked, and Maggie was sitting by her. Vinnie left us a moment, and I whispered to Maggie, and asked her what it was.

"Only Stebbins's bam, Emily"; but I knew that the right and left of the village was on the arm of Stebbins's barn. I could hear buildings falling, and oil exploding, and people walking and talking gayly, and cannon soft as velvet from parishes that did not know that we were burning up.

And so much lighter than day was it, that I saw a caterpillar measure a leaf far down in the orchard; and Vinnie kept saying bravely, "It's only the fourth of July."

It seemed like a theatre, or a night in London, or perhaps like chaos. The innocent dew falling "as if it thought no evil," . . . and sweet frogs prattling in the pools as if there were no earth.

At seven people came to tell us that the fire was stopped, stopped by throwing sound houses in as one fills a well.

Mother never waked, and we were all grateful; we knew she would never buy needle and thread at Mr. Cutler's store, and if it were Pompeii nobody could tell her.

The post-office is in the old meeting-house where L——— and I went early to avoid the crowd, and——— fell asleep with the bumble-bees and the Lord God of Elijah.

Vinnie's "only the fourth of July" I shall always remember. I think she will tell us so when we die, to keep us from being afraid.

Footlights cannot improve the grave, only immortality.

Forgive me the personality; but I knew, I thought, our peril was yours.

Love for you each.

EMILY

To Mrs. Henry Hills
(February, 1879)

The power to console is not within corporeal reach—though its attempt is precious.

To die before it feared to die, may have been a boon.

To the same
(March, 1879)

DEAR FRIEND,

The only balmless wound is the departed human life we had learned to need.

For that, even Immortality is a slow solace. All other peace has many roots and will spring again.

With cheer from one who knows.

To Mrs. Samuel Bowles
(April, 1880)

Dear Mary,

The last April that father lived, lived I mean below, there were several snow-storms, and the birds were so frightened and cold, they sat by the kitchen door. Father went to the barn in his slippers and came back with a breakfast of grain for each, and hid himself while he scattered it, lest it embarrass them. Ignorant of the name or fate of their benefactor, their descendants are singing this afternoon.

As I glanced at your lovely gift, his April returned. I am powerless toward your tenderness.

Thanks of other days seem abject and dim, yet antiquest altars are the fragrantest. The past has been very near this week, but not so near as the future—both of them pleading, the latter priceless.

David's grieved decision haunted me when a little girl. I hope he has found Absalom.

Immortality as a guest is sacred, but when it becomes as with you and with us, a member of the family, the tie is more vivid. . .

If affection can reinforce, you, dear, shall not fall.

EMILY

To Mrs. J. S. Cooper

Trusting an April flower may not curtail your February, that month of fleetest sweetness.

E. DICKINSON

To the same

Dear Friend,

Maggie was taking you a flower as you were going out.

Please accept the design, and bewail the flower, that sank of chagrin last evening.

E. DICKINSON

To the same

The founders of honey have no names.

To the same

My family of apparitions is select, though dim.

To the same

Vinnie suggests these little friends.

Would they be too grovelling? And I add a face from my garden.

Though you met it before, it might not be charmless.

E. DICKINSON

To the same
(1880)

Is sickness pathos or infamy?

While you forget to decide, please confirm this trifle.

To Louisa Norcross
(1880)

. . . Did the "stars differ" from each other in anything but "glory," there would be often envy. The competitions of the sky corrodeless ply.

To Colonel T. W. Higginson
(1880)

DEAR FRIEND,

You were once so kind as to say you would advise me. Could I ask it now?

I have promised three hymns to a charity, but without your approval could not give them.

They are short, and I could write them quite plainly, and if you felt it convenient to tell me if they were faithful, I should be very grateful, though if public cares too far fatigue you, please deny

Your Scholar

To the same
(1880)

Dear Friend,

Thank you for the advice. I shall implicitly follow it.

The one who asked me for the lines I had never seen.

He spoke of "a charity." I refused, but did not inquire. He again earnestly urged, on the ground that in that way I might "aid unfortunate children." The name of "child" was a snare to me, and I hesitated, choosing my most rudimentary, and without criterion.

I inquired of you. You can scarcely estimate the opinion to one utterly guideless. Again thank you.

Your Scholar

To the same
(Early summer, 1880)

Dear Friend,

I was touchingly reminded of (a child who had died) this morning by an Indian woman with gay baskets and a dazzling baby, at the kitchen door. Her little boy "once died," she said, death to her dispelling him. I asked her what the baby liked, and she said "to step." The prairie before the door was gay with flowers of hay, and I led her in. She argued with the birds, she leaned on clover walls and they fell, and dropped her. With jargon sweeter than a bell, she grappled buttercups, and they sank together, the buttercups the heaviest. What sweetest use of days! 'Twas noting some such scene made Vaughan humbly say,—

"My days that are at best but dim and hoary."

I think it was Vaughan. . .

To Perez Cowan
(On receiving a Life of his little daughter)
(October, 1880)

Dear Cousin,

The sweet book found me on my pillow, where I was detained, or I should have thanked you immediately.

The little creature must have been priceless—yours and not yours—how hallowed!

It may have been she came to show you Immortality. Her startling little flight would imply she did.

May I remind you what Paul said, or do you think of nothing else, these October nights, without her crib to visit?

The little furniture of loss has lips of dirks to stab us. I hope Heaven is warm, there are so many barefoot ones. I hope it is near—the little tourist was so small. I hope it is not so unlike earth that we shall miss the peculiar form—the mould of the bird. "And with what body do they come?" Then they *do* come! Rejoice! What door? What hour? Run, run, my soul! Illuminate the house!

"Body!" then real,—a face and eyes,—to know that it is them! Paul knew the Man that knew the news, He passed through Bethlehem.

With love for you, and your sweet wife, "whom seeing not, we" trust.

Cousin Emily

To Louisa and Fannie Norcross
(1880)

. . . We asked Vinnie to say in the rear of one of her mental products that we had neuralgia, but evidently her theme or her time did not admit of trifles. . . I forget no part of that sweet, smarting visit, not even the nettle that stung my rose.

When Macbeth asked the physician what could be done for his wife, he made the mighty answer, "That sort must heal itself"; but, sister, that was guilt, and love, you know, is God, who certainly "gave the love to reward the love," even were there no Browning.

. . . The slips of the last rose of summer repose in kindred soil with waning bees for mates. How softly summer shuts, without the creaking of a door, abroad for evermore.

. . . Vinnie has also added a pilgrim kitten to her flock, which besides being jet black, is, I think, a lineal descendant of the "beautiful hearse horse" recommended to Austin.

To THE SAME
(December, 1880)

. . . The look of the words (stating the death of George Eliot) as they lay in the print I shall never forget. Not their face in the casket would have had the eternity to me. Now, *my* George Eliot. The gift of belief which her greatness denied her, I trust she receives in the childhood of the kingdom of heaven. As childhood is earth's confiding time, perhaps having no childhood, she lost her way to the early trust, and no later came. Amazing human heart, a syllable can make to quake like jostled tree, what infinite for thee? . . .

To THE SAME
(February, 1881)

. . . God is rather stern with his "little ones." "A cup of cold water in my name" is a shivering legacy February mornings.

. . . Maggie's brother is killed in the mine, and Maggie wants to die, but Death goes far around to those that want to see him. If the little cousins would give her a note—she does not know I ask it—I think it would help her begin, that bleeding beginning that every mourner knows.

To THE SAME
(Spring, 1881)

The divine deposit came safely in the little bank. We have heard of the "deeds of the spirit," but are his acts gamboge and pink? A morning call from Gabriel is always a surprise.

Were we more fresh from Eden we were expecting him—but Genesis is a "far journey." Thank you for the loveliness.

We have had two hurricanes within as many hours, one of which came near enough to untie my apron—but this moment the sun shines, Maggie's hens are warbling, and a man of anonymous wits is making a garden in the lane to set out slips of bluebird. The moon grows from the seed. . . Vinnie's pussy slept in grass Wednesday—a Sicilian symptom—the sails are set for summer, East India wharf. Sage and saucy ones talk of an equinoctial, and are trying the chimneys, but I am "short of hearing," as the deaf say. Blessed are they that play, for theirs is the kingdom of heaven. Love like a rose from each one, and Maggie's a Burgundy one she ardently asks.

EMILY

To the same
(1881)

My Dear Little Cousins,

I bring you a robin who is eating a remnant oat on the sill of the barn. The horse was not as hungry as usual, leaving an ample meal for his dulcet friend. . .

Maggie was charmed with her donkeys, and has long been talking of writing, but has not quite culminated. They stand on the dining-room side-board, by the side of an orange, and a "Springfield Republican." It will please you to know that the clover in the bill of the brown one is fresh as at first, notwithstanding the time, though the only "pastures" I know gifted with that duration, are far off as the psalms.

Mr. C—— called with a twilight of you. It reminded me of a supper I took, with the pictures on Dresden china. Vinnie asked him "what he had for supper," and he said he "could easier describe the nectar of the gods." . . . We read in a tremendous Book about "an enemy," and armed a confidential fort to scatter him away. The time has passed, and years have come, and yet not any "Satan." I think he must be making war upon somemother nation.

EMILY

To the same
(1881)

The dear ones will excuse—they knew there was a cause. Emily was sick, and Vinnie's middle name restrained her loving pen.

These are my first words since I left my pillow—that will make them faithful, although so long withheld. We had another fire—it was in Phoenix Row, Monday a week ago, at two in the night. The horses were harnessed to move the office—Austin's office, I mean. After a night of terror, we went to sleep for a few moments, and I could not rise. The others bore it better. The brook from Pelham saved the town. The wind was blowing so, it carried the burning shingles as far as Tom's piazza. We are weak and grateful. The fire-bells are oftener now, almost, than the church-bells. Thoreau would wonder which did the most harm.

The little gifts came sweetly. The bulbs are in the sod—the seeds in homes of paper till the sun calls them. It is snowing now. . . "Fine sleighing we have this summer," says Austin with a scoff. The box of dainty ones—I don't know what they were, buttons of spice for coats of honey—pleased the weary mother. Thank you each for all.

The beautiful words for which L—— asked were that genius is the ignition of affection—not intellect, as is supposed,—the exaltation of devotion, and in proportion to our capacity for that, is our experience of genius. Precisely as they were uttered I cannot give them, they were in a letter that I do not find, but the suggestion was this.

It is startling to think that the lips, which are keepers of thoughts so magical, yet at any moment are subject to the seclusion of death.

. . . I must leave you, dear, to come perhaps again,—

> *We never know we go—when we are going*
> *We jest and shut the door—*
> *Fate following behind us bolts it*
> *And we accost no more.*

I give you my parting love.

EMILY

To Mrs. Samuel Bowles
(September 6, 1881)

Tuesday

Dear Mary,

I give you only a word this mysterious morning in which we must light the lamps to see each other's faces, thanking you for the trust too confiding for speech.

You spoke of enclosing the face of your child. As it was not there, forgive me if I tell you, lest even the copy of sweetness abscond; and may I trust you received the flower the mail promised to take you, my foot being incompetent?

The timid mistake about being "forgotten," shall I caress or reprove? Mr. Samuel's "sparrow" does not "fall" without the fervent "notice."

"Would you see us, would Vinnie?" Oh, my doubting Mary! Were you and your brave son in my father's house, it would require more prowess than mine to resist seeing you.

Shall I still hope for the picture? And please address to my full name, as the little note was detained and opened, the name being so frequent in town, though not an Emily but myself.

Vinnie says "give her my love, and tell her I would delight to see her"; and mother combines.

There should be no tear on your cheek, dear, had my hand the access to brush it away.

Emily

To the same
(1881)

Dear Mary,

To have been the mother of the beautiful face, is of itself fame, and the look of Arabia in the eyes is like Mr. Samuel. "Mr. Samuel" is his memorial name. "Speak, that we may see thee," and Gabriel no more ideal than his swift eclipse. Thank you for the beauty, which I reluctantly return, and feel like committing a "startling fraud" in that sweet direction. If her heart is as magical as her face, she will wreck many a spirit, but the sea is ordained.

Austin looked at her long and earnestly.

"Yes, it is Sam's child." His Cashmere confederate. It is best, dear, you have so much to do. Action is redemption.

"And again a little while and ye shall not see me," Jesus confesses is temporary.

Thank you indeed.

EMILY

To Mrs. Edward Tuckerman
(1880)

> *Love is done when love's begun.*
> *Sages say.*
> *But have sages known?*
> *Truth adjourn your boon*
> *Without day.*

EMILY

To the same
(After Professor Root's death, December, 1880)

Dear Friend,

I thought of you, although I never saw your friend.

> *Brother of Ophir,*
> *Bright adieu.*
> *Honor the shortest*
> *Route to you.*

EMILY

To the Reverend F. F. Emerson
(1880)

A blossom, perhaps, is an introduction, to whom, none can infer.

To the same

Though tendered by a stranger, the fruit will be forgiven.
　Valor in the dark is my Maker's code.

E. Dickinson

To Mrs. Edward Tuckerman
(New Year's Day, 1881)

Saturday

My bird, who is "today"?
　"Yesterday" was a year ago, and yet

> *The stem of a departed flower*
> *Has still a silent rank.*
> *The bearer from an emerald court*
> *Of a despatch of pink.*

Thank you for the lovely love.

Emily

To Mrs. George Montague

Dear Cousin,
　The "Golden Rule" is so lovely, it needs no police to enforce it.

Cousin

To the same

To have "been faithful in a few things" was the delicate compliment paid one by God. Could I not commend a rarer candidate for his approval in my loyal Cousin?

To the same
(December, 1881)

Dear Friend,
　Vinnie asked me if I had any message for you, and while I was picking it, you ran away.

Not seeing, still we know.
Not knowing, guess;
Not guessing, smile and hide
And half caress,
And quake and turn away;
Seraphic fear!
Is Eden's innuendo
"If you dare"?

EMILY

To Mrs. J. S. Cooper

How strange that Nature does not knock, and yet does not intrude!

To the same

"Give me thine heart" is too peremptory a courtship for earth, however irresistible in Heaven.

To the same

DEAR FRIEND,
So valiant is the intimacy between Nature and her children, she addresses them as "comrades in arms."

E. DICKINSON

To the same

DEAR FRIEND,
Nothing inclusive of a human heart could be "trivial." That appalling boon makes all things paltry but itself.

To the same

Give us half the thorn—then it will tear you less. To divulge itself is sorrow's right, never its presumption.

Faithfully
E. DICKINSON

To Mrs. Henry Hills
(1881)

With a kiss and a flower, one of which will endure, I am whom you infer.

To the same
(1882)

Only a pond lily that I tilled myself.

To the same

Dear Friends,

Even the simplest solace, with a loved aim, has a heavenly quality.

Emily

To Mrs. W. F. Stearns
(October, 1882)

Dear Friend,

Affection wants you to know it is here. Demand it to the utmost.

Tenderly
E. Dickinson

To Mrs. J. G. Holland
(On the death of Dr. Holland)
(October, 1881)

We read the words, but know them not. We are too frightened with sorrow. If that dear, tired one must sleep, could we not see him first?

Heaven is but a little way to one who gave it, here. "Inasmuch," to him, how tenderly fulfilled!

Our hearts have flown to you before—our breaking voices follow. How can we wait to take you all in our sheltering arms?

Could there be new tenderness, it would be for you, but the heart is full—another throb would split it—nor would we dare to speak to those whom such a grief removes, but we have somewhere heard "A little child shall lead them."

EMILY

To the same

Thursday

After a while, dear, you will remember that there is a heaven—but you can't now. Jesus will excuse it. He will remember his shorn lamb.

The lost one was on such childlike terms with the Father in Heaven. He has passed from confiding to comprehending—perhaps but a step.

The *safety* of a beloved lost is the first anguish. With you, that is peace.

I shall never forget the Doctor's prayer, my first morning with you—so simple, so believing. *That* God must be a friend—*that* was a different God—and I almost felt warmer myself, in the midst of a tie so sunshiny.

I am yearning to know if he knew he was fleeing—if he spoke to you. Dare I ask if he suffered? Someone will tell me a very little, when they have the strength. . . Cling tight to the hearts that will not let you fall.

EMILY

To the same

Panting to help the dear ones and yet not knowing how, lest any voice bereave them but that loved voice that will not come, if I can rest them, here is down—or rescue, here is power.

One who only said "I am sorry" helped me the most when father ceased—it was too soon for language.

Fearing to tell mother, someone disclosed it unknown to us. Weeping bitterly, we tried to console her. She only replied "I loved him so."

Had he a tenderer eulogy?

EMILY

To the same

. . . I know you will live for our sake, dear, you would not be willing to for your own. That is the duty which saves. While we are trying for others, power of life comes back, very faint at first, like the new bird, but by and by it has wings.

How sweetly you have comforted me—the toil to comfort you, I hoped never would come. A sorrow on your sunny face is too dark a miracle—but how sweet that he rose in the morning— accompanied by dawn. How lovely that he spoke with you, that memorial time! How gentle that he left the pang he had not time to feel! Bequest of darkness, yet of light, since unborne by him. "Where thou goest, *we* will go"—how mutual, how intimate! No solitude receives him, but neighborhood and friend.

Relieved forever of the loss of those that must have fled, but for his sweet haste. Knowing he could not spare *them*, he hurried like a boy from that unhappened sorrow. Death has mislaid his sting—the grave forgot his victory. Because the flake fell not on him, we will accept the drift, and wade where he is lain.

Do you remember the clover leaf? The little hand that plucked it will keep tight hold of mine.

Please give her love to Annie, and Kate, who also gave a father.

EMILY

To the same
(On the marriage of her daughter Annie, December 7, 1881)

SWEET SISTER,

We were much relieved to know that the dear event had occurred without overwhelming any loved one, and perhaps it is sweeter and safer so. I feared much for the parting, to you, to whom parting has come so thickly in the last few days. I knew all would be beautiful, and rejoice it was. Few daughters have the immortality of a father for a bridal gift. Could there be one more costly?

As we never have ceased to think of you, we will more tenderly, now. Confide our happiness to Annie, in her happiness. We hope the unknown balm may ease the balm withdrawn.

You and Katie, the little sisters, lose her, yet obtain her, for each new width of love largens all the rest. Mother and Vinnie think and speak. Vinnie hopes to write. Would that mother could, but her poor hand is idle. Shall I return to you your last and sweetest words—"But I love you all"?

EMILY

TO THE SAME
(Christmas, 1881)

Dare we wish the brave sister a sweet Christmas, who remembered us punctually in sorrow as in peace?

The broken heart is broadest. Had it come all the way in your little hand, it could not have reached us perfecter, though had it, we should have clutched the hand and forgot the rest.

Fearing the day had associations of anguish to you, I was just writing when your token came. Then, humbled with wonder at your self-forgetting, I delayed till now. Reminded again of gigantic Emily Brontë, of whom her Charlotte said "Full of ruth for others, on herself she had no mercy." The hearts that never lean, must fall. To moan is justified.

To thank you for remembering under the piercing circumstances were a profanation.

God bless the hearts that suppose they are beating and are not, and enfold in His infinite tenderness those that do not know they are beating and are.

Shall we wish a triumphant Christmas to the brother withdrawn? Certainly he possesses it.

> *How much of Source escapes with thee—*
> *How chief thy sessions be—*
> *For thou hast borne a universe*
> *Entirely away.*

With wondering love
EMILY

"Whom seeing not, we" clasp.

EMILY

To Mrs. Edward Tuckerman
(March, 1880)

The robin is a Gabriel
In humble circumstances,
His dress denotes him socially
Of transport's working classes.
He has the punctuality
Of the New England farmer—
The same oblique integrity,
A vista vastly warmer.
A small but sturdy residence,
A self-denying household,
The guests of perspicacity
Are all that cross his threshold.
As covert as a fugitive,
Cajoling consternation
By ditties to the enemy,
And sylvan punctuation.

EMILY

To the same

We shall find the cube of the rainbow,
Of that there is no doubt;
But the arc of a lover's conjecture
Eludes the finding out.

Confidingly
EMILY

To Professor J. K. Chickering

How charming the magnanimity which conferring a favor
on others, by some mirage of valor considers itself receiving
one!

Of such is the kingdom of knights!

E. DICKINSON

To Mr. Thomas Niles
(1880?)

Dear Friend,

I bring you a chill gift—"My Cricket"* and "The Snow."†
A base return, indeed, for the delightful book which I infer
from you, but an earnest one.

To Professor J. K. Chickering
(Autumn, 1882)

Dear Friend,

I do not know the depth of my indebtedness. Sorrow,
benighted with fathoms, cannot find its mind.

Thank you for assisting us.

We were timidly grateful.

E. Dickinson

To the same

Dear Friend,

Thank you for being willing to see me, but may I defer
so rare a pleasure till you come again? Grief is a sable
introduction, but a vital one, and I deem that I knew you
long since through your shielding thought.

I hope you may have an electrical absence, as life never
loses its startlingness, however assailed. "Seen of angels" only,
an enthralling aim.

Thank you for the kindness, the fervor of a stranger the
latest forgot.

E. Dickinson

---

* *Poems*, Second Series, page 167.
† *Poems*, Second Series, page 174.

Dear Friend,

I had hoped to see you, but have no grace to talk, and my own words so chill and burn me that the temperature of other minds is too new an awe.

> *We shun it ere it comes,*
> *Afraid of joy,*
> *Then sue it to delay,*
> *And lest it fly*

> *Beguile it more and more,*
> *May not this be,*
> *Old suitor Heaven,*
> *Like our dismay at thee?*

Earnestly
E. Dickinson

To Mr. Samuel Bowles 4th
(August 2,1882)

Dear Friend,

Our friend your father was so beautifully and intimately recalled today that it seemed impossible he had experienced the secret of death.

A servant who had been with us a long time, and had often opened the door for him, asked me how to spell "genius" yesterday. I told her and she said no more. Today she asked me what "genius" meant. I told her none had known.

She said she read in a Catholic paper that Mr. Bowles was "the genius of Hampshire," and thought it might be that past gentleman. His look could not be extinguished to any who had seen him, for "because I live, ye shall live also," was his physiognomy.

I congratulate you upon his immortality, which is a

constant stimulus to my household, and upon your noble perpetuation of his cherished "Republican."

Please remember me tenderly to your mother.

With honor
EMILY DICKINSON

TO THE SAME
(1882)

DEAR FRIEND,

A tree your father gave me bore this priceless flower. Would you accept it because of him—

Who abdicated ambush
And went the way of dusk,
And now, against his subtle name,
There stands an asterisk
As confident of him as we;
Impregnable we are—
The whole of Immortality
Secreted in a star.

E. DICKINSON

TO THE SAME
(1882)

DEAR FRIEND,

My mother and sister hoped to see you, and I, to have heard the voice in the house that recalls the strange music of your father's. A little bin of blossoms I designed for your breakfast also went astray.

I hope you are in strength, and that the passengers of peace exalt, not rend, your memory. Heaven may give them rank, it could not give them grandeur, for that they carried with themselves.

With fresh remembrance
E. DICKINSON

To Miss Maria Whitney
(November, 1882)

Sweet Friend,

Our mother ceased. While we bear her dear form through the wilderness, I am sure you are with us.

Emily

To Louisa and Fannie Norcross
(November, 1882)

Dear Cousins,

I hoped to write you before, but mother's dying almost stunned my spirit.

I have answered a few inquiries of love, but written little intuitively. She was scarcely the aunt you knew. The great mission of pain had been ratified—cultivated to tenderness by persistent sorrow, so that a larger mother died than had she died before. There was no earthly parting. She slipped from our fingers like a flake gathered by the wind, and is now part of the drift called "the infinite."

We don't know where she is, though so many tell us.

I believe we shall in some manner be cherished by our Maker—that the One who gave us this remarkable earth has the power still farther to surprise that which He has caused. Beyond that all is silence. . .

Mother was very beautiful when she had died. Seraphs are solemn artists. The illumination that comes but once paused upon her features, and it seemed like hiding a picture to lay her in the grave; but the grass that received my father will suffice his guest, the one he asked at the altar to visit him all his life.

I cannot tell how Eternity seems. It sweeps around me like a sea. . . Thank you for remembering me. Remembrance—mighty word.

"Thou gavest it to me from the foundation of the world."

Lovingly
Emily

To the same
(Spring, 1883)

Thank you, dears, for the sympathy. I hardly dare to know that I have lost another friend, but anguish finds it out.

> *Each that we lose takes part of us;*
> *A crescent still abides,*
> *Which like the moon, some turbid night,*
> *Is summoned by the tides.*

. . . I work to drive the awe away, yet awe impels the work.

I almost picked the crocuses, you told them so sincerely. Spring's first conviction is a wealth beyond its whole experience.

The sweetest way I think of you is when the day is done, and L—— sets the "sunset tree" for the little sisters. Dear F—— has had many stormy mornings;

. . . I hope they have not chilled her feet, nor dampened her heart. I am glad the little visit rested you. Rest and water are most we want.

I know each moment of Miss W—— is a gleam of boundlessness. "Miles and miles away," said Browning, "there's a girl"; but "the colored end of evening smiles" on but few so rare.

Thank you once more for being sorry. Till the first friend dies, we think ecstasy impersonal, but then discover that he was the cup from which we drank it, itself as yet unknown. Sweetest love for each, and a kiss besides for Miss W——'s cheek, should you again meet her.

EMILY

To Miss Maria Whitney
(1883?)

DEAR FRIEND,

Has the journey ceased, or is it still progressing, and has Nature won you away from us, as we feared she would?

Othello is uneasy, but then Othellos always are, they hold such mighty stakes.

Austin brought me the picture of Salvini when he was last in Boston.

The brow is that of Deity—the eyes, those of the lost, but the power lies in the *throat*—pleading, sovereign, savage—the panther and the dove!

Each, how innocent!

I hope you found the mountains cordial—followed your meeting with the lakes with affecting sympathy. Changelessness is Nature's change.

The plants went into camp last night, their tender armor insufficient for the crafty nights.

That is one of the parting acts of the year, and has an emerald pathos—and Austin hangs bouquets of corn in the piazza's ceiling, also an omen, for Austin believes.

The "golden bowl" breaks soundlessly, but it will not be whole again till another year.

Did you read Emily Brontë's marvellous verse?

> *"Though earth and man were gone,*
> *And suns and universes ceased to be,*
> *And Thou wert left alone,*
> *Every existence would exist in Thee."*

To SAMUEL BOWLES 4TH
(Upon announcement of his engagement to Miss Hoar)
(October, 1883)

DEAR FRIEND,

> *The clock strikes one that just struck two—*
> *Some schism in the sum;*
> *A sorcerer from Genesis*
> *Has wrecked the pendulum.*

With warmest congratulation
E. DICKINSON

To Mr. Thomas Niles
(1883?)

Thank you, Mr. Niles.

I am very grateful for the mistake. I should think it irreparable deprivation to know no farther of her here, with the impregnable chances.

The kind but incredible opinion of "H. H." and yourself I would like to deserve.

Would you accept a pebble I think I gave to her, though I am not sure.

With thanks
E. Dickinson

How happy is the little stone
That rambles in the road alone,
And doesn't care about careers,
And exigencies never fears;
Whose coat of elemental brown
A passing universe put on;
And independent as the sun,
Associates, or glows alone,
Fulfilling absolute decree
In casual simplicity.

To Mrs. J. G. Holland
(1883?)

Concerning the little sister, not to assault, not to adjure, but to obtain those constancies which exalt friends, we followed her to St. Augustine, since which the trail was lost, or says George Stearns of his alligator, "there was no such aspect."

The beautiful blossoms waned at last, the charm of all who knew them, resisting the effort of earth or air to persuade them to root, as the great florist says "The flower that never will in other climate grow."

To thank you for its fragrance would be impossible, but then its other blissful traits are more than can be numbered. And the beloved Christmas, too, for which I never thanked you. I hope the little heart is well,—*big* would have been the width,—and the health solaced; any news of her as sweet as the first arbutus.

Emily and Vinnie give the love greater every hour.

To Miss Maria Whitney
(1883)

Dear Friend,

The guilt of having sent the note had so much oppressed me that I hardly dared to read the reply, and delayed my heart almost to its stifling, sure you would never receive us again. To come unto our own and our own fail to receive us, is a sere response.

I hope you may forgive us.

All is faint indeed without our vanished mother, who achieved in sweetness what she lost in strength, though grief of wonder at her fate made the winter short, and each night I reach finds my lungs more breathless, seeking what it means.

> *To the bright east she flies,*
> *Brothers of Paradise*
> *Remit her home,*
> *Without a change of wings,*
> *Or Love's convenient things,*
> *Enticed to come.*
>
> *Fashioning what she is,*
> *Fathoming what she was,*
> *We deem we dream—*
> *And that dissolves the days*
> *Through which existence strays*
> *Homeless at home.*

The sunshine almost speaks, this morning, redoubling the division, and Paul's remark grows graphic, "the *weight* of glory."

I am glad you have an hour for books, those enthralling friends, the immortalities, perhaps, each may pre-receive. "And I saw the Heavens opened."

I hope that nothing pains you except the pang of life, sweeter to bear than to omit.

With love and wonder

EMILY

TO THE SAME

(1883?)

DEAR FRIEND,

Is not an absent friend as mysterious as a bulb in the ground, and is not a bulb the most captivating floral form? Must it not have enthralled the Bible, if we may infer from its selection? "The lily of the field!"

I never pass one without being chagrined for Solomon, and so in love with "the lily" anew, that were I sure no one saw me, I might make those advances of which in after life I should repent.

The apple-blossoms were slightly disheartened, yesterday, by a snow-storm, but the birds encouraged them all that they could—and how fortunate that the little ones had come to cheer their damask brethren!

You spoke of coming "with the apple-blossoms"—which occasioned our solicitude.

The ravenousness of fondness is best disclosed by children. . .

Is there not a sweet wolf within us that demands its food?

I can easily imagine your fondness for the little life so mysteriously committed to your care. The bird that asks our crumb has a plaintive distinction. I rejoice that it was possible for you to be with it, for I think the early spiritual influences about a child are more hallowing than we know. The angel begins in the morning in every human life. How small the furniture of bliss! How scant the heavenly fabric!

No ladder needs the bird but skies
To situate its wings,
Nor any leader's grim baton
Arraigns it as it sings.
The implements of bliss are few—
As Jesus says of Him,

"Come unto me" the moiety
That wafts the cherubim.

EMILY

To the same

DEAR FRIEND,

You are like God. We pray to Him, and he answers "No." Then we pray to Him to rescind the "no," and He don't answer at all, yet "Seek and ye shall find" is the boon of faith.

You failed to keep your appointment with the apple-blossoms—the japonica, even, bore an apple to elicit you, but that must be a silver bell which calls the human heart.

I still hope that you live, and in lands of consciousness.

It is Commencement now. Pathos is very busy.

The past is not a package one can lay away. I see my father's eyes, and those of Mr. Bowles—those isolated comets. If the future is mighty as the past, what may vista be?

With my foot in a sling from a vicious sprain, and reminded of you almost to tears by the week and its witness, I send this sombre word.

The vane defines the wind.

Where we thought you were, Austin says you are not. How strange to change one's sky, unless one's star go with it, but yours has left an astral wake.

Vinnie gives her hand.

Always with love
EMILY

To the same
(1883?)

DEAR FRIEND,

Your sweet self-reprehension makes us look within, which is so wild a place we are soon dismayed, but the seed sown in the lake bears the liquid flower, and so of all your words.

I am glad you accept rest.

Too many disdain it. I am glad you go to the Adiron- dacks.

To me the name is homelike, for one of my lost went every year with an Indian guide, before the woods were broken. Had you been here it would be sweet, but that, like the peach, is later. With a tomorrow in its cupboard, who would be "an hungered"?

Thank you for thinking of Dick. He is now the horse of association.

Men are picking the grass from father's meadow to lay it away for winter, and it takes them a long time. They bring three horses of their own, but Dick, ever gallant, offers to help, and bears a little machine like a top, which spins the grass away.

It seems very much like a gentleman getting his own supper— for what is his supper winter nights but tumblers of clover?

You speak of "disillusion." That is one of the few subjects on which I am an infidel. Life is so strong a vision, not one of it shall fail.

Not what the stars have done, but what they are to do, is what detains the sky.

We shall watch for the promised words from the Adirondacks, and hope the recess will all be joy. To have been made alive is so chief a thing, all else inevitably adds. Were it not riddled by partings, it were too divine.

I was never certain that mother had died, except while the students were singing. The voices came from another life. . .

Goodnight, dear. Excuse me for staying so long. I love to come to you. To one who creates, or consoles, thought, what an obligation!

EMILY

Her friendship with Mr. Clark began in 1882 through the death of one dear to them both. To him she wrote of the man always living in her deathless memory, proving her own statement that forgetting was a guile of which she was incapable.

To Mr. J. D. Clark
(1882)

. . . He never spoke of himself, and encroachment I know would have slain him. . . He was a dusk gem, born of troubled waters, astray in any crest below. Heaven might give him peace, it could not give him grandeur, for that he carried with himself to whatever scene. . .

Obtaining but his own extent
In whatsoever realm,
'Twas Christ's own personal expanse
That bore him from the tomb.

TO THE SAME
(Late autumn, 1882)

DEAR FRIEND,

It pains us very much that you have been more ill. We hope you may not be suffering now. Thank you for speaking so earnestly when our mother died. We have spoken daily of writing you, but have felt unable. The great attempt to save her life had it been successful would have been fatigueless, but failing, strength forsook us.

No verse in the Bible has frightened me so much from a child as "from him that hath not, shall be taken even that he hath." Was it because its dark menace deepened our own door? You speak as if you still missed your mother. I wish we might speak with you. As we bore her dear form through the wilderness, light seemed to have stopped.

Her dying feels to me like many kinds of cold—at times electric, at times benumbing,—then a trackless waste love has never trod. . .

The letter from the skies, which accompanied yours, was indeed a boon. A letter always seemed to me like Immortality, for is it not the mind alone, without corporeal friend?

I hope you may tell us that you are better.

Thank you for much kindness. The friend anguish reveals is the slowest forgot.

E. DICKINSON

TO THE SAME
(March, 1883)

DEAR FRIEND,

In these few weeks of ignorance of you, we trust that you are growing stronger, and drawing near that sweet physician, an approaching spring, for the ear of the heart hears bluebirds already, those enthralling signals. . . The great confidences of life are first disclosed by their departure, and I feel that I ceaselessly ought to thank you. . . Our household is scarcely larger than yours—Vinnie and I and two servants composing our simple realm, though my brother is with us often each day. I wish I could show you the hyacinths that embarrass us by their loveliness, though to cower before a flower is perhaps unwise, but beauty is often timidity—perhaps oftener pain.

A soft "Where is she?" is all that is left of our loved mother, and thank you for all you told us of yours. . .

Faithfully

E. Dickinson

To the same
(1883)

Dear Friend,

To thank you is impossible, because your gifts are from the sky, more precious than the birds, because more disembodied. I can only express my rejoiced surprise by the phrase in the Scripture, "And I saw the Heavens opened." . . .

Fathoms are sudden neighbors.

Ignorant till your note that our President's dying had defrauded you, we are grieved anew, and hasten to offer you our sorrow.

We shall make Mrs. Chadbourne's acquaintance in flowers after a few days. "Displeasure" would be a morose word toward a friend so earnest, and we only fear when you delay, that you feel more ill. Allow us to hear the birds for you, should they indeed come.

E. D.

To Mr. C. H. Clark
(April 18, 1883)

Dear Friend,

Would it be possible you would excuse me if I once more inquire for the health of the brother whom association has made sacred?

With the trust that your own is impairless, and that fear for your brother has not too much depressed you, please accept the solicitude of myself and my sister.

E. DICKINSON

To THE SAME
(April 22, 1883)

DEAR FRIEND,

The sorrowful tidings of your note almost dissuade reply, lest I for one moment take you from your brother's bedside. I have delayed to tell my sister till I hear again, fearing to newly grieve her, and hoping an encouraging word by another mail.

Please be sure we are with you in sorrowing thought, and take your brother's hand for me, if it is still with you. Perhaps the one has called him of whom we have so often talked during this grieved year.

With sympathy
E. DICKINSON

To THE SAME
(May 1, 1883)

DEAR FRIEND,

The temptation to inquire every morning for your sufferer is almost irresistible, but our own invalid taught us that a sick-room is at times too sacred a place for a friend's knock, timid as that is.

I trust this sweet May morning is not without its peace to your brother and you, though the richest peace is of sorrow.

With constant and fervent anxiousness, and the hope of an early word, please be sure we share your suspense.

E. DICKINSON

To THE SAME
(May 21, 1883)

DEAR FRIEND,

We have much fear, both for your own strength and the health of your brother, having heard nothing since we last asked, many days ago. Will you not, when possible, give us but a syllable, even a cheering accent, if no more be true? We think of you and your sufferer with intense anxiety, wishing some act or word of ours might be hope or help. The humming-birds and orioles fly by me as I write, and I long to guide their enchanted feet to your brother's chamber.

Excuse me for knocking. Please also excuse me for staying so long. Spring is a strange land when our friends are ill.

With my sister's tenderest alarm, as also my own

E. DICKINSON

To the same
(June 7, 1883)

I had, dear friend, the deep hope that I might see your brother before he passed from life, or rather life we know, and can scarcely express the pang I feel at its last denial.

His rare and hallowed kindness had strangely endeared him, and I cannot be comforted not to thank him before he went so far.

I never had met your brother but once. An unforgotten once—to have seen him but once more would have been almost like an interview with my "Heavenly Father" whom he loved and knew. I hope he was able to speak with you in his closing moment. One accent of courage as he took his flight would assist your heart. I am eager to know all you may tell me of those final days. We asked for him every morning, in heart, but feared to disturb you by inquiry aloud. I hope you are not too far exhausted from your "loved employ."

To know of you when possible would console us much, and every circumstance of him we had hoped to see. . .

E. D.

To the same
(June 16, 1883)

DEAR FRIEND,

Thank you for the paper. I felt it almost a bliss of sorrow that the name so long in Heaven on earth, should be on earth in Heaven.

Do you know if either of his sons have his mysterious face or his momentous nature?

The stars are not hereditary. I hope your brother and himself resumed the tie above, so dear to each below.

Your bond to your brother reminds me of mine to my sister—early, earnest, indissoluble. Without her life were fear, and Paradise a cowardice, except for her inciting voice.

Should you have any picture of your brother, I should rejoice to see it at some convenient hour—and though we cannot know the last, would you sometime tell me as near the last as your grieved voice is able? . . .

Are you certain there is another life? When overwhelmed to know, I fear that few are sure.

My sister gives her grief with mine. Had we known in time, your brother would have borne our flowers in his mute hand. With tears,

E. Dickinson

To the same
(July 9, 1883)

Dear Friend,

While I thank you immediately for the invaluable gift, I cannot express the bereavement that I am no more to behold it. Believing that we are to have no face in a farther life, makes the look of a friend a boon almost too precious.

The resemblance is faithful—the scholarly gentleness— the noble modesty—the absence of every dross, quite there. What a consoling prize to you, his mate through years of anguish so much sharper to see because endured so willingly.

Chastening would seem unneeded by so supreme a spirit.

I feel great grief for you—I hope his memory may help you, so recently a life. I wish I might say one liquid word to make your sorrow less. Is not the devotion that you gave him an acute balm? Had you not been with him how solitary the will of God!

Thank you for every word of his pure career. I hope it is nearer us than we are aware. Will you not still tell us of yourself and your home—from which this patient guest has flown? I am glad he lies near us—and thank you for the tidings of our other fugitive, whom to know was life. I can scarcely tell you how deeply I cherish your thoughtfulness. To still know of the dead is a great permission, and you have almost enabled that. With the ceaseless sympathy of myself and my sister, and the trust that our sufferer rests,

E. Dickinson

To the same
(January 4, 1884)

Dear Friend,

I have been very ill since early October, and unable to thank you for the sacred kindness, but treasured it each day, and hasten with my first steps, and my fullest gratitude. . . I never can thank you as I feel. That would be impossible. The effort ends in tears. You seem, by some deep accident, to be the only tie between the Heaven that evanesced, and the Heaven that stays. I hope the winged days that bear you to your brother are not too destitute of song, and wish that we might speak with you of him and of yourself, and of the third member of that sundered trio. Perhaps another spring would call you to Northampton, and memory might invite you here. . .

With a deep New Year

Your friend
E. Dickinson

To the same
(Enclosing pressed flowers, February 22, 1884)

Dear Friend,

I hoped it might gratify you to meet the little flower which was my final ministry to your brother, and which even in that faint hour, I trust he recognized, though the thronged spirit had not access to words.

These are my first out, and their golden trifles are too full of association to remain unshared.

With faithful thought of yourself and your brother, brothers in bereavement even as myself,

E. Dickinson

To the same
(April 21, 1884)

Never unmindful of your anxiety for your father, dear friend, I refrained from asking, lest even the moment engrossed by reply, might take you from him.

The peril of a parent is a peculiar pang, and one which my sister and myself so long experienced,—oh, would it were longer, for even fear for them were dearer than their absence,—that we cannot resist to offer you our earnest sympathy. I most sincerely trust that the sight is redeemed, so precious to you both, more than vicariously to you—even filially—and that the added fear has not exhausted you beyond the art of spring to cheer.

I have lost, since writing you, another cherished friend, a word of whom I enclose—and how to repair my shattered ranks is a besetting pain. Be sure that my sister and myself never forget your brother, nor his bereaved comrade.

To be certain we were to meet our lost would be a vista of reunion who of us could bear? . . .

Faithfully
E. DICKINSON

To the same
(April 22, 1884)

DEAR FRIEND,

These thoughts disquiet me, and the great friend is gone who could solace them. Do they disturb you?

> The spirit lasts, but in what mode—
> Below, the body speaks,
> But as the spirit furnishes—
> Apart it never talks.
> The music in the violin
> Does not emerge alone
> But arm in arm with touch, yet touch
> Alone is not a tune.

The spirit lurks within the flesh
Like tides within the sea
That make the water live; estranged
What would the either be?
Does that know now, or does it cease.
That which to this is done.
Resuming at a mutual date
With every future one?
Instinct pursues the adamant
Exacting this reply—
Adversity, if it may be.
Or wild prosperity,
The rumor's gate was shut so tight
Before my mind was sown.
Not even a prognostic's push
Could make a dent thereon.

With the trust you live
E. DICKINSON

To the same
(January 18, 1885)

DEAR FRIEND,

Though no New Year be old, to wish yourself and your honored father a new and happy one is involuntary, and I am sure we are both reminded of that sacred past which has forever hallowed us.

I trust the years which they behold are also new and happy, or is it a joyous expanse of year, without bisecting months—untiring Anno Domini? Had we but one assuring word, but a letter is a joy of earth—it is denied the gods. Vivid in our immortal group we still behold your brother, and never hear Northampton bells without saluting him. . .

Have you blossoms and books, those solaces of sorrow? That, I would also love to know, and receive for yourself and your father the forgetless sympathy of

Your friend
E. DICKINSON

To the same
(April 21, 1885)

Dear Friend,

The flower for which your brother cared resumes its siren circuit, and choosing a few for his name's sake, I enclose them to you. Perhaps from some far site he overlooks their transit, and smiles at the beatitudes so recently his own. Ephemeral, eternal heart!

I hope you are in health, and that the fragile father has every peace that years possess. . .

We think of your small mansion with unabated warmth, though is not any mansion vast that contains a father?

That this beloved spring inspirit both yourself and him, is our exceeding wish.

E. Dickinson

To Miss Maria Whitney
(Probably 1884)

Dear Friend,

I cannot depict a friend to my mind till I know what he is doing, and three of us want to depict you. I inquire your avocation of Austin, and he says you are "engaged in a great work!" That is momentous but not defining. The thought of you in the great city has a halo of wilderness.

Console us by dispelling it. . .

Vinnie is happy with her duties, her pussies, and her posies, for the little garden within, though tiny, is triumphant.

There are scarlet carnations, with a witching suggestion, and hyacinths covered with promises which I know they will keep.

How precious to hear you ring at the door, and Vinnie ushering you to those melodious moments of which friends are composed.

This also is fiction.

I fear we shall care very little for the technical resurrection, when to behold the one face that to us comprised it is too much for us, and I dare not think of the voraciousness of that only gaze and its only return.

Remembrance is the great tempter.

Emily

To Dr. and Mrs. T. P. Field
(Who had sent flowers)
(1884?)

Expulsion from Eden grows indistinct in the presence of flowers so blissful, and with no disrespect to Genesis, Paradise remains.

Beaconsfield says "the time has now come when it must be decided forever, who possesses the great gates to India."

I think it must be my neighbor.

With delicate gratitude
E. Dickinson

To Miss Louisa Norcross

I send a violet, for L——. I should have sent a stem, but was overtaken by snow-drifts. I regret deeply not to add a butterfly, but have lost my hat, which precludes my catching one.

To —— ——, with flowers

With the leave of the bluebirds, without whose approval we do nothing.

E. Dickinson

To Mr. Theodore Holland
(1885)

Dear Sir,

Your request to "remain sincerely" mine demands investigation, and if after synopsis of your career all should seem correct, I am tersely yours. I shall try to wear the unmerited honor with becoming volume.

Commend me to your kindred, for whom, although a stranger, I entertain esteem.

I approve the paint—a study of the Soudan, I take it, but the Scripture assures us our hearts are all Dongola.

E. DICKINSON

To —— ——
(1885)

. . . If you saw a bullet hit a bird, and he told you he wasn't shot, you might weep at his courtesy, but you would certainly doubt his word. Thomas's faith in anatomy was stronger than his faith in faith. . . Vesuvius don't talk—Ætna don't. One of them said a syllable, a thousand years ago, and Pompeii heard it and hid forever. She couldn't look the world in the face afterward, I suppose. Bashful Pompeii! . . .

To ——

DEAR FRIEND,

I thank you with wonder. Should you ask me my comprehension of a starlight night, awe were my only reply, and so of the mighty book. It stills, incites, infatuates, blesses and blames in one. Like human affection, we dare not touch it, yet flee, what else remains?

But excuse me—I know but little. Please tell me how it might seem to you.

How vast is the chastisement of beauty, given us by our Maker! A word is inundation, when it comes from the sea.

Peter took the marine walk at the great risk.

E. DICKINSON

To COLONEL T. W. HIGGINSON
(1884)

DEAR FRIEND,

May I ask the delight in advance, of sending you the "Life of Mrs. Cross," by her husband, which the papers promise for publication?

I feared somether pupil might usurp my privilege.

Emblem is immeasurable—that is why it is better than fulfilment, which can be drained.

EMILY

TO LOUISA AND FANNIE NORCROSS
(July, 1884)

DEAR COUSINS,

I hope you heard Mr. Sanborn's lecture. My "Republican" was borrowed before I waked, to read till my own dawn, which is rather tardy, for I have been quite sick, and could claim the immortal reprimand, "Mr. Lamb, you come down very late in the morning." Eight Saturday noons ago, I was making a loaf of cake with Maggie, when I saw a great darkness coming and knew no more until late at night. I woke to find Austin and Vinnie and a strange physician bending over me, and supposed I was dying, or had died, all was so kind and hallowed. I had fainted and lain unconscious for the first time in my life. Then I grew very sick and gave the others much alarm, but am now staying. The doctor calls it "revenge of the nerves"; but who but Death had wronged them? F——'s dear note has lain unanswered for this long season, though its "Goodnight, my dear," warmed me to the core. I have all to say, but little strength to say it; so we must talk by degrees. I do want to know about L——, what pleases her most, book or tune or friend.

I am glad the housekeeping is kinder; it is a prickly art. Maggie is with us still, warm and wild and mighty, and we have a gracious boy at the barn. We remember you always, and one or the other often comes down with a "we dreamed of F—— and L—— last night"; then that day we think we shall hear from you, for dreams are couriers.

The little boy we laid away never fluctuates, and his dim society is companion still. But it is growing damp and I must go in. Memory's fog is rising.

The going from a world we know
To one a wonder still

Is like the child's adversity
Whose vista is a hill,
Behind the hill is sorcery
And everything unknown.
But will the secret compensate
For climbing it alone?

Vinnie's love and Maggie's, and mine is presupposed.

EMILY

To THE SAME
(January 14, 1885)

Had we less to say to those we love, perhaps we should say it oftener, but the attempt comes, then the inundation, then it is all over, as is said of the dead.

Vinnie dreamed about F—— last night, and designing for days to write dear L——, —dear, both of you, —indeed, with the astounding nearness which a dream brings, I must speak this morning. I do hope you are well, and that the last enchanting days have refreshed your spirits, and I hope the poor little girl is better, and the sorrow at least adjourned.

L—— asked "what books" we were wooing now—watching like a vulture for Walter Cross's life of his wife. A friend sent me "Called Back." It is a haunting story, and as loved Mr. Bowles used to say, "greatly impressive to me." Do you remember the little picture with his deep face in the centre, and Governor Bross on one side, and Colfax on the other? The third of the group died yesterday, so somewhere they are again together.

Moving to Cambridge seems to me like moving to Westminster Abbey, as hallowed and as unbelieved, or moving to Ephesus with Paul for a next-door neighbor.

Holmes's "Life of Emerson" is sweetly commended, but you, I know, have tasted that. . . But the whistle calls me—I have not begun—so with a moan, and a kiss, and a promise of more, and love from Vinnie and Maggie, and the half-blown carnation, and the western sky, I stop.

That we are permanent temporarily, it is warm to know, though we know no more.

EMILY

TO MRS. EDWARD TUCKERMAN
(January, 1884)

DEAR FRIEND:

> *To try to speak, and miss the way.*
> *And ask it of the tears,*
> *Is gratitude's sweet poverty.*
> *The tatters that he wears.*
>
> *A better coat, if he possessed.*
> *Would help him to conceal.*
> *Not subjugate, the mutineer*
> *Whose title is "the soul."*

EMILY, with love

TO THE SAME
(February, 1884)

Do "men gather grapes of thorns"?

No, but they do of *roses*, and even the classic fox hushed his innuendo, as we unclasped the little box.

Sherbets untold, and recollection more sparkling than sherbets!

How wondrous is a friend, the gift of neither Heaven nor earth, yet coveted of both!

If the "archangels veil their faces," is not the sacred diffidence on this sweet behalf?

EMILY

TO THE SAME
(April, 1884)

Be encouraged, sweet friend! How cruel we did not know! But the battles of those we love are often unseen.

"If Thou hadst been here," Mary said, "our brother had not died." Hanging my head and my heart with it, that you sorrowed alone.

Late, but lovingly
EMILY

To the same
(April, 1885)

DEAR FRIEND,

We want you to wake—Easter has come and gone.

Morning without you is a dwindled dawn.

Quickened toward all celestial things by crows I heard this morning, accept a loving caw from a

Nameless friend
"SELAH"

To the same
(May, 1885)

We trust the repairs of the little friend are progressing swiftly, though shall we love her as well, revamped?

Anatomical dishabille is sweet to those who prize us.

A chastened grace is twice a grace. Nay, 'tis a holiness.

With a sweet May day
EMILY

To Mrs. Joseph Sweetser
(November, 1884)

SWEET AND GRACIOUS AUNT KATIE,

The beloved lilies have come, and my heart is so high it overflows, as this was mother's week, Easter in November.

Father rose in June, and a little more than a year since, those fair words were fulfilled, "and a little child shall lead them"—but boundlessness forbids me. . .

It is very wrong that you were ill, and whom shall I accuse? The enemy, "eternal, invisible, and full of glory"—but He declares himself a friend! It is sweet you are better.

More beating that brave heart has to do before the emerald recess.

With sorrow for Emma's accident, and love for all who cherish you, including the roses, your velvet allies,

Tenderly
EMILY

Many letters missing that would have been of rare interest—most notably those to the Lords and Helen Hunt—were supposed to have been burned in accordance with a mutual bond. Their loss was silently accepted on this understanding.

To "H. H."
(March, 1885)

DEAR FRIEND,

To reproach my own foot in behalf of yours is involuntary, and finding meagre solace in "whom He loveth He chasteneth," your valor astounds me. It was only a small wasp, said the French physician, repairing the sting, but the strength to perish is sometimes withheld—though who but you can tell a foot.

Take all away from me
But leave me ecstasy.
And I am richer then
Than all my fellow-men.
Is it becoming me
To dwell so wealthily.
When at my very door
Are those possessing more.
In abject poverty?

That you glance at Japan as you breakfast, not in the least surprises me, thronged only with music, like the decks of birds.

Thank you for hoping I am well. Who could be ill in March, that month of proclamation? Sleighbells and jays contend in my matinée, and the north surrenders instead of the south, a reverse of bugles.

Pity me, however, I have finished "Ramona." Would that like Shakespeare it were just published!

Knew I how to pray, to intercede for your foot were intuitive, but I am but a pagan.

To ——

Of God we ask one favor, that we may be forgiven. For what, He is presumed to know. The crime, from us, is hidden.

Immured the whole of life
Within a magic prison,
We reprimand the happiness
That too competes with Heaven.

May I once more know, and that you are saved?

Yours
E. DICKINSON

After Mrs. Jackson's death, August 12, 1885, Emily wrote of her:

Helen of Troy will die, but Helen of Colorado, never. Dear friend, can you walk, were the last words that I wrote her.

Dear friend, I can fly—
Her immortal reply.

To——

SWEET FRIENDS,
I send a message by a mouth that cannot speak.

The ecstasy to guess
Were a receipted bliss
If grace could talk.

With love

To ——

. . . What a hazard an accent is! When I think of the hearts it has scuttled or sunk, I almost fear to lift my hand to so much as a punctuation.

To Mr. Samuel Bowles 4th on the
birth of a son
(August, 1885)

Dear Friend,

I did not know.

God bless you indeed!

Extend to that small hand my own "right hand of fellowship," and guide the woman of your heart softly to my own.

I give "his angels charge"—well-remembered angels, whose absence only dims our eyes. The magnanimity I asked, you how freely gave!

If ever of any act of mine you should be in need, let me reply with the laureate, "Speak that I live to hear."

Vitally
E. Dickinson

To Mrs. E. P. Crowell
(When about to sail for Europe)
(March 2, 1885)

Is it too late to touch you, dear?
We this moment knew.
Love marine and love terrene,
Love celestial too.

I give his angels charge.

Emily

To Miss Eugenia Hall
(1885?)

Let me thank the little cousin in flowers, which, without lips, have language.

Somewhat cousin
Emily

To THE SAME
(With a wedding gift, October 20, 1885)

Will the sweet cousin who is about to make the Etruscan
experiment, accept a smile which will last a life, if ripened in
the sun?

COUSIN EMILY

To MRS. J. C. GREENOUGH

The flower keeps its appointment—should the heart be tardy?
When Memory rings her bell, let all the thoughts run in.

EMILY

To THE SAME
(After her Mother's death, October, 1885)

DEAR FRIEND,

I had the luxury of a mother a month longer than you, for
my own mother died in November, but the anguish also was
granted me to see the first snow upon her grave the following
day, which, dear friend, you were spared.

But Remembrance engulfs me, and I must cease.

I wish I could speak a word of courage, though that
love has already done. Who could be motherless who has a
mother's grave within confiding reach?

Let me enclose the tenderness born of bereavement.

To have had a mother—how mighty!

EMILY

To MRS. EDWARD TUCKERMAN
(October, 1885)

DEAR FRIEND,

I thought of you on your lonely journey, certain the
hallowed heroine was gratified, though mute. I trust you
return in safety and with closer clutch for that which remains,
for dying whets the grasp.

October is a mighty month, for in it little Gilbert died.
"Open the door," was his last cry, "the boys are waiting for me."

Quite used to his commandment, his little aunt obeyed, and still two years and many days, and he does not return.

Where makes my lark his nest?

But Corinthians' bugle obliterates the birds', so covering your loved heart to keep it from another shot.

Tenderly
EMILY

To Professor J. K. Chickering
(1885)

DEAR FRIEND,

The Amherst heart is plain and whole and permanent and warm.

In childhood I never sowed a seed unless it was perennial—and that is why my garden lasts.

We dare not trust ourselves to know that you indeed have left us.

The fiction is sufficient pain. To know you better as you flee, may be our recompense.

I hope that you are well, and nothing mars your peace but its divinity—for ecstasy is peril.

With earnest recollection
E. DICKINSON

To Mrs. Hanson Read
(One year after the drowning of her two only sons)

MY DEAR MRS. READ,

We have often thought of you today, and almost spoken with you, but thought you might like to be alone—if one can be alone with so thronged a Heaven.

E. DICKINSON

To Mr. Thomas Niles
(1885)

DEAR FRIEND,

Thank you for the kindness. I am glad if the bird seemed true to you.

Please efface the others, and receive these three, which are more like him—"A Thunder Storm," "A Humming Bird," and "A Country Burial."

The life of Marian Evans had much I never knew—a doom of fruit without the bloom, like the Niger fig:

> *Her losses make our gains ashamed—*
> *She bore life's empty pack*
> *As gallantly as if the East*
> *Were swinging at her back.*
> *Life's empty pack is heaviest.*
> *As every porter knows—*
> *In vain to punish honey.*
> *It only sweeter grows.*

(Almost the only record of her giving a title to any poem.)

To Mrs. Tuckerman
(After the death of Professor Tuckerman, March 15, 1886)

Dear One,

"Eye hath not seen nor ear heard." What a recompense! The enthusiasm of God at the reception of His sons! How ecstatic! How infinite! Says the blissful voice, not yet a voice, but a vision, "I will not let thee go, except I bless thee."

Emily

To Louisa and Fannie Norcross
(March, 1886)

I scarcely know where to begin, but love is always a safe place. I have twice been very sick, dears, with a little recess of convalescence, then to be more sick, and have lain in my bed since November, many years, for me, stirring as the arbutus does, a pink and russet hope; but that we will leave with our pillow. When your dear hearts are quite convenient, tell us of their contents, the fabric cared for most, not a fondness wanting.

Do you keep musk, as you used to, like Mrs. Morene of Mexico? Or cassia carnations so big they split their fringes of berry? Was your winter a tender shelter—perhaps like Keats's bird, "and hops and hops in little journeys"?

Are you reading and well, and the W——s near and warm? When you see Mrs. French and Dan give them a tear from us.

Vinnie would have written, but could not leave my side. Maggie gives her love. Mine more sweetly still.

EMILY

To Mr. C. H. Clark
(April 5, 1886)

DEAR FRIEND,

Are you living and well, and your father in peace, and the home in —— Street without effacing change? I received your very kind message, I think in November, since which I have been very ill, and begin to roam in my room a little, an hour at a time.

Do you, as time steals on, know anything of the W—— whom Mr. —— so loved, and of whom he said with a smile, "Should he find a gold watch in the street he would not pick it up, so unsullied was he"? . . .

My sister gives her faithful remembrance to yourself and your father, the brother so cherished never once forgot.

You will recall the flower sacred to your brother.

No sloth has memory.

E. DICKINSON

To Mrs. Currier
(April 10, 1886)

. . . Mr. Hunt was tinning a post this morning, and told us L—— didn't feel quite as well as usual, and I haven't felt quite as well as usual since the chestnuts were ripe, though it wasn't the chestnuts' fault, but the crocuses are so martial and the daffodils to the second joint, let us join hands and recover.

"I do remember an apothecary," said that sweeter robin than Shakespeare, was a loved paragraph which has lain on my pillow all winter, but perhaps Shakespeare has been "up street" oftener than I have, this winter.

Would father's youngest sister believe that in the "Shire town" where he and Blackstone went to school, a man was hung yesterday, for the murder of a man by the name of Dickinson, and that Miss M—— was poisoned by a strolling juggler to be tried in the Supreme Court next week?

Don't you think fumigation ceased when father died?

Poor, romantic Miss M——! But perhaps a "Police Gazette" was better for you than an essay.

I hope you are both stronger, and ask a word of gain with these ecstatic days. I give my anxious love, and Vinnie's faithfulness with mine.

Your Emily

To Mr. C. H. Clark
(April 15, 1886)

Thank you, dear friend, I am better. The velocity of the ill, however, is like that of the snail. I am glad of your father's tranquillity, and of your own courage. Fear makes us all martial.

I could hardly have thought it possible that the scholarly stranger to whom my father introduced me, could have mentioned my friend, almost itself a vision, or have still left a legend to relate his name. With the exception of —— . . . your name alone remains.

"Going home," was he not an aborigine of the sky?

The last time he came in life I was with my lilies and heliotropes. Said my sister to me, "The gentleman with the deep voice wants to see you, Emily "—hearing him ask of the servant.

"Where did you come from?" I said, for he spoke like an apparition. "I stepped from my pulpit to the train," was his simple reply; and, when I asked, "how long?"—"twenty years," said he, with inscrutable roguery.

But the loved voice has ceased; and to someone who heard him "going home" it was sweet to speak. . . Thank you for each circumstance, and tell me all you love to say. . .

Excuse me for the voice, this moment immortal.

E. DICKINSON

To LOUISA AND FANNIE NORCROSS
(The day before her death, May 15,1886)

LITTLE COUSINS
   Called back.

EMILY

THE END

A Note About the Authors

Martha Dickinson Bianchi (1866–1943) was the niece of Emily Dickinson and the only daughter of Austin and Susan Dickinson. In a life marked with tragedy, Bianchi excelled as a pianist and received her formal education at the Smith College School of Music, had a short marriage to Captain Alexander Bianchi, before finally pursuing a career as a poet and novelist in her late 30s. While she would go on to write *The Cuckoo's Nest*, *A Cossack Lover* and *The Kiss of Apollo*, Bianchi was best known for collecting and editing her aunt's poetry, in particular, 1914's *The Single Hound*, which led to a revival of interest in her aunt's work.

Emily Dickinson (1830–1886) was an American poet. Born in Amherst, Massachusetts, Dickinson was raised in a prominent family of lawyers and politicians alongside two siblings. For seven years, she studied at Amherst Academy, excelling in English, classics, and the sciences. Dickinson suffered from melancholy and poor health from a young age, taking several breaks from school to stay with family in Boston. After graduation, Dickinson enrolled at Mount Holyoke Female Seminary, withdrawing ten months later to return home to Amherst. Through her friend Benjamin Franklin Newton, she was introduced to the poetry of William Wordsworth and Ralph Waldo Emerson, whose influence would prove profound as she embarked on a literary life of her own. Despite her status as one of the greatest American poets of the nineteenth century, Dickinson published only ten poems and one letter during her lifetime, only a sampling of nearly two thousand poems discovered after her death. Cast as an eccentric by contemporaries and later critics alike, Dickinson was an enigmatic figure whose experimental forms and extensive use of symbols have inspired generations of readers and poets. By the 1870s, following the death of her father, Dickinson had largely withdrawn from public life. Spending much of her time caring for her ailing mother, she still managed to write poems and send letters to friends and family. In 1886, following her death, Dickinson's younger sister Lavinia discovered her collection of poems and began the long and arduous process of bringing them to print.

A Note from the Publisher

Spanning many genres, from non-fiction essays to literature classics to children's books and lyric poetry, Mint Edition books showcase the master works of our time in a modern new package. The text is freshly typeset, is clean and easy to read, and features a new note about the author in each volume. Many books also include exclusive new introductory material. Every book boasts a striking new cover, which makes it as appropriate for collecting as it is for gift giving. Mint Edition books are only printed when a reader orders them, so natural resources are not wasted. We're proud that our books are never manufactured in excess and exist only in the exact quantity they need to be read and enjoyed. To learn more and view our library, go to minteditionbooks.com

bookfinity & MINT
EDITIONS

Enjoy more of your favorite classics with Bookfinity,
a new search and discovery experience for readers.
With Bookfinity, you can discover more vintage
literature for your collection, find your Reader Type,
track books you've read or want to read,
and add reviews to your favorite books.
Visit www.bookfinity.com, and click on
Take the Quiz to get started.

Don't forget to follow us
@bookfinityofficial and @mint_editions

CPSIA information can be obtained
at www.ICGtesting.com
Printed in the USA
JSHW032301150822
29281JS00001B/4